21 Visual Thinking Tools for the Classroom

This resource is for any busy teacher looking to enrich their lesson planning and support the development of critical thinking, problem-solving, and metacognition skills. Designed for use in Grades 5–10, each of these 21 tools is paired with a real-world issue or ethical dilemma to guide students through complex social, emotional, and intellectual topics and can even be used within your existing lessons.

Every chapter introduces a different visual thinking tool and a step-by-step approach for a range of topics from challenging bias and promoting self-awareness to reflecting on social interactions. Stories from the classroom and world, a range of ethical issues, and student and educator examples illustrate how the tools can be used.

Ideal for in-service teachers in Grades 5–10 across content areas regardless of curriculums, these tools will inspire your students to be open-minded and actively engage in classroom discussions while developing new and different perspectives about themselves, your lessons and the world around them.

The 21 Harbord & Khan Thinking Tools© featured in the book are available to download for classroom use at www.routledge.com/9781032662923.

Meredith J. Harbord is an adjunct professor for the International Graduate Programs for Educators SUNY, Buffalo State University and Core 21 Education Services US, teaching courses in holistic curriculum, the reflective teacher, design thinking, maker spaces and game-based learning together with ethical leadership and navigating gender in a global world. She also teaches middle and high school. Meredith is the co-founder of Harbord & Khan Educational Consultants.

Sara Riaz Khan is an educator and visual artist who has taught middle years program art and design. She has been a school artist-in-residence and exhibited internationally since 2004. Sara has developed community art projects as well as supported hospital outreach, disaster relief, and literacy initiatives. Sara is the co-founder of Harbord & Khan Educational Consultants.

21 Visual Thinking Tools for the Classroom

Developing Real-World Problem Solvers in Grades 5–10

Meredith J. Harbord and Sara Riaz Khan

Routledge
Taylor & Francis Group
NEW YORK AND LONDON

Designed cover image: Renee Gross-Zylbersztajn

First published 2025
by Routledge
605 Third Avenue, New York, NY 10158

and by Routledge
4 Park Square, Milton Park, Abingdon, Oxon, OX14 4RN

Routledge is an imprint of the Taylor & Francis Group, an informa business

ISBN: 978-1-032-66292-3 (hbk)
ISBN: 978-1-032-62622-2 (pbk)
ISBN: 978-1-032-66498-9 (ebk)

DOI: 10.4324/9781032664989

Typeset in Palatino
by Apex CoVantage, LLC

Access the Support Material: www.routledge.com/9781032662923

The following tools were first published in articles for Intrepid ED News: The Circles Tool©, The Detective Tool©, The Go Earth Tool©, The Knowledge Twister Tool©, The Time Tunnel Tool©, The Transfer Tool© and The Zig-Zag Tool©.

Contents

About the Authors

Harbord & Khan Educational Consultants
website https://harbordandkhan.com
Email: info@harbordandkhan.com

Meredith J. Harbord, EdD, and Sara Riaz Khan are global educators who use ethical dilemmas to enrich and transform curriculum. Their student-centric approach is driven by an ethical model and visual thinking tools that support critical thinking, creativity and student well-being.

Meredith and Sara's collaboration as design teachers at an international school in Muscat, focused on sustainability, ethical design and global-mindedness and inspired them to establish Harbord & Khan Educational Consultants. Meredith and Sara develop units of work based on real-world issues to engage and challenge students for diverse curriculums (IB, problem-based learning, Common Core and Australian). Projects they have collaborated on include curriculum resources for marginalized communities in Fort Worth, Texas, as well as creating innovative units of work for design technology for DATTA Vic. They have presented at international workshops and conferences, including ECIS and MAIS, and provide professional development to meet the specific needs of schools.

Being curious about real-world issues and learning from others is an integral part of Meredith and Sara's work practice. Projects and organizations they have supported include Edible Schoolyard NYC and those relating to sanitation, mental health, sustainable materials and climate emergency awareness. Meredith and Sara have authored two teacher curriculum books: *Interdisciplinary Thinking for Schools: Ethical Dilemmas MYP 1, 2 & 3* and *Interdisciplinary Thinking for Schools: Ethical Dilemmas MYP 4 & 5* (2020).

Online Support Material

Available to download at www.routledge.com/9781032662923

Introduction

Developing Real-World Problem Solvers in Grades 5–10

Who We Are

Harbord & Khan Educational Consultants—Meredith and Sara are global educators who use ethical dilemmas to enrich and transform curriculum.

Why Did We Write This Book?

Education is always in the spotlight, and educators are considered 'first responders' in terms of help. Our primary reason for writing this book was to support teachers and students who are under pressure. As teachers, we understand the stress of being in the classroom, particularly in these challenging times, with students having many disrupted experiences.

The climate emergency, the global displacement of people and the post-pandemic world have exacerbated the demand for sustainable ways of thinking and living.

Schools have been placed at the forefront to navigate the complex and sensitive emotional and mental health challenges faced by their communities due to the many world crises.

DOI: 10.4324/9781032664989-1

Students want to see change. There are high instances of depression and isolation for many young people, and what we can offer them is a lifeline to a better future.

As we negotiate new technologies such as artificial intelligence (AI), there is increasing evidence of a need for schools to teach and develop creative and critical thinking skills in order to prepare students for an unknown future. Our visual thinking tools can fulfill this need.

Overview

Our 21 visual thinking tools (Harbord & Khan Thinking Tools©—HKTT©) have been designed for students to foster empathy, provoke curiosity, inform emotional regulation and promote higher-order thinking skills. In each chapter we have included a table in which we have aligned the tools with critical and creative thinking skills, as well as aspects of social emotional learning. The table can be used as a guide for teachers and give students a fresh perspective on what being critical and creative looks like in your subject.

In each chapter we have made suggestions about tools that can complement each other and included definitions of key words. Our 'Stories From the Classroom' and 'Stories From the World' sections have authentic examples and experiences. Online support material includes worksheet and templates as well as a 'pack' of 21 HKTT© cards. This book is curriculum neutral and can be used in any curriculum.

Some students, teachers and participants have requested their full names be used, while others have requested to be anonymous or just use their initials.

How Can This Book Help You and Your Students?

- Provides teachers holistic and engaging ways to develop deep thinking, metacognition, self-awareness and empathy.
- Offers young people a 'game plan' to develop their higher-order thinking skills in order to have strategies to discuss, analyze and formulate personal opinions on ethical issues and dilemmas through real-world scenarios.
- Gives insights about how students are thinking through conversations that develop when the class is using the tools.

- Helps with class collaboration and communication through the sharing of ideas and bridges gaps in both understanding and self-awareness e.g. reflecting on important issues such as identity and gender.
- Can inspire students to be curious, open-minded and actively engage in discussions, developing new and different perspectives about themselves and the world around them.
- Gives students opportunities to imagine and create their own novel ideas and solutions.
- Can act as an icebreaker when working with new students.
- Provides opportunities to embed higher thinking skills and ethical components in the planning stages of the curriculum.
- Can help you connect and collaborate with your colleagues and use the tools as a first step, not as a final step.
- Provides opportunities for personal and professional development e.g. to write an article inspired by your use of the tools, as a topic for your annual appraisal or review.
- Includes templates and worksheets.
- Provides samples and stories from the classroom.

Although the tools range from Grades 5 to 10, many of the tools could be used throughout elementary, middle and high school.

Who Else Can Use This Book?

This is a teacher and student resource written by teachers; however, it would be useful in other contexts:

- **Professional development (PD)**—Focusing on whole-school PD could make a big impact on the school culture.
- **Leadership teams** have found the Thinking Generator Tool useful for resolving faculty discontent and The Ethical Charter Tool helpful for planning, for example, the support dog program.
- **Substitute teachers**—This is an attractive addition to their lesson toolbox, and it can give faculty an easy activity for these unexpected replacement teacher days.
- **Parents**—Interested in their children's learning and understand the importance of preparing them for an unknown future.

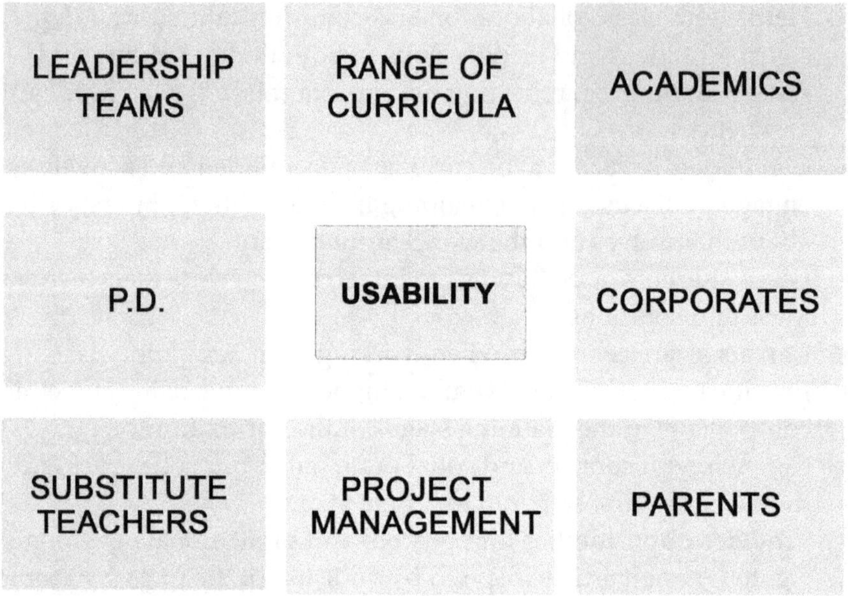
LEADERSHIP TEAMS
RANGE OF CURRICULA
ACADEMICS
P.D.
USABILITY
CORPORATES
SUBSTITUTE TEACHERS
PROJECT MANAGEMENT
PARENTS

Figure 0.1 Other potential book users.
Source: Graphic created by the authors.

- **Variety of curriculums**—Accessible for broad audiences, the book does not require a background in critical thinking or pedagogy.
- **Teacher education resource**—Any academic interested in promoting critical and creative thinking skills, well-being and self-awareness.
- **Project management**—The 'Stories From the World' section provides examples of how the tools could be used in real-life situations e.g. implementing a local emotional therapy dog program in schools.

Thinking Tools and the Harbord & Khan Ethical Educational Model©

We developed the Harbord & Khan Ethical Educational Model© to inspire other educators to embed ethical components into their curriculum. The model is a conceptual framework of our philosophy and can be used with all curriculum.

The Harbord & Khan Ethical Educational Model© is divided into six components, including Thinking Tools, that overlap and can work together.

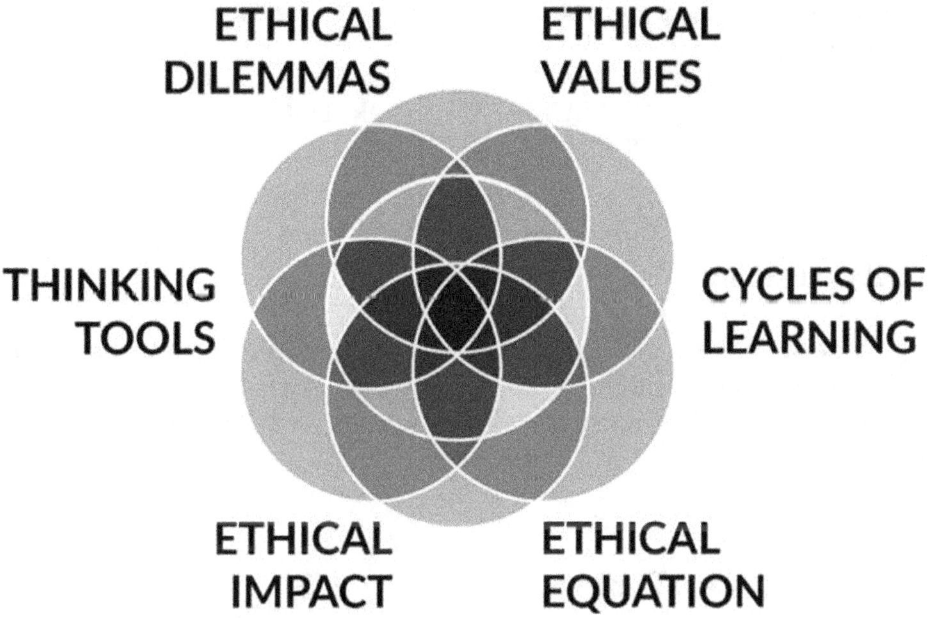
ETHICAL DILEMMAS
ETHICAL VALUES
THINKING TOOLS
CYCLES OF LEARNING
ETHICAL IMPACT
ETHICAL EQUATION

Figure 0.2 The Harbord & Khan Ethical Educational Model©.

Ethical Dilemmas

Ethical dilemmas can engage students on an emotional level. They are crucial to the model and are explicitly explored in many of the thinking tools.

Ethical Values

Ethical values e.g. empathy, fairness, inclusion, open-mindedness, etc., are embedded in the design of many of the thinking tools.

The Ethical Equation Tool (p 114)

This is a novel planning tool that uses a mathematical formula to generate ideas. It supports the development of an ethical mindset by integrating the ethical dilemma, values and impact into the curriculum from the start. The Ethical Equation Tool consists of an ethical value, a real-world inquiry, subject skills and purposeful impact and can also be used for interdisciplinary planning.

ETHICAL VALUE + REAL WORLD INQUIRY +
SUBJECT SKILLS = PURPOSEFUL IMPACT

Cycles of Learning

Our model includes cycles and processes that can inspire learning and understanding and promote higher-order thinking skills. We have deliberately not included a specific learning cycle so you can slot in the one that your school system uses.

The Harbord & Khan Thinking Tools©

The HKTT© were intentionally created as visual organizers to guide student reflection about big ideas relating to their metacognition, self-understanding, self-awareness and well-being. Graphic elements of the tools, such as color, shape and line, provide students with visual clues to guide their inquiry, in addition to the written content.

Testing of the tools and feedback have been conducted in a range of international schools and by independent students in Australia, Brazil, China, Columbia, India, Ireland, Kazakhstan, Mexico, Malaysia, New Zealand, Norway, Oman, Pakistan, Philippines, Sweden, Thailand, Türkiye, the United Kingdom and the United States.

- The Bias & Fairness Tool
- The Building Blocks Tool
- The Circles Tool
- The Clock Tool
- The Design for the Need Tool
- The Detective Tool
- The Ethical Charter Tool
- The Ethical Equation Tool
- The Go Earth Tool
- The Inquiry Builder Tool
- The Knowledge Twister Tool
- The Myself Tool
- The Orange Sun Tool

- The Plus-Minus Tool
- The Points of View Tool
- The Polka Dot Tool
- The Snowman Tool
- The Thinking Generator Tool
- The Time Tunnel Tool
- The Transfer Tool
- The Zig-Zag Tool

Key Themes Explored in This Book

AI, adaptability, assumption, bias, collaboration, communication, community, connections, conflict resolution, creative thinking, critical thinking, curiosity, decision-making, design, divergent thinking, diversity, DEIJ (diversity, equity, inclusion, and justice), empathy, ethical dilemmas, ethical mindset, ethical perspectives, environment, fake news, flexibility, flow, global skills, global themes, holistic, human impact, idea generation, inquiry generation, inclusion, inquiry, imagination, innovation, intuition, logic, long-term thinking, open-mindedness, manipulation of information, metacognition, mindfulness, multiculturalism, multiple perspectives, perseverance, problem-solving, relationships, responsibility, reflection, (builds) resilience, self-awareness, self-regulation, service, social awareness, social conformity, storytelling, sustainability, stereotypes, real-world issues, time and transfer.

Important Key Themes

Global Skills

Global skills such as creative and critical thinking, collaboration, intercultural competence and citizenship, emotional self-regulation, well-being and digital literacies are considered an integral part of an educational experience in today's world. Leading organizations such the United Nations Educational, Scientific and Cultural Organization (UNESCO) and the Organisation for Economic Co-operation and Development (OECD), as well as departments of education, are starting to encourage the inclusion of global skills in a more holistic school curriculum. They believe these global skills should be assessed and seriously addressed in school curriculum. One of the main reasons is that not only are the skills transferable across school disciplines but, more importantly, they encourage really strong lifelong skills. These can be used when the student finishes school, as this will equip them to fully participate in the future.

Global Themes

World issues are worrying our students and may cause disconnection from the world around them and can cause a lack of empathic understanding. Many of these tools can support a growth of empathy through the process of examining and considering these themes through the use of ethical dilemmas.

Storytelling

> *"We tell stories because we are human. But we are also made more human because we tell stories."*
>
> —Amanda Gorman

www.nytimes.com/2022/12/08/special-series/the-big-question-why-do-we-tell-stories.html ret 8/oct 23

Storytelling is a powerful way to learn used by people from different cultures all over the world throughout the centuries. Stories engage an emotional reaction and because of that the ideas are anchored in our mind. Real-world issues and imaginative exploration are vital for students to develop a wider perspective and greater understanding. Artist Linda Weil's inventive interpretation of the HKTT© both enhance the content and add another layer of storytelling.

Multiculturalism

Some of the ways the tools support multiculturalism is by having different language examples. This provides students with opportunities to express themselves in their mother tongue e.g. the Spanish examples of both The Inquiry Builder Tool and The Snowman Tool and a Mandarin version of The Myself Tool. The Myself Tool gives students opportunities to discuss different cultural perspectives between their family, friends and school.

We drew our inspiration from many different places and cultures e.g. the Ethical Charter Tool was inspired by Italian design principles and has been translated.

The stories from both the classroom and the world are all sourced globally.

Time

We can think of time as a key theme to foster student understanding and empathy. Although contemporary culture has seen a focus on living in the moment and being present and bringing our attention to the here and now, our tools encourage a multifaceted approach to the idea of time.

- The Orange Sun Tool—students reflect on 'What just happened to me', 'What happened to me some time ago' and 'My hopes and dreams'.
- The Time Tunnel Tool—can be used as a starting point for discussions about our impact on future generations and learning from the past.
- The Go Earth Tool—can encourage students to research and track changes using the '*Time Lapse*' option in Google Earth e.g. to viewing changing forests.
- The Clock Tool—uses the mechanism of reading and telling time to investigate actions and consequences. This focuses on learning from the past to make decisions about the future.
- The Building Blocks Tool—memory is used as a way of reflecting on past experiences to inform the present and future.

Ethical Dilemmas

The use of an ethical dilemma focuses the inquiry on the ethical and moral real-world dilemmas that challenge society today.

The ethical dilemma involves the exploration of at least two different perspectives, usually with neither view being absolutely right. Exploring ethical dilemmas fosters students' critical thinking and often provokes an emotional response.

Human behavior can be ethical or unethical, depending on whose perspective is being considered. Positive impact for one community may be discriminatory for another. Debating and discussing provocative ethical dilemmas can engage students more deeply with their learning.

How Can the Tools Complement Each Other?

- **Self-Regulation and Identity:**
  The Bias and Fairness Tool, The Circles Tool, The Myself Tool, The Orange Sun Tool, The Plus-Minus Tool, The Polka Dot Tool, The Points of View Tool, The Snowman Tool, The Thinking Generator Tool, The Transfer Tool
- **Inquiry Generation:**
  The Inquiry Builder Tool, The Detective Tool, The Ethical Equation Tool
- **Ethical Mindset:**
  The Bias and Fairness Tool, The Building Blocks Tool, The Circles Tool, The Clock Tool, The Design for the Need Tool, The Detective Tool, The Ethical Charter Tool, The Ethical Equation Tool, The Plus-Minus Tool, The Thinking Generator, The Time Tunnel Tool

- **Design:** The Design for the Need Tool, The Ethical Charter Tool
- **Multiple Perspectives**:
  The Building Blocks Tool, The Clock Tool, The Detective Tool, The Knowledge Twister Tool, The Points of View Tool, The Time Tunnel Tool, The Zig-Zag Tool
- **Multiculturalism:** The Bias and Fairness Tool, The Go Earth Tool
- **Time:** The Clock Tool, The Detective Tool, The Orange Sun Tool, The Time Tunnel Tool, The Zig-Zag Tool

You Know Your Students

After using the tools, as experts, you will know what the best course of action is and when and how to follow up with students e.g. discussing challenging and complex issues in a safe space where situations relating to identity, well-being and conflict may arise.

1

The Bias & Fairness Tool

Mindset Measure

Suggested Grade Level: 6–10

Key Takeaway—Fostering ethical thinking: Students can think about how biased or fair they believe they are and how their mindset impacts their behavior.

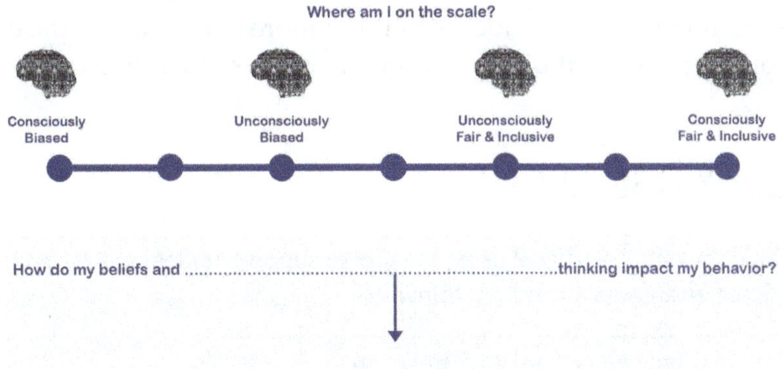
Where am I on the scale?
Consciously Biased
Unconsciously Biased
Unconsciously Fair & Inclusive
Consciously Fair & Inclusive
How do my beliefs and
thinking impact my behavior?

Figure 1.1 The Bias and Fairness Tool.
Source: Graphic created by the authors.

DOI: 10.4324/9781032664989-2

Global Skills and Key Themes

Skills: Critical thinking, creative thinking, open-mindedness, problem-solving, reflection and open-mindedness.
Themes: Assumption, bias, diversity, DEIJ, empathy, ethical mindset, ethical perspectives, mindfulness, identity, inclusion, prejudice, self-awareness, social justice and stereotypes.

Stories

FROM THE CLASSROOM: Student reflections on personal bias.
FROM THE WORLD: The SHIFT app design concept—developed by Manu Revi to combat misinformation and the editor of Intrepid ED News, Joel Backon.
DEFINITIONS: Affinity bias, assumption, behavior, bias, confirmation bias, empathy, fairness, prejudice and stereotypes (p 25).

What Does the Bias and Fairness Tool Do?

The Bias and Fairness Tool can be used to support students in exploring how biased or fair they may be and the factors that can influence their behavior. It can be a starting point for students to think more deeply and critically about their implicit and explicit biases in different areas of their lives.

Benefits for Your Students

Table 1.1 Table showing benefits of using the tool to support student metacognition, well-being, self-awareness and ethical thinking.

The Bias and Fairness Tool can help me:	
Metacognition Support critical thinking, open-mindedness and problem-solving.	• Be more aware of the complex issues that impact me based on my beliefs and opinions on race, religion, ethnicity, physical abilities, sexual orientation or gender identities. • Examine my bias in more analytical ways. • Develop a deeper understanding of what being open-minded is.

(*Continued*)

Table 1.1 (Continued)

The Bias and Fairness Tool can help me:	
Well-being Support self-management.	• Be aware of how my beliefs and emotions can influence my reactions and actions. • Guide me in how to self-regulate and grow my resilience.
Self-awareness Reflect critically on what we believe, why we believe it and how accurate our beliefs might be.	• Understand how easy or difficult it is to put bias aside and be open-minded to new ideas. • Become more aware of my unconscious beliefs.
Ethical thinking Support thinking about ethical issues and values e.g. empathy, fairness, caring, integrity, open-mindedness, etc.	• Be more aware of my bias and be more inclusive. • See how easy or difficult it is for me to rethink and review my beliefs and biases. • Think about how I can be more empathetic to others.

How to Use It

1. Choose your topic.
2. Define terms such as bias, fairness, inclusion, prejudice and stereotypes.
3. Discuss your understanding of what bias is. Do you hold beliefs that affect your behavior based on stereotypical understandings of groups and situations? Give an example of this.
4. Mark a cross where you think you are on the scale from 'Consciously Biased' to 'Consciously Fair & Inclusive'.
5. In the box, write about how your thinking (e.g. 'Consciously Biased') affects your behavior.

Activity 1: Bias & Fairness

To make sure your students understand all the ideas that are implied in this tool, have them complete the following exercise.

Look at the following examples and explain how each one can impact someone's actions:

Mindset ◉Consciously Biased *I am aware of my biases and choose to be biased.*
IMPACT ....
....

Mindset ◉Unconsciously Biased *I am prejudiced towards some people based on a stereotype (e.g. race, religion, ethnicity, physical abilities, sexual orientation or gender identities) but am not aware of my bias.*
IMPACT ....
....

Mindset ◉Unconsciously Fair & Inclusive *I am fair and inclusive in my thinking without realizing that I am.*
IMPACT ....
....

Mindset ◉Consciously Fair & Inclusive *I choose to be fair and inclusive towards others.*
IMPACT ....
....

Activity 2: Using the Tool

1. Ask your students to think about a particular topic and mark a cross on the scale that reflects their mindset. If students need help, there are some topic ideas in 'Applications' (p 19).
2. Students can use the box to write about how their mindset impacts their behavior.

Student Discussion

- How can you use your problem-solving skills to be more open-minded?
- If you are conscious of your bias, how willing are you to change your behavior or make different choices?
- Does your behavior change, depending on who you are with?
- How does the way you think affect how much empathy you have?

STORIES FROM THE CLASSROOM

Some students, teachers and participants have requested their full names be used, while others have requested to be anonymous or just use their initials

A student reflected on being consciously biased towards pro-choice.

EXAMPLE 1 Topic: Abortion Rights. A Pro-choice Stance.
Mindset: Consciously biased in favor of pro-choice rights.

How do my beliefs and thinking impact my behavior?

The tool encouraged me to think deeply about other perspectives on this topic and also to think about the argument from multiple perspectives. I reached my final conclusion after thinking over these perspectives and my own viewpoint. Being consciously biased means I have thought about the topic from various perspectives but, ultimately, my choices will remain the same as will my behavior because I feel strongly about women being able to make decisions about their own bodies. Regardless of who I am with, as previously stated, I am going to stay true to my convictions and present my viewpoint in the same way always. I like to think using multiple perspectives which allows me to see other's viewpoints and sympathize with their emotions but only to a certain extent. I will always put my opinion and perspective over others, which is why my empathy will be limited, as I have such strong feelings on this subject.

Reflection

I am aware of my biases; however, the tool encouraged me to think more deeply about them and I consciously choose to be biased about this topic. I know my strong feelings on this subject will impact my behavior by making me more likely to argue with someone regarding my transparent support of pro-choice decisions. My viewpoint on this topic and my bias towards pro-choice makes me more comfortable sticking to my convictions and beliefs as I firmly believe in a woman's right to make decisions about her own body.

Anger: Decisions made by men in power about women's bodies and the generalization of those decisions that can lead to illegal and possibly fatal outcomes is what angers me and makes me determined to continue to support my pro-choice beliefs (Student A, personal communication, November 24, 2023).

Grade 11 student Nuriya Zaki reflected on her unconscious bias towards people who are more attractive.

EXAMPLE 2 Topic: Being more inclined towards attractive people.
Mindset: Unconsciously biased in favor of attractive people.

1. How do my beliefs and thinking impact my behavior?
   While my bias is unconscious, it has still made me more likely to favor attractive people in given situations. I am more likely to engage with, befriend and extend support to people based on how their looks appeal to me and less likely to befriend people I consider less attractive. My bias is more likely to affect my behavior and encourage me to be friends with someone I find attractive and be more inclined to engage with them. I am willing to change my bias. It is unconscious so I don't actively think about it. If I was to think about it, my bias would lessen and be more even.

2. Was the tool useful in helping you think about whether you are biased; if so, how?
   This tool was useful as it opened my mind and made me acknowledge an unconscious bias within me. In the future, I believe it will help identify situations when my bias would usually come into play and will also make me reflect on how I can react differently.

3. Did the tool get you to think about fairness in new and different ways, and do you think this would affect your actions?
   It did make me think about how my unconscious bias is unfair and hopefully, I will treat people more fairly in the future, now that I have thought about it. Seeing as I do have an unconscious bias, I am likely to show less empathy for those I see as less appealing to me. At the same time, being aware I have this bias may make me more empathetic if I reflect on it in a particular situation (N. Zaki, personal communication, November 26, 2023).

Student Rafey Abdullah reflected on his conscious bias against people who don't stand up for their rights.

EXAMPLE 3 Topic: Not taking a stand for your rights.
Mindset: Consciously biased against those who don't take a stand for their rights.

1. How do my beliefs and thinking impact my behavior?
   I am aware that I have a bias against anyone who refuses to take a stand for their rights or voices any opposition. My bias tends to make me question people when they refuse to fight for their rights or to make strong

statements in favor of them. I do tend to judge them and to question those whom I am able to. I don't ever take an aggressive stand but I do ask why when I can (depending on my relationship with the concerned person), and I admit to perhaps thinking less of anyone who is not vocal on this topic.

This is a conscious bias that I have reflected on after discussing it and will try to continue this reflection whenever I am faced with an example of someone backing off from opposing an infringement of their rights. Discussing this bias has helped me to understand that there are always different reasons for why people don't find it easy to fight for a cause. They may be constrained by family or community. They may have already tried and been burned. They may see failure around them and not want to take a risk. There are many reasons other than just being cowardly or playing it safe.

2. **Was the tool useful in helping you think about whether you are biased; if so, how?**
   The tool did get me thinking about my bias and whether I am being totally fair in my thinking and opinions. I agree that my bias does tend to make me more likely to be judgmental of anyone who does not passionately and vociferously voice their opinions and take a heated stand. The tool has been useful in that it actually made me consider my bias from a different perspective, something I have not always been inclined to do in the past. I hope, with continued reflection, that I can be more open to analyzing a person or group's motivation and reasons before passing judgment on them.

3. **Did the tool get you to think about fairness in new and different ways, and do you think this would affect your actions?**
   Yes, I did reflect more on my bias and whether it is totally fair and do hope to be more conscious in the future. I may end up, in some situations, being more judgmental but I feel that talking about my bias from different perspectives has stretched my thinking to encompass the reality that not everyone can take a stand, and those who don't want to may do so from a place of insecurity or fear or oppression (R. Abdullah, personal communication, November 26, 2023).

STORIES FROM THE WORLD

App Developer

Manu Revi developed the concept for SHIFT, an app that can help people access digital images from different perspectives, time frames and locations. He described using SHIFT to be "like lending someone else's eyes, words and thoughts to understand an image".

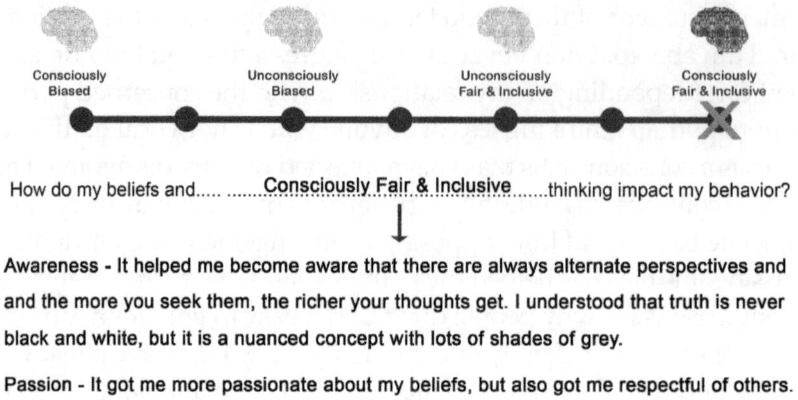
Consciously Biased
Unconsciously Biased
Unconsciously Fair & Inclusive
Consciously Fair & Inclusive
How do my beliefs and..... ....Consciously Fair & Inclusive.......thinking impact my behavior?
Awareness - It helped me become aware that there are always alternate perspectives and and the more you seek them, the richer your thoughts get. I understood that truth is never black and white, but it is a nuanced concept with lots of shades of grey.
Passion - It got me more passionate about my beliefs, but also got me respectful of others.

Figure 1.2 Manu Revi's tool result.
Source: Graphic created by the authors.

Using The Bias & Fairness Tool, Manu chose the point 'Consciously Fair & Inclusive' on the scale.

Being Open-Minded

You can always blame the algorithm for feeding into your biases. But it is just one part of the problem, and I believe the deeper part is still human. Lately, I have been trying to keep myself informed of voices that are against my beliefs.

What I understood is, it is hard to be open to opposing point of views. It is like tight rope walking where you have to keep your left and right at check. Moreover, you can't expect people to go mining for alternate perspectives. I want to make this tight rope walking an easy affair—at least when it comes to visual imagery.

Reflecting on what you see shouldn't be as hard as reverse image searching that in Google. It should be as easy as a left and right swipe. Or in SHIFT, panning through an image or moving it across a map. SHIFT is an attempt to reduce this friction in the search of alternate perspectives (M. Revi, personal communication, August 19, 2023).

Editor, Intrepid ED News

Joel Backon, former editor of Intrepid ED News, described an implicit bias exercise he collaborated on with Tanya Sheckley to encourage educators to reflect on their unconscious preferences. This could be something to try with your students.

Intrepid ED News is a lighthouse for educators and parents and is published by OESIS Network, Inc.

Basically, we have everyone list the 10 people (outside of family) they really trust. After they make the list, we have them look at it from different perspectives. The columns represent some of the angles we have them look at. The idea is that each person will be able to get a sort of personal analysis of where they may have unconscious biases ("Wow . . . all my trusted people are women." or "Hmmm . . . everyone on my list is straight & white."). It allows everyone to have an individual a-ha & can then set up a pretty rich conversation that can include some of the points we may want to bring in about education, income level, etc. We'll do this in a turn-and-talk format with a neighbor. In this context, it will be designed to uncover some personal truths that they can keep in mind as we move through the rest of the material (J. Backon, personal communication, November 14, 2023).

Applications

- ◆ Reflecting on what assumptions students make when they collaborate.
- ◆ Supporting the development of school values and mission.
- ◆ Examining bias in AI tools and technologies.
- ◆ Being more able to listen and be more open-minded about the views of people whose beliefs are different from their own (advisory, SEL).
- ◆ Discussion of issues relating to civic education, multiculturalism (cultural pluralism) in increasingly polarized times (social studies).
- ◆ What does it mean to be a digital citizen?
- ◆ Reflecting on prejudice and assumption towards subjects students find more challenging at the start of the semester.
- ◆ Generating ideas for projects and community activities—are

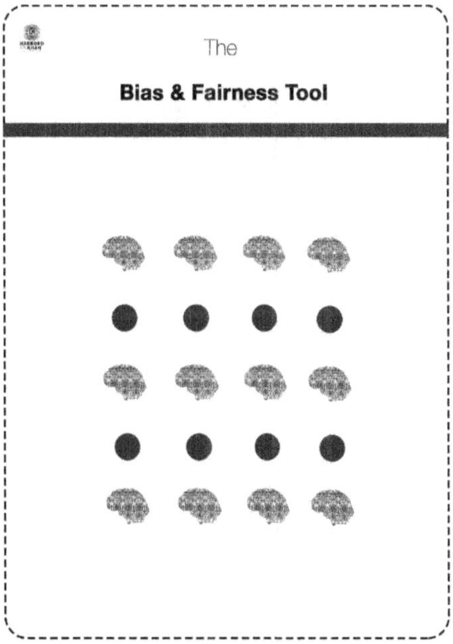
The
Bias & Fairness Tool

Figure 1.3 The Bias & Fairness Tool card.
Source: Graphic created by the authors.

students thinking about age, gender, race, the differently abled, DEIJ and social justice issues?

- Critically thinking about prejudice in their interactions with others (online and offline).
- Evaluating resources with a focus on fake news, misrepresentation and sponsorship e.g. 'greenwashing'.
- Questioning the accuracy of research—this is most often done on WEIRD (white, educated, industrialized, rich and democratic) populations.
- Stereotypes in advertising, media and online platforms (visual arts, media arts, English language arts: literacy).

Suggestions to Align Skills with the Tools

Teachers can share this checklist with students to support them in identifying their higher-order thinking and social emotional skills.

Table 1.2 Suggestions to align higher-order thinking and social emotional learning skills with the tool.

Critical and Creative Thinking Skills for Problem-Solving		Social Emotional Learning Skills
☐ I can analyze and evaluate issues and my ideas. ☐ I can recognize unstated assumptions and bias. ☐ I can check the facts and interpretations. ☐ I can revise my understanding based on new information and evidence. ☐ I can analyze and evaluate my emotions and how they affect others. ☐ I reflect on my own possible bias and compare that to the bias of others.	☐ I can use different creative strategies that make thinking visible. ☐ I use brainstorming and visual diagrams to create and develop ideas, connections and inquiries.	☐ I can recognize and examine my emotions and understand how they impact other people. ☐ I can understand and explore bias and prejudice. ☐ I can manage and communicate my emotions in a thoughtful way. ☐ I understand that I have a responsibility to behave in an ethical way. ☐ I can plan for and evaluate what the consequences of my actions will be. ☐ I understand what empathy is and can empathize with others. ☐ I can make decisions that are fair and impartial. ☐ I care about others' feelings and the impact of my actions on them.

Source: Graphic created by the authors.

Questions for Students to Support Higher-Order Thinking Skills

1. Was the tool useful in helping you think about whether you are biased; if so, how?
2. Did the tool get you to think about fairness in new and different ways, and do you think this would affect your actions?

Teacher Reflection

KEY TAKEAWAY: Fostering ethical thinking—students can think about how biased or fair they believe they are and how their mindset impacts their behavior.

- Describe the scenario and classroom context—what was the problem you wanted to address with this tool?
- Did you achieve your goal?
- How did you use the tool to support students' higher-order thinking skills (HOTS)?

Complement with Other Tools

Self-regulation and identity: The Myself Tool, The Orange Sun Tool and The Points of View Tool.
Ethical mindset: The Ethical Charter Tool, The Ethical Equation Tool and The Thinking Generator Tool.

Chapter Notes

Use this space to plan and write your personal thoughts, ideas and questions here:

Create your mind-map or sketch out your ideas

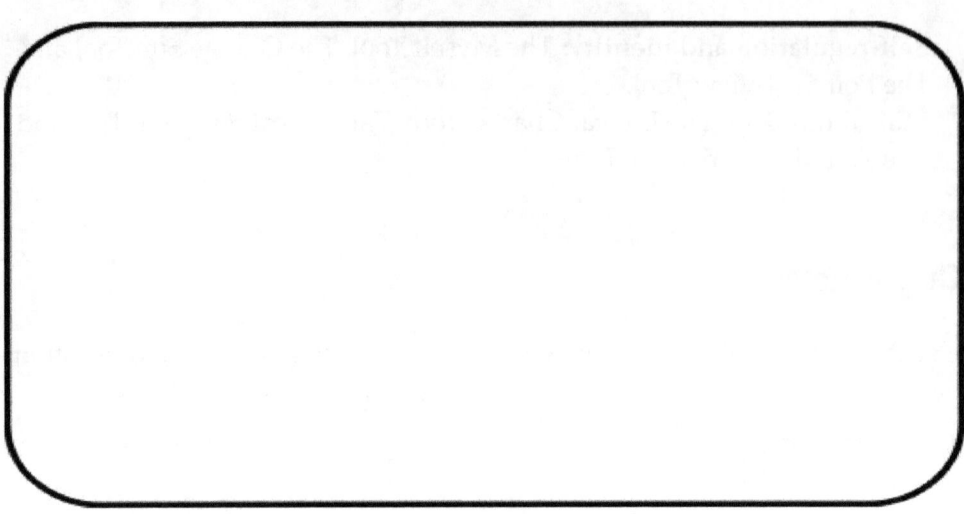

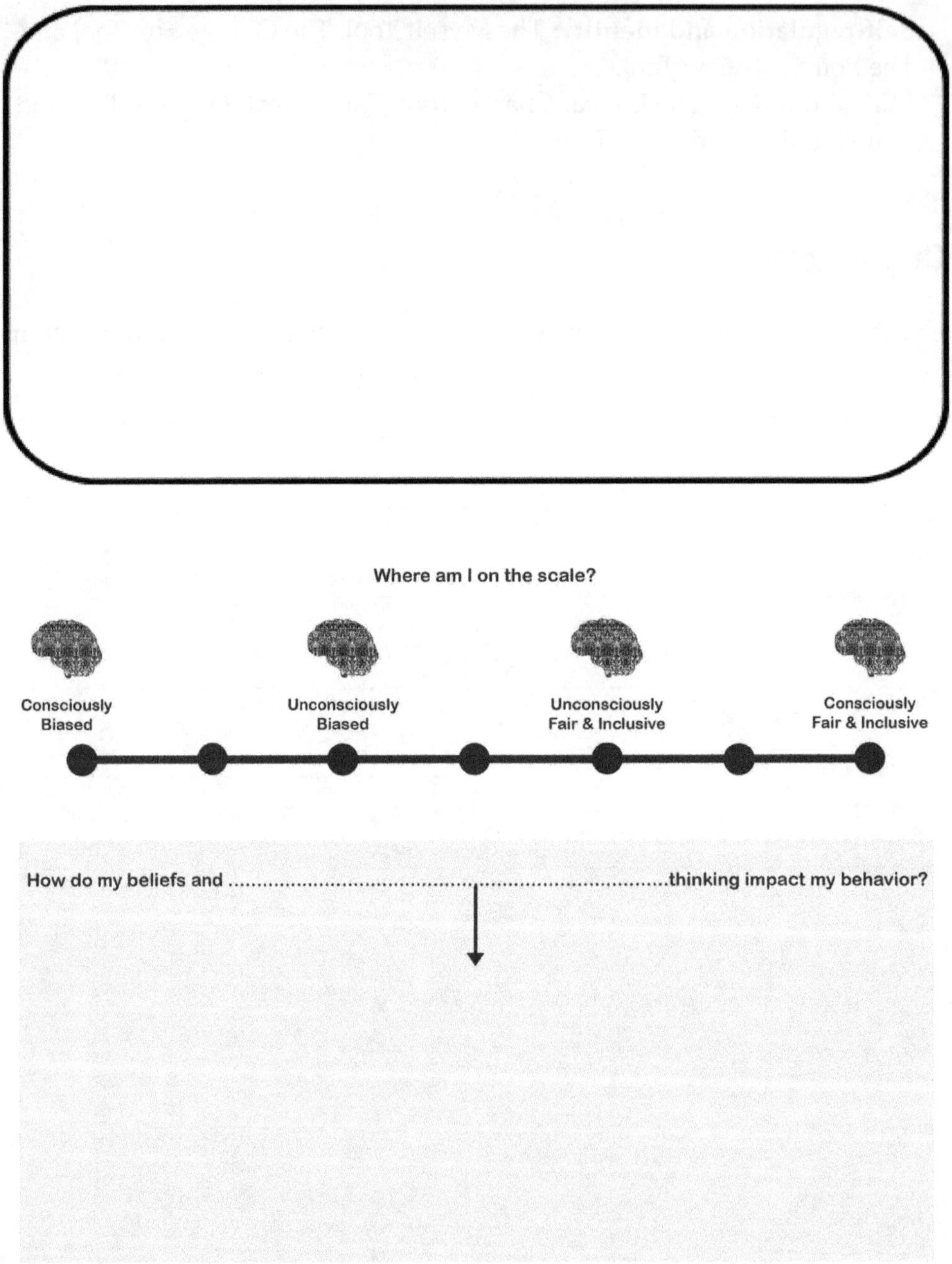
Where am I on the scale?
Consciously Biased
Unconsciously Biased
Unconsciously Fair & Inclusive
Consciously Fair & Inclusive
How do my beliefs and ....thinking impact my behavior?

Figure 1.4 The Bias & Fairness Tool blank template.
Source: Graphic created by the authors.

Definitions

Affinity bias: also known as similarity bias; the tendency to prefer people who have similar backgrounds, interests and beliefs.
Assumption: something that you accept as true without question or proof.
Behavior: the way in which someone behaves, especially towards others.
Bias: a strong feeling in favor of or against one group of people or one side in an argument, often not based on fair judgment.
Confirmation bias: the tendency to intentionally seek out information that confirms our existing beliefs while ignoring information that contradicts them.
Empathy: the ability to understand and share the feelings of another.
Fairness: the quality of treating people equally or in a way that is right or reasonable.
Prejudice: an unfair and unreasonable opinion or feeling, especially when formed without enough thought or knowledge.
Stereotypes: a set idea that people have about what someone or something is like, especially an idea that is wrong.

The definitions in this list have been sourced from the Cambridge Online Dictionary (2023) and Wolf (2023).

References

Cambridge University Press & Assessment (Ed.). (2023). *Cambridge online dictionary*. Retrieved November 14, 2023, from https://dictionary.cambridge.org/

Wolf, J. (2023). *Bias: Definition, examples, & types*. Berkeley Wellbeing. Retrieved November 14, 2023, from www.berkeleywellbeing.com/bias.htmL

2

The Building Blocks Tool

Understanding My World

Suggested Grade Levels: 8–10

Key Takeaway—Using ways in which we know and understand our world to create purposeful change e.g. using our imagination to design more inclusive ways of living.

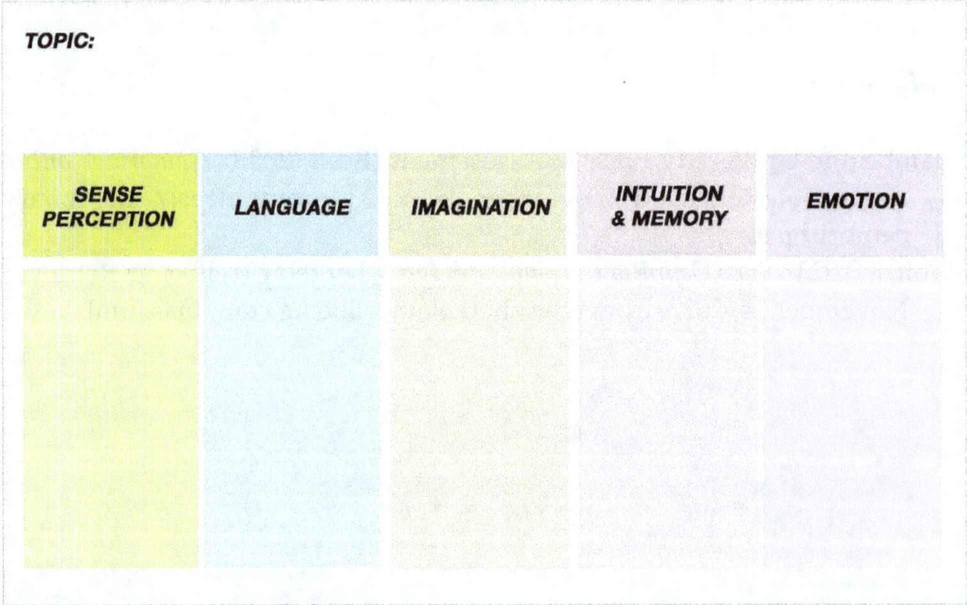

TOPIC:
SENSE PERCEPTION
LANGUAGE
IMAGINATION
INTUITION & MEMORY
EMOTION

Figure 2.1 The Building Blocks Tool.
Source: Graphic created by the authors.

DOI: 10.4324/9781032664989-3

Global Skills and Key Themes

Skills: Critical thinking, creative thinking, problem-solving and reflection.
Themes: Communication, curiosity, ethical dilemmas, ethical perspectives, empathy, holistic and identity.

Stories

FROM THE WORLD: Two experts reflect on their work practice. Special Effects & Virtual Reality—Craig Springett and Registered Dietitian—Aalia Khan.
DEFINITIONS: Sense perception, empathy, intuition and imagination (p 41).

What Does the Building Blocks Tool Do?

It can help students to develop empathy and encourage a multifaceted understanding of our world. The Building Blocks Tool is a way to navigate social and emotional states and give students structure as they think about sense perception, language, imagination, intuition and memory and emotion. This tool was inspired by the International Baccalaureate Ways of Knowing (pre-2020) Theory of Knowledge course.

How can you use sense perception, language, imagination, intuition and memory and emotion to understand yourself and your world?

Here are some themes from the ways of knowing that could connect to your topic:

SENSE PERCEPTION	Visuals Sounds Textures Scent Taste Prorioception (Understanding where we are in space. Sensing movement and action)
LANGUAGE	Words Ideas Songs Stories Culture Tone Pitch Communication Connection Multi-lingualism Translation Script direction Code
IMAGINATION	Visualization New ideas Unusual connections Unreal Possibilities
INTUITION & MEMORY	Gut feeling Hunch Instinct Without reason Perception Subconscious Past experiences and events History
EMOTION	Feelings Beliefs Values Actions Reactions Identity Meaning Relationships Communication Experience Expression Self-Regulation

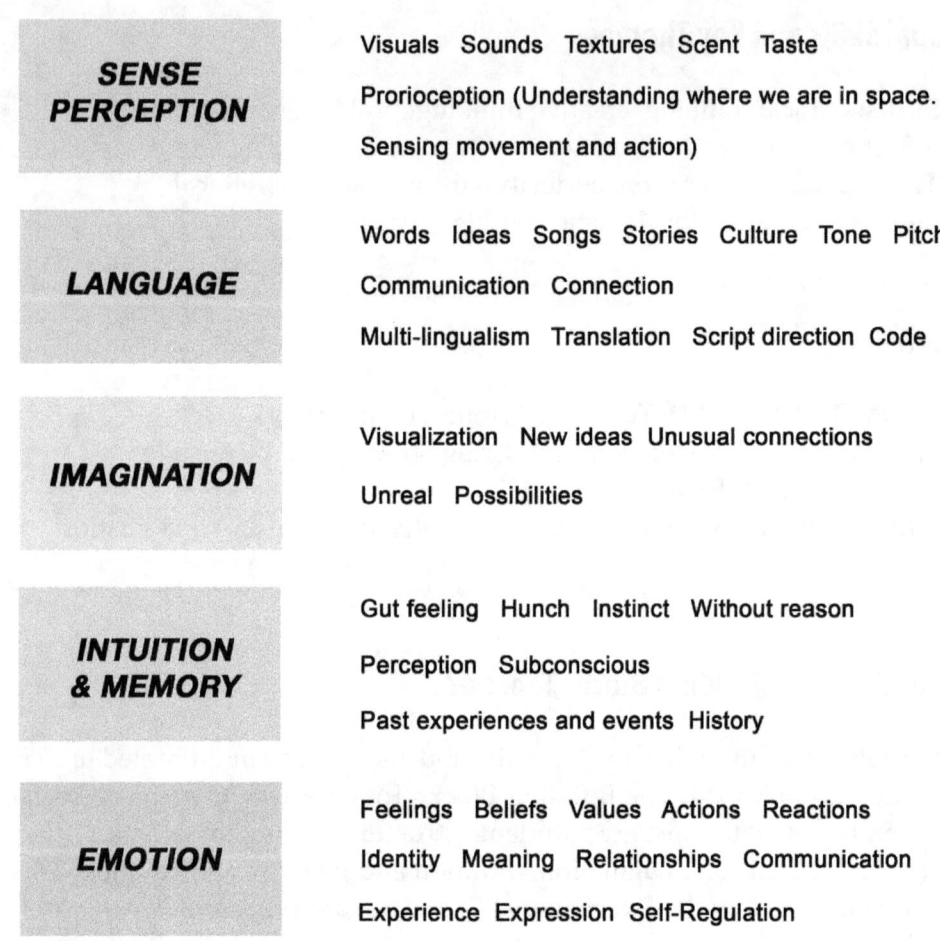

Figure 2.2 Themes in the Building Blocks Tool.
Source: Graphic created by the authors.

How to Use It

1. Choose your topic.
2. Connect your topic to relevant themes from the ways of knowing to generate inquiry. Sometimes you will use all of these, but other times you may only select a few.

EXAMPLE 1 Topic: Should we hold the Olympic Games or cancel them because of scandals?

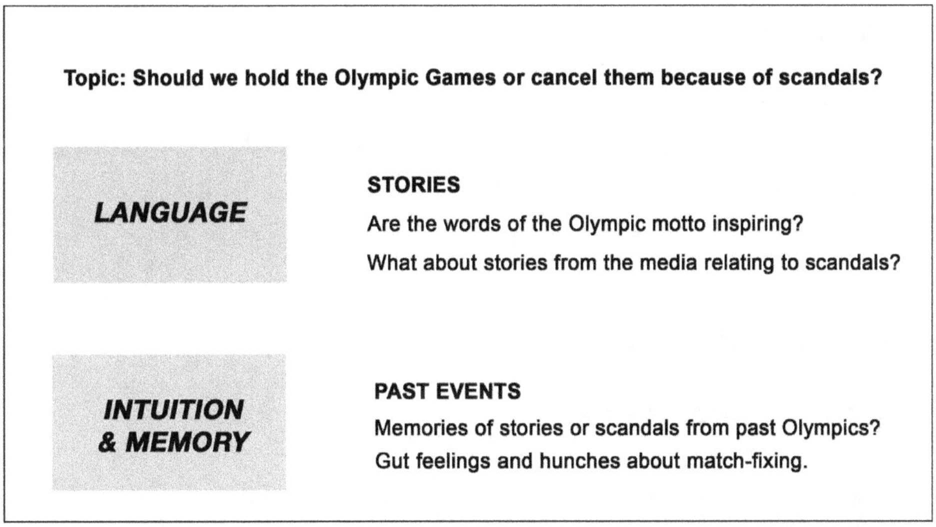
Topic: Should we hold the Olympic Games or cancel them because of scandals?
LANGUAGE
STORIES
Are the words of the Olympic motto inspiring?
What about stories from the media relating to scandals?
INTUITION & MEMORY
PAST EVENTS
Memories of stories or scandals from past Olympics?
Gut feelings and hunches about match-fixing.

Figure 2.3 Selected themes to explore the Olympic Games topic.
Source: Graphic created by the authors.

Exploring the topic through language and intuition and memory.

Language
Theme: Stories
Inquiry: Are the words of the Olympic motto and ideals inspiring? What about stories from the media relating to scandals and corruption?

Intuition and Memory Theme: Past Events
Inquiry: Do other people I know remember stories or scandals about past Olympics or sporting events? What does my gut feeling tell me about match fixing?

EXAMPLE 2 Topic: Designing a space to bring people together.

This tool can also help us in designing architectural models, planning community events and presentations. Reflecting on emotion and how we feel in a space can make us more self-aware of the impact of our physical environment on our well-being.

Exploring the topic through sense perception and imagination

Sense perception—Visual
Inquiry: How can I use visuals to make people feel at ease with themselves and others in the space?

Imagination—Visualization
Inquiry: How can I use my imagination to imagine a space that brings people together?

STORIES FROM THE WORLD

Visual Effects and Production

Craig Springett, master of design technology, visual effects technical artist and virtual production stage operator, reflected on his work through the lens of the Building Blocks Tool.

Creating believable fantasy worlds requires a designer to consider what you wish the audience to experience, with particular focus on their relation to each element and the human experience. Due to this, it clearly requires all aspects of the "Building Blocks Tool" to have been evaluated in the process. Whether they are attempting to create believable worlds with grounded characters, or fantastical vistas with no characters at all, the designer must always consider and balance the way in which we, as humans, experience the real world around us, and the boundaries that can be pushed and pulled to successfully communicate their ideas to their audience.

Sense Perception

We live in an almost infinitely detailed world, so being able to compartmentalize, deconstruct, and optimize what we see is vital as in the current day we cannot process an infinite amount of data digitally at a reasonable rate.

As always, this means understanding the scope and visibility of what the designer is attempting to create is an important step to consider throughout development of a scene. At whatever scale discernible to the audience, a useful method to understand is shape distribution and density: Breaking the scene into primary (large), secondary (medium), and tertiary (small) shapes, it can then be determined that progressively more of each shape exists, in proximity to the previously higher tier shape. Additionally, it should be observed whether these shapes are placed naturally (non-uniformly), or in a constant, potentially man-made, pattern (uniformly). It is worth noting the term 'shape' in this context is used loosely, as it is not limited to just geometry, and can equally be applied to color, or texture and pattern, potentially all at the same time.

Exceptions to these rules should also be evaluated to understand why they are considered realistic or possible, e.g. What makes Giant's Causeway in Scotland a natural landscape, when such unnatural patterning exists? How does this help explain the existence and use of unnatural shapes in natural contexts when creating fantasy environments?

Language

Whether working alone or in a team of people, we rely on many forms of language to share ideas and intentions, therefore, having a clear and common understanding is vital. Revision notes received orally can be influenced by the tone of the delivery, whilst when written, might require more precise vocabulary to reach the same effect. Is what I am being asked to do achievable? Is there a more efficient or clearer way I can describe this problem/solution? How might someone else misinterpret me?

Imagination

Often the scope of a project is as wide as it is deep, meaning ideas could be infinite, and why limitations should always be applied. By limiting variables, it forces the designer to fit their ideas into a cohesive product, often forming unusual and novel solutions to problems that would otherwise be solved in a typical and unsurprising fashion. It can also help with idea generation, as sometimes too broad of a topic can become overwhelming with possibilities.

Starting with an overarching log line of what the idea is can help to focus future ideas by way of reference; does it fit within these central elements? The designer can then outline those central elements with key adjectives. Typically, conflicts arise from these descriptions, or something relevant can now be created: Is it between the character and themselves? Others? The environment? By using these questions, a detailed summary of variables can be produced to help guide the designer's imaginative process.

Intuition and Memory

One of the greatest tools every designer has is the knowledge that can be drawn upon from memory. Past experiences hold clues and answers to present problems, typically guiding decision-making in the process. Using this, the designer can leverage our natural ability to compare things to each other for their advantage. If something feels 'off' or 'wrong', it is worth taking a moment to step back and evaluate what is causing that feeling. It might be that the past is trying to inform the present by asking, have I experienced what I'm attempting to create, and is there some sort of mismatch? Or perhaps more broadly, is the scene missing something/is it too busy, and the original intention is lost?

Emotion

When designing fiction, some of the best stories originate from real-life situations that have strong emotional connections. This can be used to enhance many aspects of a production, but importantly, the emotional response in the audience. This requires thought into the different perspectives and worldviews any person might have and defining the emotional beats required. The relationships between the characters, objects, and environments of a scene should be considered too. What overall emotional response do I want to elicit from the audience after they've experienced this? And on a more scene-to-scene level, how can I get the audience to connect with the situation, and understand the thoughts and feelings of the scene? How should everything interact to reflect this? (C. Springett, personal communication, November 17, 2023).

Dietitian

Aalia Khan, RD, reflected on how she uses language and emotion to support her patients with their nutritional requirements.

Language

As a dietitian, what I say, how I say it, and when I say it to my patients all play a critical role in impacting their health.

Everything we do as dietitians is based on our nutritional aim and language is used as a tool to achieve this. A nutritional aim needs to be realistic—it could be for a malnourished patient to gain a certain amount of weight, or it may just be to minimize (inevitable) nutritional losses. I often tailor the language I use with patients based on how receptive they appear to be, how knowledgeable they are about the role of nutrition in their condition, and what the goal of my nutritional intervention is going to be.

A critical element of empowering patients to enact the changes they need to achieve these goals is to ensure that they have an understanding of the 'diet-disease' link, which often requires me to describe complex physiological processes in a digestible way.

I need to select the language I use to describe the diet-disease link carefully, which can vary.

If a patient demonstrates a clear interest in the role of nutrition and some knowledge about food groups and organs, I could delve deeper, saying something like 'your body needs a minimum of 50 grams of carbohydrates in a snack before you sleep, because when your liver is impaired, it's unable to convert its stored glucose into energy while you're "fasting" overnight which causes your body to break down and metabolize your muscle mass instead'. I would let the patient explain their understanding of the situation and importance of nutrition before explaining this. This provides the patient with the necessary information to make sense of the reasoning behind the nutritional advice given and may increase adherence to advice. In this case, my nutritional aim might be to maximize nutritional status.

On the other hand, if a patient is extremely poorly, not engaging with the conversation nor maintaining eye contact, and displays a lack of interest in their condition, then I may keep this very short and simple in order to emphasize the key point e.g. 'try your best to eat something sugary before you sleep so your body can use that as fuel while you sleep' without burdening the patient with too much complicated information during a difficult time. In this case, my nutritional aim would likely be to minimize the nutritional deficit. It wouldn't be appropriate to elaborate on the role of the liver in converting glycogen to glucose as this may overwhelm the patient and possibly act as a barrier to adhering to nutritional advice.

Emotion

You can't be a dietitian if you can't understand how people are feeling. Empathizing with people and picking up on verbal as well as non-verbal cues, for example, being able to perceive what someone's mental state is, and being able to respond in a way that is appropriate is crucial (A. Khan, personal communication, November 25, 2023).

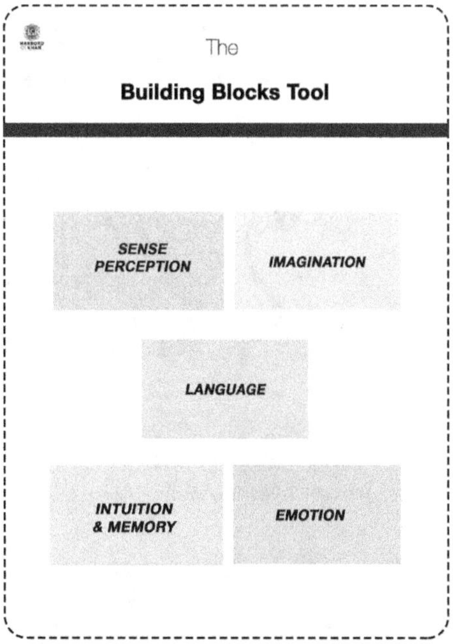
The
Building Blocks Tool
SENSE PERCEPTION
IMAGINATION
LANGUAGE
INTUITION & MEMORY
EMOTION

Figure 2.4 The Building Blocks Tool card.
Source: Graphic created by the authors.

Applications

There are a range of different topics that we have included as examples, but you can write your own topics that are relevant for your students' needs.

- **Sense perception**—physical sports or gaming.
- **Language**—advertising, posters and plays.
- **Imagination**—growing and cooking food and analyzing text.
- **Intuition and memory**—debating and theater.
- **Emotion**—listening to music or expression through dance.

I can use my existing knowledge to create novel concepts, products or processes.

Figure 2.5 Rabbit building with blocks.
Source: Artwork by Linda Weil©

Suggestions to Align Skills with the Tools

Teachers can share this checklist with students to support them in identifying their higher-order thinking and social emotional skills.

Table 2.1 Suggestions to align higher-order thinking and social emotional learning skills with the tool

Critical and Creative Thinking Skills for Problem-solving	Social Emotional Learning Skills
Critical Thinking Skills ☐ I can analyze and evaluate issues and my ideas. ☐ I can break up complicated ideas into different parts and reassemble them to develop new understanding. **Creative Thinking Skills** ☐ I use brainstorming and visual diagrams to create and develop ideas, connections and inquiries. ☐ I can create new solutions to genuine problems. ☐ I can use my existing knowledge to create novel concepts, products or processes. ☐ I create innovative works and ideas. ☐ I transform existing ideas and works and find innovative uses for them. ☐ I can use different creative strategies that make thinking visible.	☐ I am curious and open-minded. ☐ I understand what empathy is and can empathize with others. ☐ I can reflect on my own, my family's and my community's well-being. ☐ I can make decisions that are fair and impartial. ☐ I care about others' feelings and the impact of my actions on them. ☐ I take action to support others' well-being.

Source: Graphic created by the authors.

Questions for Students to Support Higher-Order Thinking Skills

Table 2.2 Questions for students.

1. Did the tool help you break up complicated ideas and think about the topic in different ways to help you develop new understandings?
2. How are your relationships impacted by the language you use e.g. what you say or don't say and how you say it? Did this tool give you any insights into how you communicate with others?
3. Can you think of ways in which using this tool could help you plan projects and/or take action to build a sense of community in your school?

Source: Graphic created by the authors.

Teacher Reflection

KEY TAKEAWAY: Using ways in which we know and understand our world to create purposeful change.

- Describe the scenario and classroom context—what was the problem you wanted to address with this tool?
- Did you achieve your goal?
- How did you use the tool to support students' higher-order thinking skills (HOTS)?

Complement with Other Tools

Multiple perspectives: The Detective Tool.

Chapter Notes

Use this space to plan and write your personal thoughts, ideas and questions here:

Create your mind-map or sketch out your idea

Table 2.3 The Building Blocks tool table.

TOPIC:	
SENSE PERCEPTION	
LANGUAGE	
IMAGINATION	
INTUITION & MEMORY	
EMOTION	

Source: Graphic created by the authors.

The Building Blocks Tool Template

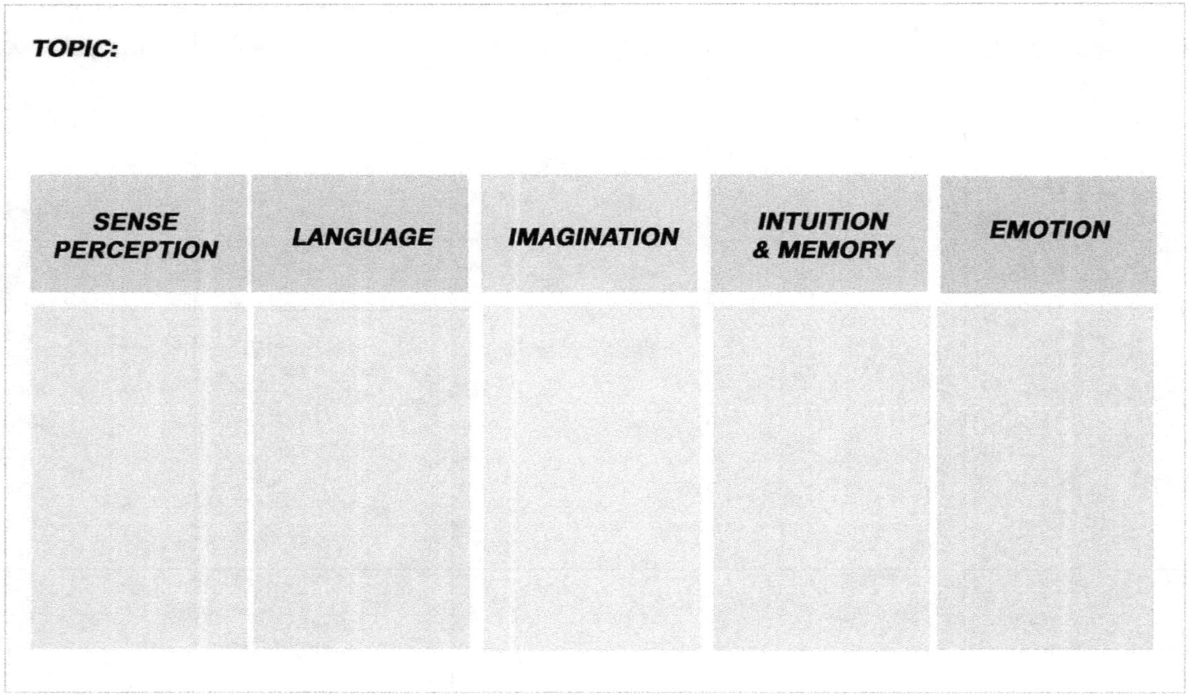
TOPIC:
SENSE PERCEPTION
LANGUAGE
IMAGINATION
INTUITION & MEMORY
EMOTION

Figure 2.6 The Building Blocks Tool template.
Source: Graphic created by the authors.

Definitions

Sense perception: the use of our senses to acquire information about and to understand the world around us. Traditionally, there are five senses: sight, touch, hearing, smell and taste.
Empathy: the ability to understand and share the feelings of another.
Intuition: an ability to understand or know something immediately based on your feelings rather than facts.
Imagination: the ability to form pictures, ideas or situations in the mind.

The definitions in this list are sourced from Cambridge Online Dictionary (2023), Merriam-Webster Dictionary (2023) and Oxford Learners Dictionaries (2023).

References

Cambridge University Press & Assessment (Ed.). (2023). *Cambridge online dictionary*. Retrieved November 14, 2023, from https://dictionary.cambridge.org/

Merriam-Webster, Incorporated (Ed.). (2023). *Merriam-Webster dictionary*. Merriam-Webster.com. Retrieved November 15, 2023, www.merriam-webster.com/

Oxford University Press (Ed.). (2023). *Oxford learners dictionaries*. Retrieved November 15, 2023, from https//www.oxfordlearnersdictionairies.com

3

The Circles Tool

Digging Into Dilemmas

Suggested Grade Level: 9–10

Key Takeaway—Supporting students develop their self-awareness and personal ethics through the exploration of an ethical dilemma.

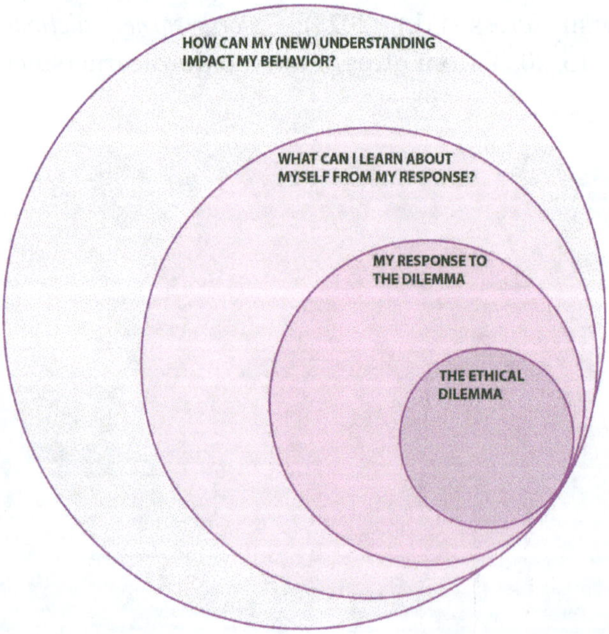

HOW CAN MY (NEW) UNDERSTANDING IMPACT MY BEHAVIOR?
WHAT CAN I LEARN ABOUT MYSELF FROM MY RESPONSE?
MY RESPONSE TO THE DILEMMA
THE ETHICAL DILEMMA

Figure 3.1 The Circles Tool.
Source: Graphic created by the authors.

DOI: 10.4324/9781032664989-4

Global Skills and Key Themes

Skills: Critical thinking, problem-solving and reflection.
Themes: Bias, emotion, empathy, ethical dilemmas, identity and self-awareness.

Stories

FROM THE CLASSROOM: Grade 8 students from ABA Oman International School.
FROM THE WORLD: Wildlife photography—Bill Mulholland
DEFINITIONS: Beliefs, bias, ethical dilemma, personal ethics, self-awareness and values (p 55).

What Does the Circles Tool Do?

The Circles Tool provides students with a step-by-step process to guide their responses to ethical dilemmas. Through a voyage of self-awareness, they can develop their higher-order thinking strategies as they reflect, evaluate and modify their ideas and opinions while developing their personal ethics.

While thinking about their values, beliefs and biases, students can reshape their initial thoughts to create solutions to the dilemma. The Circles Tool can be used to reflect on personal as well as global dilemmas.

An ethical dilemma is a situation or problem where you have two different perspectives and both points of view have ethical issues.

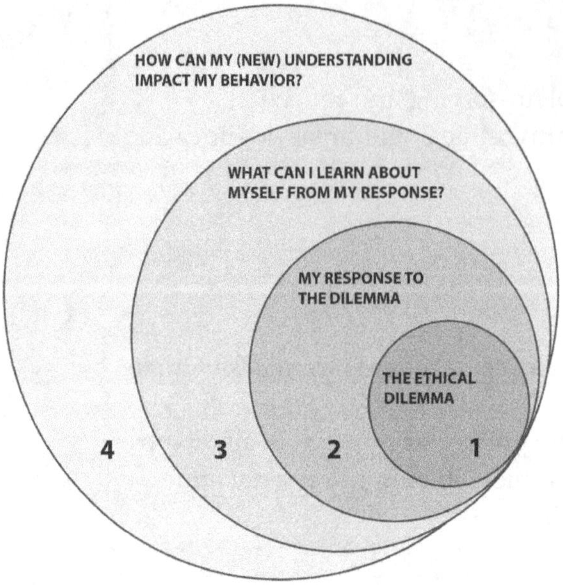
HOW CAN MY (NEW) UNDERSTANDING
IMPACT MY BEHAVIOR?
WHAT CAN I LEARN ABOUT
MYSELF FROM MY RESPONSE?
MY RESPONSE TO
THE DILEMMA
THE ETHICAL
DILEMMA
4
3
2
1

Figure 3.2 The Circles Tool with numbered circles.
Source: Graphic created by the authors.

How to Use It

1. Choose your topic—the ethical dilemma.
2. Start at the smallest circle and work through each graduated circle to explore ethical issues and dilemmas.

Circle 1—ETHICAL DILEMMA
What is the ethical dilemma? Your teacher may provide you with an ethical dilemma or you can write your own.

Circle 2
MY RESPONSE TO THE ETHICAL DILEMMA
Respond to the ethical dilemma being addressed. What are your views and beliefs about it?

Circle 3
WHAT CAN I LEARN ABOUT MYSELF FROM MY RESPONSE?
Reflect on your response to the ethical dilemma. What does this reveal about what and how you think and who you are? Did you gain any new insights about your beliefs, values and opinions?

Circle 4
HOW CAN THIS NEW UNDERSTANDING ABOUT MYSELF IMPACT MY BEHAVIOR?
Consider how your new understanding and self-awareness could impact your behavior.
Some students may find Circles 3 and 4 more challenging and will benefit from teachers taking the time to talk them through these ideas.

EXAMPLE 1: Using Mobile Phones Versus Cheating

Circle 1
THE ETHICAL DILEMMA
Using mobile phones in school versus concerns about cheating.

Circle 2
MY RESPONSE TO THE ETHICAL DILEMMA
I should be allowed to use my phone in school because I want to be connected to everybody. I also need to let my parents know about changes in my extracurricular activities. There are ways for teachers to check if anyone has been cheating; they don't need to not allow me to bring my phone.

Circle 3
WHAT CAN I LEARN ABOUT MYSELF FROM MY RESPONSE?
I am being thoughtful about my parents, as they have to drive a long way. As a student I believe I have a right to have access to my phone. I think I am also annoyed about not being trusted.

Circle 4
HOW CAN THIS NEW UNDERSTANDING ABOUT MYSELF IMPACT MY BEHAVIOR?
It's not just about the phone. Feeling not trusted has made me more annoyed than I thought I could get, so I need to keep that in mind.

EXAMPLE 2: Needing a Phone Versus Use of Child Labor in Making Phones

Circle 1
ETHICAL DILEMMA
Use of child labor in cobalt mining (Democratic Republic of the Congo [DRC]) for manufacture of phones versus the necessity of having a phone.

Circle 3
WHAT CAN I LEARN ABOUT MYSELF FROM MY RESPONSE?
It is so hard to make a decision about this as I think that my phone is needed; it isn't just a want. My parents need to know I'm safe, and I use it to chat with my friends and want to listen to my music.

Circle 2
MY RESPONSE TO THE ETHICAL DILEMMA

I want a phone so how do I feel about the child labor used in the DRC? Maybe I don't care; my needs are greater and I can't see evidence myself, so how do I know it's true? I did some research and according to Amnesty International there are over 40,000 children used in mining the poisonous mineral. However, I need my phone and I feel bad about the children but what can I do? How would my phone make a difference?

Circle 4
HOW CAN THIS NEW UNDERSTANDING ABOUT MYSELF IMPACT MY BEHAVIOR?

This is really hard to decide because I now have new knowledge about how phones are manufactured and this information is really disturbing but I don't think this will change my behavior because I need to have a phone. Maybe I could see if there is some way in which I could make a difference?

STORIES FROM THE CLASSROOM

Grade 8 students from ABA International School Muscat exploring natural disasters used the tool to reflect on the following ethical dilemma:

> When people are displaced by a natural disaster (e.g. volcanic eruption/tsunami/earthquake/hurricane), should the government pay for their resettlement?
> **OR**
> Are the people responsible, as they choose to live in an environmentally dangerous area?

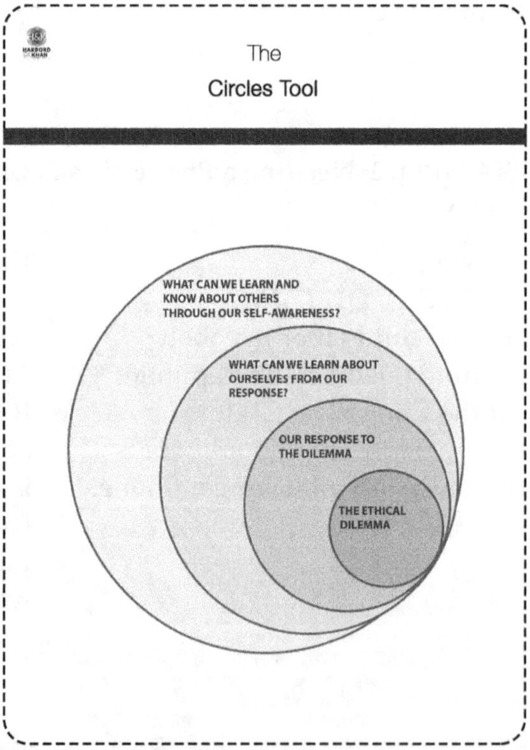
The
Circles Tool
WHAT CAN WE LEARN AND KNOW ABOUT OTHERS THROUGH OUR SELF-AWARENESS?
WHAT CAN WE LEARN ABOUT OURSELVES FROM OUR RESPONSE?
OUR RESPONSE TO THE DILEMMA
THE ETHICAL DILEMMA

Figure 3.3 (adapted) The Circles Tool card.
Source: Graphic created by the authors.

A Grade 8 student from ABA Oman International school, Gabriel Diaz da Silva, used his critical thinking skills to reflect on the following questions:

Circle 1—ETHICAL DILEMMA
Who is responsible for compensation for the displacement of natural disasters: the government or the citizens?

Circle 2—MY RESPONSE TO THE ETHICAL DILEMMA
I believe that the government should compensate for their citizens' displacement.

Circle 3—WHAT CAN I LEARN ABOUT MYSELF FROM MY RESPONSE?
This allows me to learn that I believe that others should take initiative for their actions and reap the consequences of their own doing.

Circle 4—HOW CAN THIS NEW UNDERSTANDING ABOUT MYSELF IMPACT MY BEHAVIOR?
This new knowledge impacts me by educating me that I rely on others to lead the way and to take the initiative.

Reflection

Was the Circles Tool useful in helping you think about the ethical dilemma and, if so, how?

I believe that the Circles Tool was helpful in breaking down ethical dilemmas into smaller parts, allowing me to view the dilemma and my answers in a new light, further allowing me to learn about not only how I will respond to dilemmas but also how I view problems, in other words, my perspective on the world around me.

2. Did using the Circles Tool give you a better understanding of what an ethical dilemma is?
I believe that this task did not help me understand the ethical dilemma, I believe that it merely helped me break it down so that I could find the 'answer'. This might be a biased opinion as I already knew what ethical dilemmas were, so to learn more about them further would be challenging (G. D. da Silva, personal communication, November 2, 2023).

A Grade 8 student from ABA Oman International School, Burhanuddin Dairkee, used his critical thinking skills to reflect on the topic:

Circle 1—ETHICAL DILEMMA
Government responsibility versus fault of people.

2—MY RESPONSE TO THE ETHICAL DILEMMA

I think the government should make evacuation plans and ways to mitigate the tsunami; this is because some people may not be able to afford to live in a safer area like the main city and have to live near the coastal region where it is prone to tsunamis.

Circle 3—WHAT CAN I LEARN ABOUT MYSELF FROM MY RESPONSE?

My response to the ethical dilemma shows that I care about other people's lifestyle and not everybody is fortunate.

Circle 4—HOW CAN THIS NEW UNDERSTANDING ABOUT MYSELF IMPACT MY BEHAVIOR?

Understanding that I care about other people's way of living, this can mean that I like helping people that are in need (B. Dairkee, personal communication, November 2, 2023).

STORIES FROM THE WORLD

Photography

Bill Mulholland is an amateur nature and wildlife photographer who loves exploring the world and our own backyards. He uses a Sony RX10mIV camera, though anything with a good zoom lens will do. Bill believes there are wonders all around us and loves to capture and share these moments. He used the tool to reflect on and explore ethical dilemmas surrounding photographing wildlife.

Figure 3.4 Image of a swan reflected in the water.
Source: Photograph credit Bill Mulholland.

Circle 1—ETHICAL DILEMMA

What are the ethics involved when you photograph wildlife?
By being present within the animal's environment to take photographs, any impact is unavoidable, but how best to minimize it? By taking and sharing photographs, am I encouraging others to do the same, thereby leading to increased impact to the area?

Circle 2—MY RESPONSE TO THE ETHICAL DILEMMA

I minimize my impact on the environment, remaining quiet, respectful of the natural balance of an area. 'Take only photographs, leave only footprints' (attributed to Baltimore Grotto).
When sharing information on the location, I only provide general information. If there are nesting birds or breeding animals, obfuscate (to intentionally make something less clear) any identifying location markers and/or delay the sharing of images.

Circle 3—WHAT CAN I LEARN ABOUT MYSELF FROM MY RESPONSE?
I grow more mindful of and care about the world around me, the impact I have on the world and, by extension, our collective impact as a species. By minimizing my impact around me, I avoid the impact some photographers have when staging and setting up interesting foregrounds and backgrounds and luring animals.

Circle 4—HOW CAN THIS NEW UNDERSTANDING ABOUT MYSELF IMPACT MY BEHAVIOR?
I become much more aware of natural habitat destruction around me and the world, the impacts of climate change and the ongoing changes seen in our local and broader environments. It becomes even more important to me to document and capture these moments before they disappear, being aware of the dilemma that this can lead to further impacts (B. Mulholland, personal communication, November 7, 2023).

Suggestions to Align Skills with the Tools

Teachers can share this checklist with students to support them in identifying their higher-order thinking and social emotional skills.

Table 3.1 Suggestions to align higher-order thinking and social emotional learning skills with the tool.

Critical and Creative Thinking Skills for Problem-Solving	Social Emotional Learning Skills
Critical Thinking Skills ☐ I can analyze and evaluate issues and my ideas. ☐ I can construct reasonable conclusions and generalizations and check the accuracy of facts and interpretations. ☐ I can revise and clarify my understanding based on new information and evidence. ☐ I can develop contrary or opposing arguments. ☐ I can analyze and evaluate my emotions. **Creative Thinking Skills** ☐ I can use different creative strategies that make thinking visible. ☐ I use brainstorming and visual diagrams to create and develop ideas, connections and inquiries. ☐ I know how to think in flexible ways to develop a range of perspectives and viewpoints.	☐ I can recognize and examine my emotions and understand how they impact other people. ☐ I care about others' feelings and the impact of my actions on them. ☐ I can understand and explore bias and prejudice. ☐ I understand that I have a responsibility to behave in an ethical way.

Source: Graphic created by the authors.

Questions for Students to Support Higher-Order Thinking Skills

Table 3.2 Questions for students.

1. Was the Circles Tool useful in helping you think about the ethical dilemma; if so, how? 2. Did using the Circles Tool help you think about your personal ethics? Give reasons for your answer.

Source: Graphic created by the authors.

Teacher Reflection

KEY TAKEAWAY: Supporting students to develop their self-awareness and personal ethics through the exploration of an ethical dilemma.

– Describe the scenario and classroom context—what was the problem you wanted to address with this tool?
– Did you achieve your goal?
– How did you use the tool to support students' higher-order thinking skills (HOTS)?

Complement with Other Tools

Self-regulation and identity: The Bias and Fairness Tool, The Myself Tool, The Thinking Generator Tool and The Transfer Tool.

Chapter Notes

Use this space to plan and write your personal thoughts, ideas and questions here:

Create your mind-map or sketch out your ideas

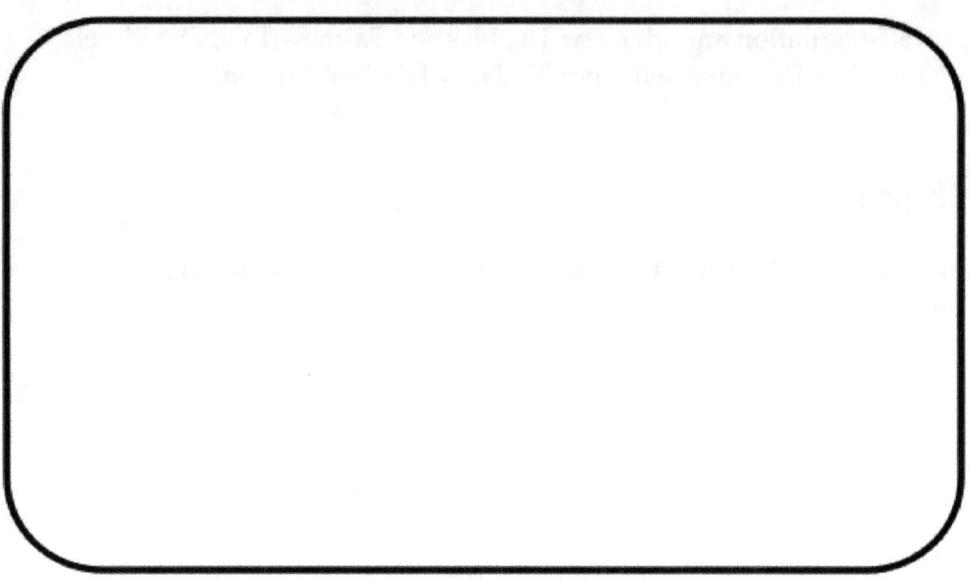

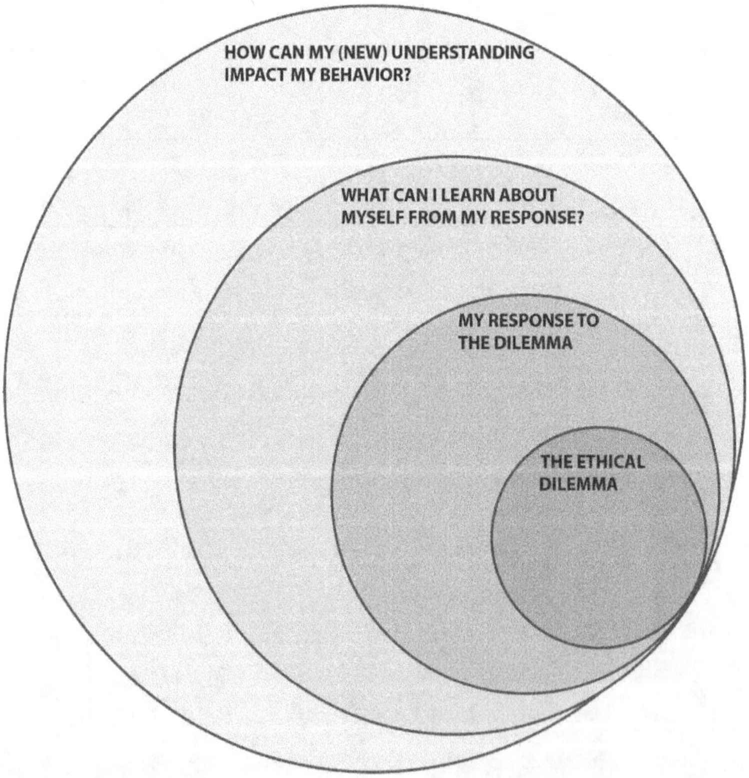
HOW CAN MY (NEW) UNDERSTANDING
IMPACT MY BEHAVIOR?
WHAT CAN I LEARN ABOUT
MYSELF FROM MY RESPONSE?
MY RESPONSE TO
THE DILEMMA
THE ETHICAL
DILEMMA

Figure 3.5 The Circles Tool template.
Source: Graphic created by the authors.

Definitions

Beliefs: the feeling of being certain that something exists or is true.
Bias: a strong feeling in favor of or against one group of people or one side in an argument, often not based on fair judgment.
Ethical dilemma: a situation or problem where you have two different perspectives and both points of view have ethical issues.
Personal ethics: related to values, beliefs, behaviors and practices that can guide you in your personal life.
Self-awareness: conscious knowledge of one's own character and feelings.
Values: the beliefs people have, especially about what is right and wrong and what is most important in life, that control their behavior.

The definitions in this list are sourced from Cambridge Online Dictionary (2023), Merriam-Webster Dictionary (2023) and Oxford Learners Dictionaries (2023).

References

Cambridge University Press & Assessment (Ed.). (2023). *Cambridge online dictionary*. Retrieved November 14, 2023, from https://dictionary.cambridge.org/

Merriam-Webster, Incorporated (Ed.). (2023). *Merriam-Webster dictionary*. Merriam-Webster.com. Retrieved November 15, 2023, from www.merriam-webster.com/

Oxford University Press (Ed.). (2023). *Oxford learners dictionaries*. Retrieved November 15, 2023, from www.oxfordlearnersdictionaries.com

4

The Clock Tool

Time Is Ticking

Suggested Grade Level: 9–10

Key Takeaway—Exploring topics and ethical dilemmas through personal, community and global perspectives. Learning from the past and looking to the future to consider our actions and their consequences.

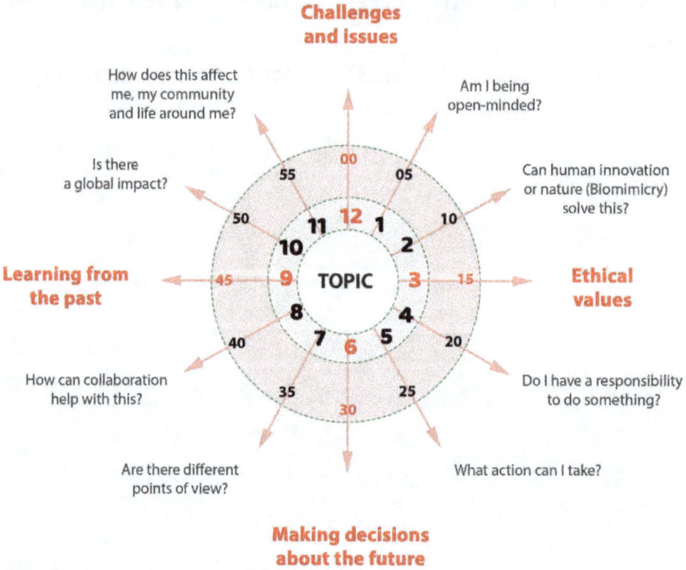

Challenges and issues
How does this affect me, my community and life around me?
Am I being open-minded?
Is there a global impact?
Can human innovation or nature (Biomimicry) solve this?
Learning from the past
TOPIC
Ethical values
How can collaboration help with this?
Do I have a responsibility to do something?
Are there different points of view?
What action can I take?
Making decisions about the future
00
05
10
15
20
25
30
35
40
45
50
55
12
1
2
3
4
5
6
7
8
9
10
11

Figure 4.1 The Clock Tool.
Source: Graphic created by the authors.

DOI: 10.4324/9781032664989-5

Global Skills and Key Themes

Skills: Collaboration, critical thinking, creative thinking, open-mindedness and problem-solving.
Themes: Multiple perspectives, real-world issues, responsibility, self-awareness, self-regulation and service.

Stories

FROM THE WORLD: Two experts share their insights.
Animal Shelter—Founder Raewyn Jeganathan and Maritime Archaeology—Amer Bazl Khan Director, MaritimEA Research.
DEFINITIONS: Biomimicry, ethical values, global impact, human innovation and open-minded (p.73).

What Does the Clock Tool Do?

The Clock Tool can support students combine themes and questions to generate inquiry about actions and consequences, through the exploration of ethical dilemmas and other topics e.g. the climate emergency. Using the tool, students can explore challenges and issues, ethical values, decision-making and learning from the past in relation to the topic they are exploring.

The Clock Tool is made up of the following:

- A central circle (topic or ethical dilemma).
- An inner donut of numbers (hours)—themes.
- An outer donut of numbers (minutes)—questions.

Benefits for Students

Table 4.1 Benefits of using the tool to support student metacognition, well-being, self-awareness and ethical thinking.

The Clock Tool can help me:	
Metacognition Support creative and critical thinking, open-mindedness and problem-solving.	• Think about issues from personal, local and global perspectives. • Imagine possible solutions inspired by nature or humankind.

(*Continued*)

Table 4.1 (Continued)

The Clock Tool can help me:	
	• Reflect on how open-minded I am regarding the issue and the value of learning from others. • Collaborate to generate ideas about action I or my community can take to make a difference.
Well-being Develop a more positive attitude.	• Think about opportunities to effect change instead of just focusing on the problem.
Self-awareness Reflect critically on the role I could play to make a positive impact.	• Be more aware about my personal, community and global well-being. • Have a greater understanding of the consequences of my actions.
Ethical thinking Support thinking about ethical issues and values e.g. empathy, justice and being responsible.	• Generate inquiry about ethical issues from multiple perspectives. • Develop my understanding about the complexity of ethical dilemmas.

How to Use It

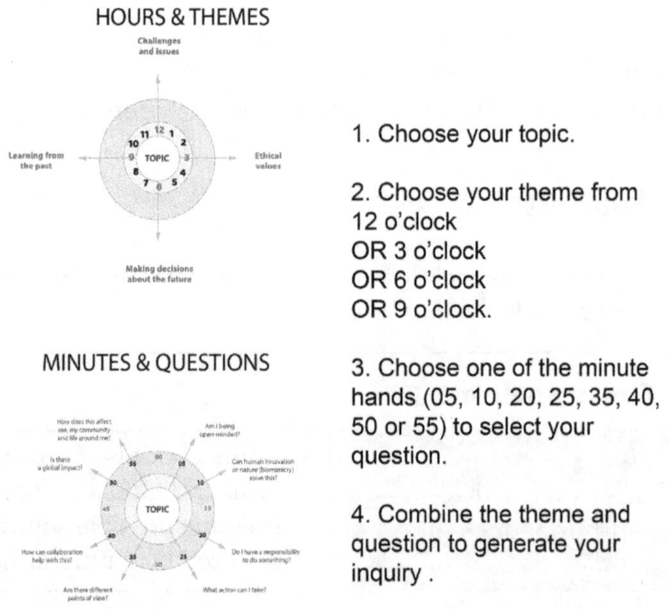
HOURS & THEMES
Challenges and issues
Learning from the past
TOPIC
Ethical values
Making decisions about the future
MINUTES & QUESTIONS
How does this affect me, my community and life around me?
Am I being open-minded?
Is there a global impact?
Can human innovation or nature (biomimicry) solve this?
TOPIC
How can collaboration help with this?
Do I have a responsibility to do something?
Are there different points of view?
What action can I take?
1. Choose your topic.
2. Choose your theme from 12 o'clock OR 3 o'clock OR 6 o'clock OR 9 o'clock.
3. Choose one of the minute hands (05, 10, 20, 25, 35, 40, 50 or 55) to select your question.
4. Combine the theme and question to generate your inquiry .

Figure 4.2 How to use the Clock Tool.
Source: Graphic created by the authors.

EXAMPLE 1 Ethical dilemma: Exploring the ethics of controlled deforestation

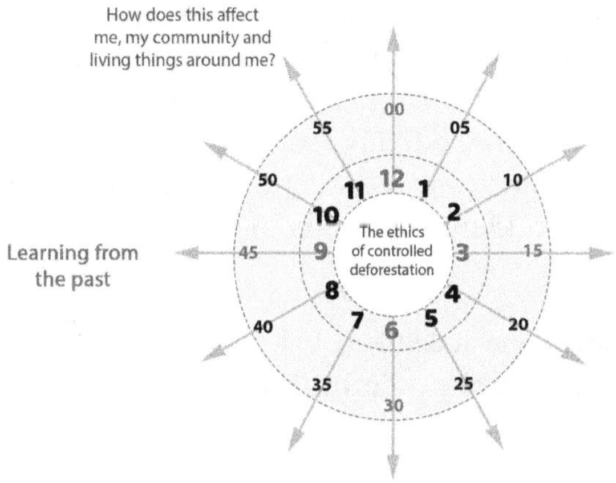
How does this affect me, my community and living things around me?
Learning from the past
00
05
10
15
20
25
30
35
40
45
50
55
12
1
2
3
4
5
6
7
8
9
10
11
The ethics of controlled deforestation

Figure 4.3 Exploring the ethics of controlled deforestation. *Source:* Graphic created by the authors.

Theme—9 o'clock
Learning from the past

Question—55 minutes
How does this affect me, my community and living things around me?

Inquiry: 9:55 + Ethical dilemma
What is the impact of controlled deforestation on me, my community and living things around me? Is deforestation acceptable if it is controlled?

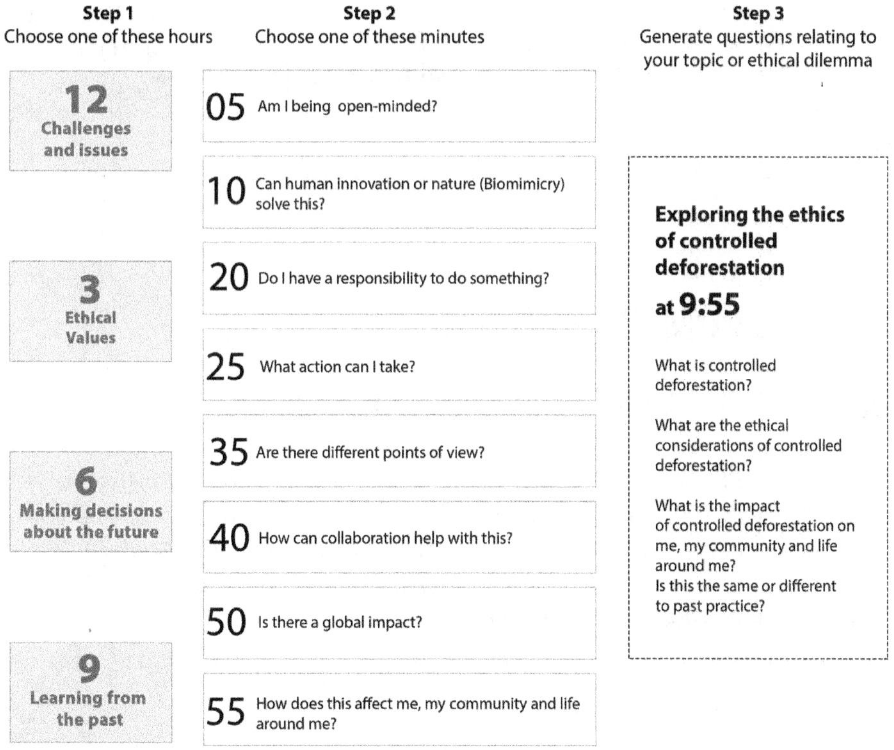
Step 1
Choose one of these hours
Step 2
Choose one of these minutes
Step 3
Generate questions relating to your topic or ethical dilemma
12 Challenges and issues
3 Ethical Values
6 Making decisions about the future
9 Learning from the past
05 Am I being open-minded?
10 Can human innovation or nature (Biomimicry) solve this?
20 Do I have a responsibility to do something?
25 What action can I take?
35 Are there different points of view?
40 How can collaboration help with this?
50 Is there a global impact?
55 How does this affect me, my community and life around me?
Exploring the ethics of controlled deforestation
at 9:55
What is controlled deforestation?
What are the ethical considerations of controlled deforestation?
What is the impact of controlled deforestation on me, my community and life around me?
Is this the same or different to past practice?

Figure 4.4 Step-by-step instructions on how to use the Clock Tool. *Source:* Graphic created by the authors.

EXAMPLE 2 Ethical dilemma: Earth's systems and eating habits

Many young people are changing traditional eating habits and are choosing to be vegetarian or vegan. With increasing population pressures, would eating more plant-based products as opposed to meat consumption be better not just for our health but also for our world? Do plant-based foods provide us with all the minerals and vitamins we need? For example, 'Eating more plant-based foods to reduce increases in meat consumption' versus 'Some vitamins such as B_{12} are only found in food from animals and are required for neural activity'.

What's happening at 6:50?

6 o'clock Making decisions about the future + **50 minutes**—is there a global impact?

Table 4.2 How to use the Clock Tool to generate time and inquiry about Earth's systems and eating habits.

TOPIC	THEME hours	QUESTION minutes	THEME + QUESTION = INQUIRY 6:50
Earth's systems and eating habits	Making decisions about the future	Is there a global impact?	

STORIES FROM THE WORLD

Waratah Wildlife Shelter Founder Raewyn Jeganathan

Waratah Wildlife Shelter is a small rescue and rehabilitation center for native Australian wildlife founded and run by Raewyn Jeganathan. We can use the Clock Tool to explore her work and the topic 'Comparing Indigenous animal and land management pre-European invasion as opposed to European animal and land management post-European settlement'.

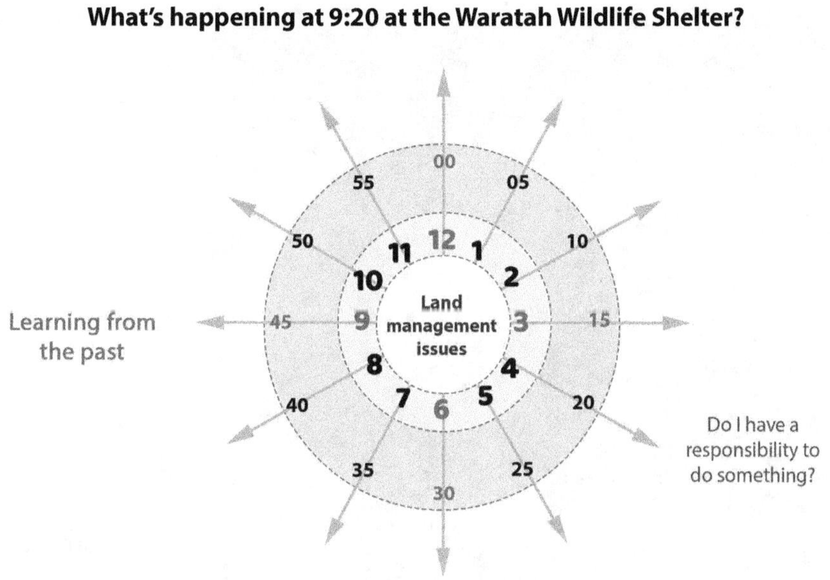
What's happening at 9:20 at the Waratah Wildlife Shelter?
Learning from the past
Do I have a responsibility to do something?
Land management issues
12
1
2
3
4
5
6
7
8
9
10
11
00
05
10
15
20
25
30
35
40
45
50
55

Figure 4.5 Exploring land management issues.
Source: Graphic created by the authors.

Table 4.3 How to use the Clock Tool to generate time and inquiry about land management issues.

TOPIC	THEME hours	QUESTION minutes	
Indigenous animal and land management issues	9 Learning from the past	20 Do I have a responsibility to do something?	THEME + QUESTION = INQUIRY 9:20

Source: Graphic created by the authors.

9 o'clock: Learning from the past

It was important to me to acknowledge the original custodians of this land. They respected and admired our unique array of native animals and lived harmoniously with them. The colonial invasion of Australia was not only devastating for our native people but for our wildlife as well.
No longer did the humans in this country live in harmony with the wildlife. They were hunted to excess for their pelts, driven out of their habitat for farms and towns and forced to compete with the introduction

Figure 4.6 A bag full of possums.
Source: Image credit Raewyn Jeganathan.

of multiple non-native animals which have wreaked absolute havoc on the ecosystem.

+ 20 minutes: Do I have a responsibility to do something?
I love animals, always have. I have always had a strong sense of social justice and found great fulfillment in feeling like I am making a difference (R. Jeganathan, personal communication, November 15, 2023).

Maritime Archaeologist Amer Khan

Amer Bazl Khan is the director of MaritimEA Research. He is a maritime archaeologist and has approximately 20 years of experience working on maritime archaeological projects in the Western Indian Ocean and broader Asia-Pacific region. Amer has also worked with United Nations Educational, Scientific and Cultural Organization (UNESCO) to develop regional capacity for the protection of underwater cultural heritage in the Asia-Pacific region. He is a member of the International Committee on the Underwater Cultural Heritage (ICUCH), an international scientific committee member for the International Council on Monuments and Sites (ICOMOS) and a member of the ICOMOS Pakistan National Committee.

Amer used the Clock Tool to reflect on ethical dilemmas and issues relating to sustainable tourism and archaeological sites.

1. Ethical Dilemma about Access to Sites versus Protecting Archaeology

In managing cultural heritage sites, visitor management is essential to ensure detrimental impacts from visitation are minimized. There is often a tension between letting the public get as close as possible to the archaeology, to maximize engagement and learning, and protecting the archaeology, to maximize conservation outcomes. Sustainable tourism ultimately aims to balance both needs, and this can pose ethical questions that require constant monitoring and recalibration of visitor management strategies.

Some ethical issues to consider: What is more important? Keeping sites undamaged or making them accessible to the most number of people?

Emerging technologies are providing solutions to enhance broader public access, while limiting the impacts of uncontrolled visitation. For instance, 3D recording of archaeological sites is increasingly becoming a standard archaeological tool for capturing a 'digital snapshot' of a site or artifact. This is done using 3D photogrammetry, a process by which hundreds of photographs are combined to create a detailed and geometrically accurate 3D model of a site. These digital copies are so accurate that archaeologists can use them to take measurements of objects within a site, without having to go back there in person. This technique can be useful when an excavation trench has been backfilled after a field season, or indeed even when a site no longer exists. Researchers can continue to ask questions and investigate the site from its digital copy.

These digital copies can also be made available to the public in the form of digital heritage trails. Such trails allow a general public audience to 'digitally visit' a site through immersive and interactive digital experiences. Think of a video game where you can control your character to move around the game world, but this time the game world is an exact copy of a real archaeological site for you to explore.

What are some ways to protect an important cultural heritage site that is being damaged by uncontrolled visitor access? Are some of your solutions likely to limit the public's access to and enjoyment of the site?

What can you do to maximize public access while ensuring the site is protected? What are some signs that a site is not being managed correctly, etc.? What can you do to prevent such things from happening e.g. trash around the site, graffiti, modern constructions on top of site remains?

What's happening at 3:40?

TOPIC	THEME hours	QUESTION minutes	THEME + QUESTION = INQUIRY
Access to sites Versus Protecting archaeology	3 Ethical Values	40 How can collaboration help with this?	3:40

Figure 4.7 How to use the Clock Tool© to generate time and inquiry about access to sites versus protecting archaeology.
Source: Graphic created by the authors.

3 o' clock: Ethical values: Respect, trust and integrity
40 minutes: How can collaboration help with this? Collaborations are essential for the protection of cultural heritage sites.

- The research archaeologist will typically work with government organizations tasked with the management of archaeological sites, and there is often an active exchange of data and information regarding research progress.
- The archaeologist also works closely with local community members, who play a key role in ensuring that management of significant cultural heritage sites is aligned with community expectations. Communities can also be involved in the day-to-day monitoring of sites that are otherwise difficult for government officials and supervisors to actively keep an eye on.
- Students can, through citizen science initiatives, also help develop a better understanding of the type and extent of archaeological sites in a given area. Actively collaborating with the community greatly increases public awareness of the importance of cultural heritage and increases the sustainability of protection programs.
- Museums and universities also play a key role in developing educational programs that can help the general public develop a greater appreciation of their heritage. Together such partnerships are based on mutual respect, trust and integrity to ensure healthy collaborations and positive heritage outcomes.

Questions for Students

- What role could students play in protecting archaeological sites?
- Would you like to be involved in field schools where you can learn about archaeology?
- Do you know of any archaeology programs in your city or area where you can volunteer to help out?

Figure 4.8 Image of a stone anchor.
Source: Image credit Amer Bazl Khan.

2. Ethical Dilemma about Salvage/Looting versus Archaeological Investigations

Archaeologists are not the only ones interested in historical sites. The RMS *Titanic* sank in 1912, when she collided with an iceberg during her maiden voyage. The exact location of the *Titanic* remained unknown until in 1985, the wreck was finally located by a joint French-American expedition led by Jean-Louis Michel and Robert Ballard of the Woods Hole Oceanographic Institution. Since the finding of the wreck there has been intense debate about the ownership of the vessel. The site is located in international waters, beyond the jurisdiction of any one country, so it has remained unclear who has a right to control access to the site. The shipwreck has therefore been subject to several looting and illegal salvage attempts where people have tried to recover items from the wreck. However, given the depth of the site (over 12,500 feet), where the pressure is over 6,000 pounds per square inch, the site is relatively difficult to reach for most people. This has given archaeologists the opportunity to investigate the site while it still remains mostly undisturbed. Some items have been recovered, not from the wreck site itself, but from the debris field around it, that have been included in museum exhibitions for the general public.

Questions for Students

- Is it okay to recover items from a shipwreck site where many people lost their lives?
- Should we recover items from such sites for the general public to learn and understand what happened, or should we leave such sites alone?

There are people who target archaeological sites for other reasons, and sometimes these can be detrimental to the integrity of the sites and can lead to the sites being destroyed. Some of these people actively seek out and salvage items from the sites and that can result in loss of information about the site and its ultimate destruction.

Some Ethical Issues to Consider

Why is salvage and looting of a site different from archaeological excavation? Who ultimately owns an archaeological site or artifact? Such sites have value to all of humanity, so is it alright for someone to take these items for themselves and sell them for their own private gain? What is wrong with recovering and selling artifacts?

What's happening at 12:10?

TOPIC	THEME hours	QUESTION minutes	THEME + QUESTION = INQUIRY
Salvage/Looting versus Archaeological investigations	12 Challenges and issues	10 Human innovation (or Biomimicry)	**12:10**

Figure 4.9 How to use the Clock Tool to generate time and inquiry about salvage/looting versus archaeological investigations.
Source: Graphic created by the authors.

12 o'clock challenges and issues + 10 minutes—Human innovation (or biomimicry)

Recent innovations have enabled heritage professionals to protect sites from being disturbed by looters. For example, certain significant shipwreck sites can have buffer zones defined around them to prevent people from going there without a permit. However, it is difficult to monitor these zones to ensure people are actually not entering them. One solution has been to install acoustic and sonar buoys over the sites to detect any vessels entering the buffer zones. The sonar buoys can measure the distance, speed and direction of an approaching vessel based on the characteristics of how sound travels through water and is very similar to how whales communicate with each other over long distances. Once a vessel is detected, a message is sent to local authorities to come and check on the site, while a camera begins recording the activities of the intruding vessel (A. B. Khan, personal communication, November 15, 2023).

Applications

- Investigating the use of renewable energy sources and the impact of these on the world carbon emissions.
- Reflecting on the impact of deforestation on Indigenous populations.
- Examining data of the rate of ice melt in Antarctica and the implications for coastal environments.
- Widening community involvement in the school recycling program.
- Investigating how effective your school's environmental policy is.
- Reflecting on what assumptions students make when they collaborate.
- Supporting the development of school values and mission.
- Examining bias in artificial intelligence (AI) tools and technologies.
- Being more open-minded about the views of people whose beliefs are different from their own (advisory, social emotional learning).
- Discussion of issues relating to civic education, multiculturalism (cultural pluralism) in increasingly polarized times (social studies).

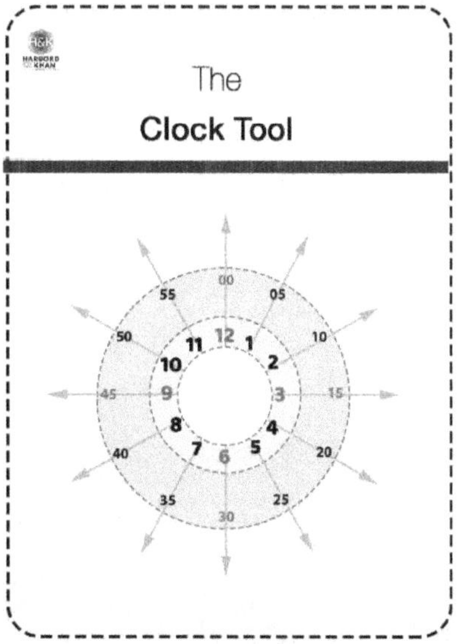
The
Clock Tool
00
05
10
15
20
25
30
35
40
45
50
55
12
1
2
3
4
5
6
7
8
9
10
11

Figure 4.10 The Clock Tool card.
Source: Graphic created by the authors.

- What does it mean to be a digital citizen?
- Reflecting on prejudice and assumption towards subjects students find more challenging at the start of the semester.
- Generating ideas for projects and community activities—are students thinking about age, gender, race, the differently abled, social justice issues, etc.?
- Critically thinking about prejudice in their interactions with others (online and offline).
- Evaluating resources with a focus on fake news, misrepresentation, sponsorship e.g. 'greenwashing'.
- Questioning the accuracy of research—this is most often done on WEIRD (white, educated, industrialized, rich, and democratic) populations.
- Stereotypes in advertising, media and online platforms (visual arts, media arts, English language arts: literacy).

Subject Suggestions

Environmental science, geography, humanities, individuals and societies, language arts, language and literature, personal, social health and economic education, science and theory of knowledge (TOK).

Suggestions to Align Skills with the Tools

Teachers can share this checklist with students to support them in identifying their higher-order thinking and social emotional skills.

I can make decisions that are fair and impartial.
12
9
3
6

Figure 4.11 Caterpillar on a clock.
Source: Artwork by Linda Weil©.

Table 4.4 Suggestions to align higher-order thinking and social emotional learning skills with the tool.

Critical and Creative Thinking Skills for Problem-Solving		Social Emotional Learning Skills
☐ I can analyze and evaluate issues and my ideas. ☐ I can consider ideas from multiple perspectives. ☐ I can break up complicated ideas into different parts and reassemble them to develop new understanding. ☐ I can check the accuracy of facts and interpretations. ☐ I can analyze and evaluate my emotions. ☐ I can verify the accuracy of research that was generated using AI tools.	☐ I can use different creative strategies that make thinking visible. ☐ I can use my existing knowledge to create novel concepts, products or processes.	☐ I am curious and open-minded. ☐ I understand that I have a responsibility to behave in an ethical way. ☐ I can find possible ways to problem-solve for myself and society. ☐ I can plan for and evaluate what the consequences of my actions will be. ☐ I understand what empathy is and can empathize with others. ☐ I can reflect on my own, my family's and my community's well-being. ☐ I can make decisions that are fair and impartial. ☐ I care about others' feelings and the impact of my actions on them. ☐ I take action to support others' well-being.

Source: Graphic created by the authors.

Questions for Students to Support Higher-Order Thinking Skills

Table 4.5 Questions for students.

1. Did combining the themes and the questions give you new ideas about your topic?
2. It's 6:25—How can 'Making decisions about the future' + 'What action can I take?' influence your choices? Give an example.

Source: Graphic created by the authors.

Teacher Reflection

KEY TAKEAWAY: Exploring topics and ethical dilemmas through personal, community and global perspectives. Learning from the past and looking to the future to consider our actions and their consequences.

- Describe the scenario and classroom context—what was the problem you wanted to address with this tool?
- Did you achieve your goal?
- How did you use the tool to support students' higher-order thinking skills (HOTS)?

Multiple perspectives: The Clock Tool, The Detective Tool, The Points of View Tool, The Time Tunnel Tool and The Zig-Zag Tool.

Chapter Notes

Use this space to plan and write your personal thoughts, ideas and questions here:

Create your mind-map or sketch out your ideas

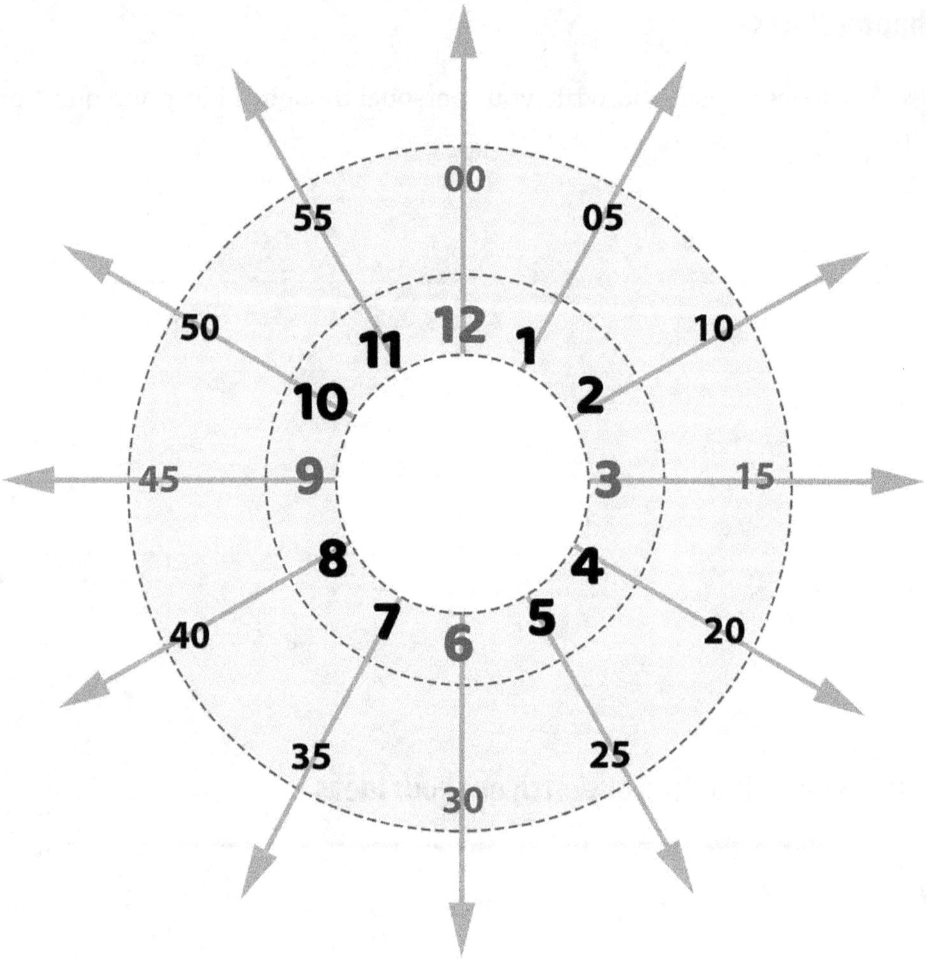
00
05
10
15
20
25
30
35
40
45
50
55
12
1
2
3
4
5
6
7
8
9
10
11

Figure 4.12 The Clock Tool template.
Source: Graphic created by the authors.

Definitions

Biomimicry: the design and production of materials, structures and systems that are modeled on biological entities and processes.
Ethical values: the beliefs people have, especially about what is right and wrong and what is most important in life, that control their behavior.
Global impact: a powerful effect relating to the whole world.
Human innovation: a new method, idea or product created by a human.
Open-minded: willing to consider ideas and opinions that are new or different from your own.

The definitions in this list are sourced from Cambridge Online Dictionary (2023), Merriam-Webster Dictionary (2023) and Oxford Learners Dictionaries (2023).

References

Cambridge University Press & Assessment (Ed.). (2023). *Cambridge online dictionary*. Retrieved November 14, 2023, from https://dictionary.cambridge.org/

Oxford University Press (Ed.). (2023). *Oxford learners dictionaries*. Retrieved November 15, 2023, from www.oxfordlearnersdictionaries.com

5

The Design for the Need Tool

Criteria Checklist

Suggested Grade Level: 6–10

Key Takeaway—Guiding students in thinking about different aspects or criteria for their projects.

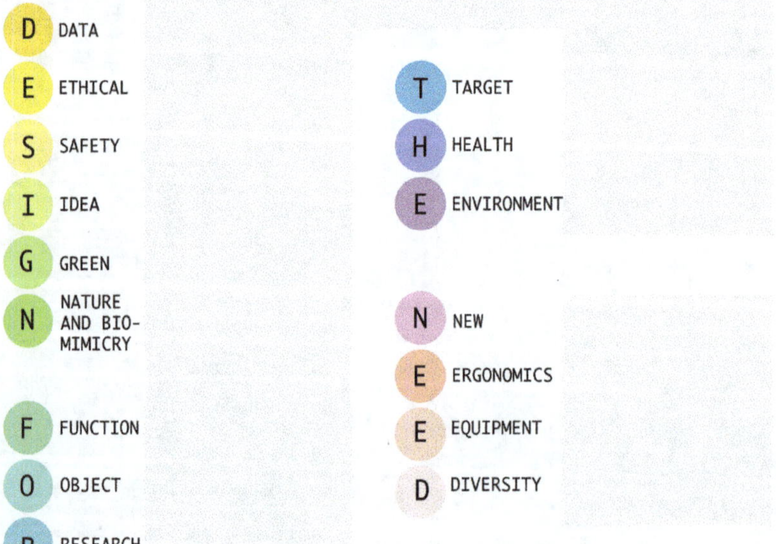
D DATA
E ETHICAL
S SAFETY
I IDEA
G GREEN
N NATURE AND BIO-MIMICRY
F FUNCTION
O OBJECT
R RESEARCH
T TARGET
H HEALTH
E ENVIRONMENT
N NEW
E ERGONOMICS
E EQUIPMENT
D DIVERSITY

Figure 5.1 The Design for the Need Tool.
Source: Graphic created by the authors.

DOI: 10.4324/9781032664989-6

Global Skills and Key Themes

Skills: Critical thinking, creative thinking, idea generation and problem-solving.
Themes: Design, diversity, inclusion, empathy, ethical perspectives, real-world issues, service and sustainability.

Stories

FROM THE CLASSROOM: Investigating natural disasters—Grade 8 students from ABA International School.
FROM THE WORLD: DIY flashlight kit of children in refugee camps and Joaquin Bur, an Autonomous Vehicle Program Manager.
DEFINITIONS: Biomimicry, diversity, criteria, design specifications ergonomics, ethical and sustainability (p. 86).

What Does the Design for the Need Tool Do?

This tool can guide students in thinking about different aspects or criteria for their projects in most subjects with a focus on inclusion, diversity, and sustainability.

This tool can be used with the design cycle or design thinking (or, in fact, any learning cycle). This is an excellent checklist to see if you have all the areas you wish to cover with your design specifications and to support the planning of the project.

Homeroom teachers can ask students to think about situations in which they might use the tool to support their critical and creative thinking skills such as community projects or celebrations, the development of unused spaces on campus, planning extracurricular activities, etc.

How to Use It

1. Choose your topic that you need to generate criteria for e.g. your product, activity or event.
2. Look at the definitions of any words you don't know or understand.
3. Use each of the words e.g. data and safety to generate ideas and design specifications/criteria.

Defining Criteria and Design Specifications for Students

Students may be familiar with these terms, but it is worth revisiting these so it is clear as to why these are used:

- Design criteria are sometimes known as success criteria, and they are similar, as they both explain the goals that a project must achieve in order to be successful.
- Design specifications detail exactly what a product or a process should have.

These terms are used in engineering projects, architectural projects, advertising, manufacturing and design (fashion, graphic, industrial, product, textile).

You probably won't use all the criteria, only what's relevant for your current project e.g. designing a toothbrush: S for Safety, F for Function, H for Health, T for Target audience and E for Ergonomics. Each letter stands for a word that can help students think about design specifications e.g. 'I' for IDEA.

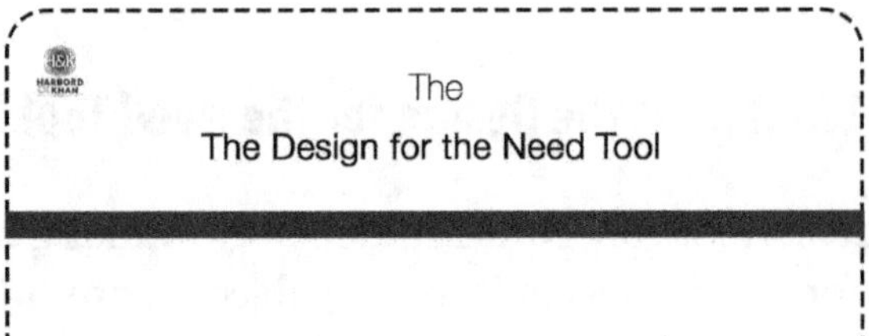
The
The Design for the Need Tool
D DATA
E ETHICAL
S SAFETY
I IDEA
G GREEN
N NATURE AND BIO-MIMICRY
F FUNCTION
O OBJECT
R RESEARCH
T TARGET
H HEALTH
E ENVIRONMENT
N NEW
E ERGONOMICS
E EQUIPMENT
D DIVERSITY

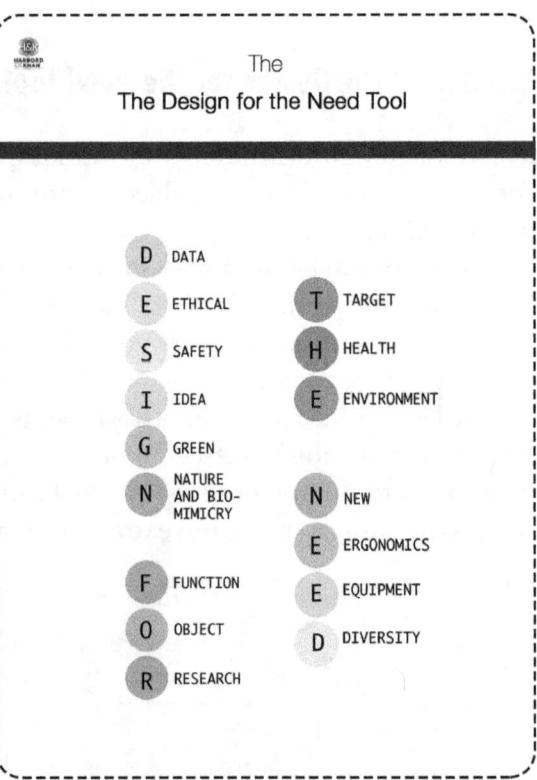

Figure 5.2 The Design for the Need Tool card.
Source: Graphic created by the authors.

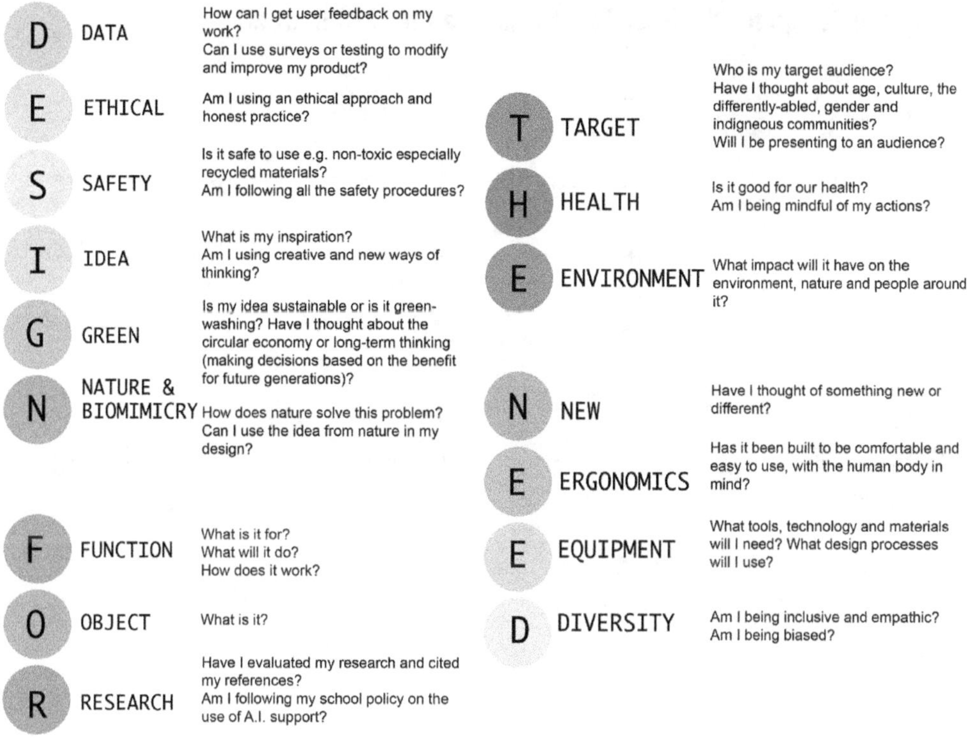
D DATA
How can I get user feedback on my work?
Can I use surveys or testing to modify and improve my product?
E ETHICAL
Am I using an ethical approach and honest practice?
S SAFETY
Is it safe to use e.g. non-toxic especially recycled materials?
Am I following all the safety procedures?
I IDEA
What is my inspiration?
Am I using creative and new ways of thinking?
G GREEN
Is my idea sustainable or is it green-washing? Have I thought about the circular economy or long-term thinking (making decisions based on the benefit for future generations)?
N NATURE & BIOMIMICRY
How does nature solve this problem?
Can I use the idea from nature in my design?
F FUNCTION
What is it for?
What will it do?
How does it work?
O OBJECT
What is it?
R RESEARCH
Have I evaluated my research and cited my references?
Am I following my school policy on the use of A.I. support?
T TARGET
Who is my target audience?
Have I thought about age, culture, the differently-abled, gender and indigneous communities?
Will I be presenting to an audience?
H HEALTH
Is it good for our health?
Am I being mindful of my actions?
E ENVIRONMENT
What impact will it have on the environment, nature and people around it?
N NEW
Have I thought of something new or different?
E ERGONOMICS
Has it been built to be comfortable and easy to use, with the human body in mind?
E EQUIPMENT
What tools, technology and materials will I need? What design processes will I use?
D DIVERSITY
Am I being inclusive and empathic?
Am I being biased?

Figure 5.3 The Design for the Need Tool with criteria questions.
Source: Graphic created by the authors.

EXAMPLE 1 Flashlight Kit for Children in Refugee Camps

Scenario: Design a DIY flashlight kit for children in refugee camps that is easy to make and teaches them about science and electricity.

Using a real-life example, let's unpack the design using The Design for the Need Tool.

Pentagram is a multidisciplinary, independently owned design studio with 22 practicing designers based in New York and London who partnered with a social enterprise group called Ambressa Play. This company makes educational science, technology, engineering and mathematics (STEM) do-it-yourself (DIY) kits and provides a free kit for a displaced child for every kit sold. The design is a flat pack kit of parts that make a small compact flashlight with a removable winder that will fit in a pocket and be made by the child. The bonus feature is that while making the kit the child will learn about electricity (Aouf, 2023; May, 2023).

Using the Design for the Need Tool to Explore the Flashlight Kit

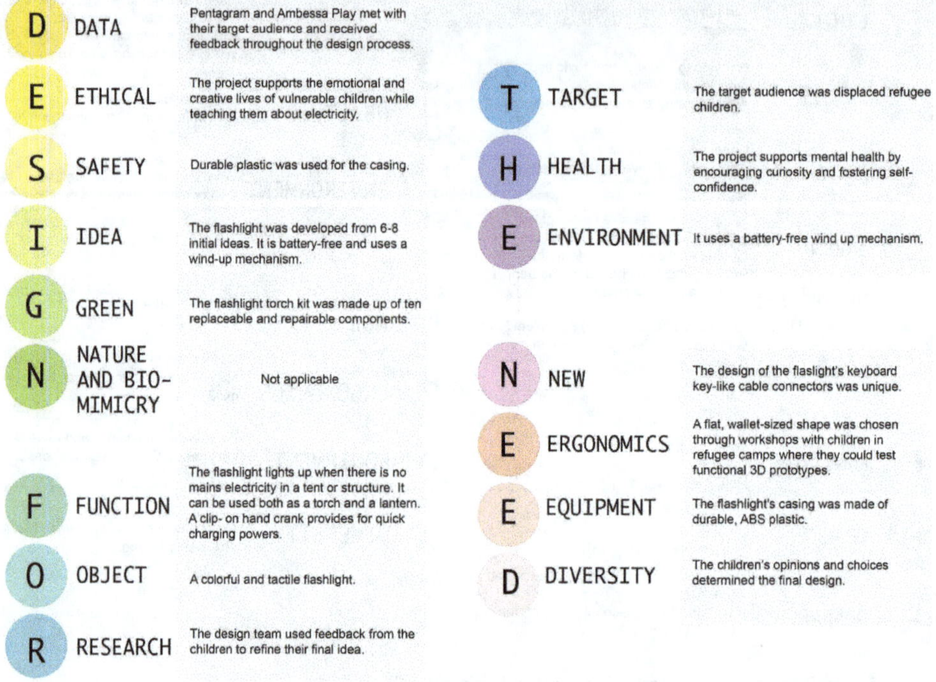
D DATA
Pentagram and Ambessa Play met with their target audience and received feedback throughout the design process.
E ETHICAL
The project supports the emotional and creative lives of vulnerable children while teaching them about electricity.
S SAFETY
Durable plastic was used for the casing.
I IDEA
The flashlight was developed from 6-8 initial ideas. It is battery-free and uses a wind-up mechanism.
G GREEN
The flashlight torch kit was made up of ten replaceable and repairable components.
N NATURE AND BIO-MIMICRY
Not applicable
F FUNCTION
The flashlight lights up when there is no mains electricity in a tent or structure. It can be used both as a torch and a lantern. A clip- on hand crank provides for quick charging powers.
O OBJECT
A colorful and tactile flashlight.
R RESEARCH
The design team used feedback from the children to refine their final idea.
T TARGET
The target audience was displaced refugee children.
H HEALTH
The project supports mental health by encouraging curiosity and fostering self-confidence.
E ENVIRONMENT
It uses a battery-free wind up mechanism.
N NEW
The design of the flaslight's keyboard key-like cable connectors was unique.
E ERGONOMICS
A flat, wallet-sized shape was chosen through workshops with children in refugee camps where they could test functional 3D prototypes.
E EQUIPMENT
The flashlight's casing was made of durable, ABS plastic.
D DIVERSITY
The children's opinions and choices determined the final design.

Figure 5.4 Using the Design for the Need Tool to explore the flashlight kit.

STORIES FROM THE CLASSROOM

Grade 8 students used the tool to generate at least six specifications for a product that will help people who have lost their homes due to natural disasters e.g. an emergency shelter, water purification or medical kits, food supplies or supply delivery drones.

A Grade 8 student from ABA Oman International School, Gabriel Diaz da Silva, generated design specifications for a portable jump-starter for cars:

- **DATA** We must run tests on the jump-starter to make sure it can survive a solar flare.
- **SAFETY** The jump-starter must have a built-in countermeasure for short circuits and solar flares.
- **FUNCTION** The jump-starter must be able to start up a car battery.
- **TARGET AUDIENCE** We should build the product with the target audience in mind.

Figure 5.5 Flooded streets.
Source: Photo credit Chris Gallagher on Unsplash.

- **ERGONOMICS** The product must be easy to use and require little prior knowledge to function.
- **EQUIPMENT** The product must not require external equipment (G. D. da Silva, personal communication, November 2, 2023).

Another Grade 8 student from ABA Oman International School, Burhanuddin Dairkee, generated design specifications for a tent for sheltering displaced people:

- **SAFETY** I will use fabric that is durable and hard to rip and tear.
- **IDEA** A tent for shelter.
- **FUNCTION** The tent will help people have a temporary roof over their head and protect them from the rain or anything like it.
- **OBJECT:** An igloo-like structure tent.
- **TARGET AUDIENCE** People who have lost their home and need somewhere to live.
- **ERGONOMICS** Uses an igloo-like shape for space, is easy to set up as you only need a rod in the middle and is easy to fold into a ball.
- **EQUIPMENT** I will need fabric and metal (B. Dairkee, personal communication, November 16, 2023).

STORIES FROM THE WORLD

Autonomous Vehicles

Joaquin Bur, an autonomous vehicle program manager from Florida, used the tool to think about designing and making a self-driving car (J. Bur, personal communication, November 4, 2023).

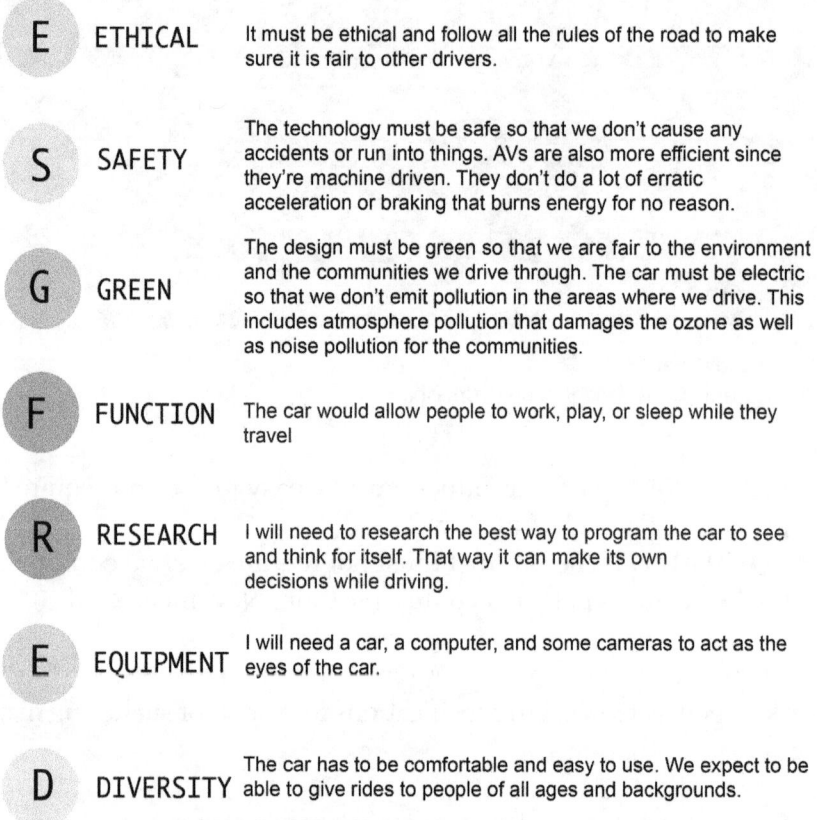

E	ETHICAL	It must be ethical and follow all the rules of the road to make sure it is fair to other drivers.
S	SAFETY	The technology must be safe so that we don't cause any accidents or run into things. AVs are also more efficient since they're machine driven. They don't do a lot of erratic acceleration or braking that burns energy for no reason.
G	GREEN	The design must be green so that we are fair to the environment and the communities we drive through. The car must be electric so that we don't emit pollution in the areas where we drive. This includes atmosphere pollution that damages the ozone as well as noise pollution for the communities.
F	FUNCTION	The car would allow people to work, play, or sleep while they travel
R	RESEARCH	I will need to research the best way to program the car to see and think for itself. That way it can make its own decisions while driving.
E	EQUIPMENT	I will need a car, a computer, and some cameras to act as the eyes of the car.
D	DIVERSITY	The car has to be comfortable and easy to use. We expect to be able to give rides to people of all ages and backgrounds.

Figure 5.6 Exploring aspects of autonomous vehicle design using The Design for the Need Tool.
Source: Graphic created by the authors.

The Design for the Need Tool was originally created when we were teaching design in middle and high school, as the students often struggled to include all the criteria needed to create their projects. This was very useful to remind them of what was needed to fulfill the requirements for 21st-century design. However, the tool has a wider application and can be used in other subjects as well, for example, in science, English language arts, engineering design and humanities—in fact, any project that requires planning.

Suggestions to Align Skills With the Tools

Teachers can share this checklist with students to support them in identifying their higher-order thinking and social emotional skills.

Table 5.1 Suggestions to align higher-order thinking and social emotional learning skills with the tool.

Critical and Creative Thinking Skills for Problem-Solving	Social Emotional Learning Skills
Critical Thinking Skills ☐ I can recognize and evaluate concepts and theories. ☐ I can investigate the design challenge and research existing products. ☐ I can propose and evaluate a variety of solutions. ☐ I can practice observing carefully in order to recognize problems and improve and modify designs. **Creative Thinking Skills** ☐ I can use different creative strategies that make thinking visible. ☐ I use brainstorming and visual diagrams to create and develop ideas, connections and inquiries. ☐ I can modify existing tools and technologies and design new ones.	☐ I can find possible ways to problem-solve for myself and society. ☐ I understand what empathy is and can empathize with others. ☐ I care about others' feelings and the impact of my actions on them. ☐ I take action to support others' well-being. ☐ I understand that I have a responsibility to behave in an ethical way.

Source: Graphic created by the authors.

Questions for Students to Support Higher-Order Thinking Skills

Table 5.2 Questions for students.

1. Did The Design for the Need Tool make writing design specifications easier?
2. Think of another project or situation that you could use The Design for the Need Tool in and explain why it would be useful.

Source: Graphic created by the authors.

Teacher Reflection

KEY TAKEAWAY—Developing inclusive and ethical criteria when designing and creating products and activities.

- Describe the scenario and classroom context—what was the problem you wanted to address with this tool?
- Did you achieve your goal?
- How did you use the tool to support students' higher-order thinking skills (HOTS)?

Complement With Other Tools

Design: The Ethical Charter Tool.

Chapter Notes

Use this space to plan and write your personal thoughts, ideas and questions here:

Create your mind-map or sketch out your idea

Generating My Specifications

I am going to design (and make) . . .

Table 5.3 Student design specifications.

DATA	
ETHICAL	
SAFETY	
IDEA	
GREEN	
NATURE/BIOMIMICRY	
FUNCTION	
OBJECT	
RESEARCH	
TARGET	
HEALTH	
ENVIRONMENT	
NEW	
ERGONOMICS	
EQUIPMENT	
DIVERSITY	

Source: Graphic created by the authors.

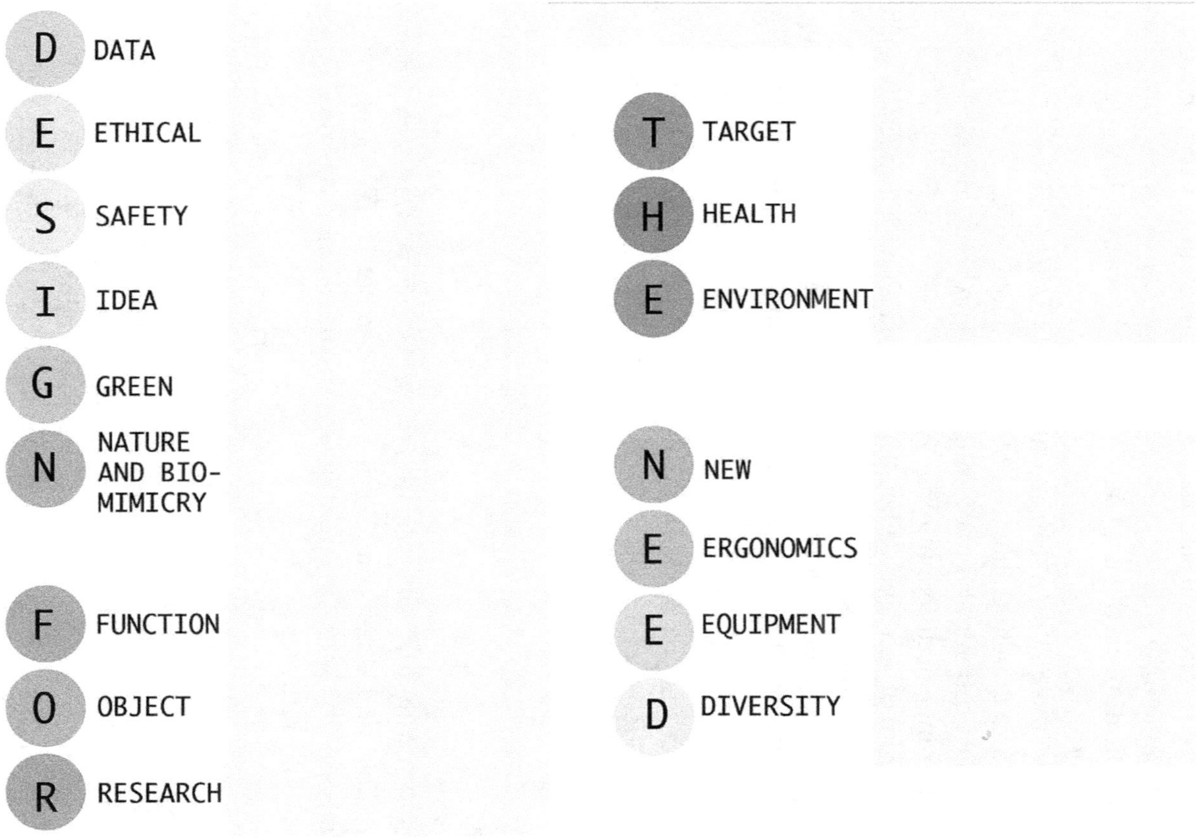
D DATA
E ETHICAL
S SAFETY
I IDEA
G GREEN
N NATURE AND BIO-MIMICRY
F FUNCTION
O OBJECT
R RESEARCH
T TARGET
H HEALTH
E ENVIRONMENT
N NEW
E ERGONOMICS
E EQUIPMENT
D DIVERSITY

Figure 5.7 The Design for the Need Tool template.
Source: Graphic created by the authors.

Definitions

Biomimicry: the design and production of materials, structures and systems that are modeled on biological entities and processes.
Criteria, plural of criterion: standards by which you judge, decide about or deal with something.
Design specifications: a detailed description of how something should be done, made, etc.
Sustainability: the quality of causing little or no damage to the environment and therefore able to continue for a long time.
Diversity: many different types of things or people being included in something; a range of different things or people.
Ethical: a system of accepted beliefs that control behavior, especially such a system based on morals.
Ergonomics: an applied science concerned with designing and arranging things people use so that the people and things interact most efficiently and safely.

The definitions in this list are sourced from Cambridge Online Dictionary (2023), Merriam-Webster Dictionary (2023) and Oxford Learners Dictionaries (2023).

References

Aouf, R. S. (2023, May 10). *Pentagram works with child refugees to design Ambessa Play flashlight kit*. Dezeen.com. Retrieved November 15, 2023, from www.dezeen.com/2023/05/10/pentagram-designs-ambessa-play-flashlight-kit-child-refugees/

Cambridge Press (Ed.). (2023, November 16). *Dictionary.Cambridge*. Cambridge Online Dictionary. Retrieved December 3, 2023, from https://dictionary.cambridge.org/

May, T. (2023, April 6). *Clever DIY flashlight offers a fun way to teach your kids and help a child refugee*. Creative boom.com. Retrieved November 15, 2023, from www.creativeboom.com/news/diy-flashlight/

Merriam-Webster (Ed.). (2023). *Merriam-Webster dictionary*. Merriam-Webster.com. Retrieved November 15, 2023, from www.merriam-webster.com/

Oxford learners dictionaries (Ed.). (2023). *Oxford learners dictionaries*. Oxford University Press. www.oxfordlearnersdictionaries.com

6

The Detective Tool

Gathering Evidence

Suggested Grade Level: 6–8

Key Takeaway—Analysis and inquiry generation to promote deeper understanding from multiple perspectives.

TOPIC	
IDENTIFY & DESCRIBE	What is the situation or context? Who or what does this involve?
REASONS	Why has this happened? Can you see it from different points of view?
PROCESSES	What are the systems or processes involved?
TIME & PLACE	Where and when?
ETHICAL VALUE	What ethical value(s) can you identify?

Figure 6.1 The Detective Tool.
Source: Graphic created by the authors.

DOI: 10.4324/9781032664989-7

Global Skills and Key Themes

Skills: Communication, critical thinking, creative thinking, problem-solving and inquiry generation.
Themes: Empathy, ethical values, multiple perspectives, real-world issues, sustainability and systems.

Stories

FROM THE CLASSROOM: Investigating natural disasters—Grade 8 student from ABA Oman International School.
FROM THE WORLD: Architecture for those displaced by natural disasters—award winning architect Dr. Yasmeen Lari.
DEFINITIONS: Detect, ethical values, evidence and fairness (p 102).

What Does The Detective Tool Do?

The Detective Tool is a versatile tool that guides and generates inquiry. It can help students to focus their initial topic ideas and research.

Often students are asked to provide evidence to support an article or justify an opinion. This graphic tool helps break up the topic so students can examine it from differing viewpoints e.g. identify and describe it, define reasons for it, reflect on the processes or systems involved, place the topic within a particular time and place and consider which ethical values can be addressed while discussing it.

Using ethical values intentionally as part of the inquiry process can generate challenging questions that evoke strong emotions. Suddenly, the topic can become more personal and relatable for students.

How to Use It

1. Choose your topic.
2. Use the five headings 'Identify & Describe', 'Reasons', 'Processes', Time & Place' and 'Ethical Value' as clues to guide your inquiry.

EXAMPLE 1 Student Activity

TOPIC: The use of water in a river.
How can this be allocated fairly between the farmers, townspeople, water sports enthusiasts and environmentalists?

IDENTIFY & DESCRIBE	What is at stake? Whose needs should be met?
REASONS	Why is there conflict? What are the issues and diffferent viewpoints?
PROCESSES	How can we allocate water fairly? How can we strike a balance?
TIME & PLACE	Present time, the river.
ETHICAL VALUE	Fairness.

Figure 6.2 Exploring the distribution of water using The Detective Tool.
Source: Graphic created by the authors.

Give your students the topic and divide them into small groups. Each group must discuss, debate and report on the group findings about the concept of fair use of water. The graphic illustrates how a particular river is allocated between all the different stakeholders who want access e.g. the farmers, townspeople, watersport enthusiasts and environmentalists. All have valid reasons for wanting their share, so what is fair?

STORIES FROM THE CLASSROOM

Figure 6.3 Volcanic eruption.
Source: Photo credit Toby Elliott on Unsplash

> *A Grade 8 student from ABA Oman International School, Mohammed Firas Al Abduwani, was investigating the eruption of Mount Vesuvius. He analyzed the processes and systems involved in this disaster and also noted that there had been warning signs prior to the big eruption.*

Reflecting on including the impact of an ethical value such as trust in his inquiry, Firas commented, "I think trust could have been a major value to help because some people did evacuate due to the signs before the big eruption, which were mini eruptions and earthquakes. I think other people didn't believe in these warnings because of the lack of knowledge; however, if they trusted others they could have avoided all these deaths" (M. F. Al Abduwani, personal communication, November 16, 2023).

STORIES FROM THE WORLD

Dr. Yasmeen Lari—Global Visionary—Building Homes, Building Lives

Architect and philanthropist Dr. Yasmeen Lari promotes low-cost, zero-carbon and zero-waste methodologies based on vernacular heritage and renewable materials, such as earth, lime and bamboo. Her awards include the Pakistani national awards Sitara-i-Imtiaz and Hilal-i-Imtiaz, the Fukuoka Prize and Jane Drew Prize as well as the Royal Gold Medal in architecture from the Royal Institute of British Architects.

TOPIC: How can sustainable architecture support people who have been displaced through natural disasters?

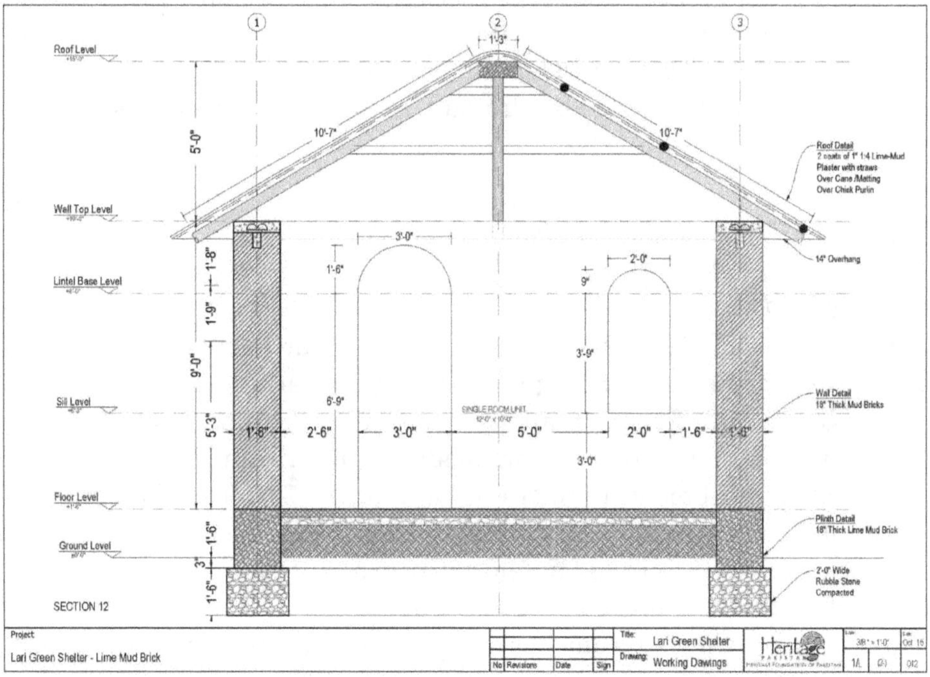

Roof Level
Wall Top Level
Lintel Base Level
Sill Level
Floor Level
Ground Level
SECTION 12
5'-0"
9'-0"
1'-8"
1'-9"
5'-3"
1'-6"
3"
10'-7"
1'-3"
3'-0"
1'-6"
6'-9"
2'-6"
5'-0"
2'-0"
9"
3'-9"
SINGLE ROOM UNIT
Roof Detail
2 coats of 1" 1:4 Lime-Mud
Plaster with straws
Over Cane /Matting
Over Chick Purlin
14" Overhang
Wall Detail
18" Thick Mud Bricks
Plinth Detail
18" Thick Lime Mud Brick
2'-0" Wide
Rubble Stone
Compacted
Project
Lari Green Shelter - Lime Mud Brick
No
Revisions
Date
Sign
Title:
Lari Green Shelter
Drawing:
Working Dawings
Heritage
Oct 15
012

Figure 6.4 Lari green shelter—lime brick conical roof.
Source: Image courtesy ©Heritage Foundation of Pakistan

Identify and Describe

Dr. Lari's greatest concern in her work is the issue of displacement of people through natural disasters. "Every time a disaster happens, people have to leave, women and children especially are the worst sufferers. Anyone who hasn't experienced displacement cannot understand the depth of anguish, pain and helplessness when you have to move from your own home to somewhere else. People have to leave for many months before they can restart living their lives, because if you are displaced you can't live your life."

Reasons

Why Sustainable Architecture?

Since her retirement from architectural practice in 2000, Dr. Lari has engaged in heritage management and humanitarian architecture with a focus on sustainability. She has been published among 60 women who have contributed the most toward United Nations Educational, Scientific and Cultural Organization' (UNESCO's) objectives. The climate emergency has exacerbated flooding, drought and earthquakes all over the world. Dr. Lari commented that "Water disasters are the most common disasters in the world today, more than 50% of all disasters are water related, either floods, tsunamis, rising sea levels, rains themselves and also drought, as that means there is no water".

Processes

Testing and Prototypes

Dr. Lari explained, "My first effort is to see how I can avoid displacement for everybody, whether by flooding or as a result of earthquakes. We have different models for different situations; our earthquake model is tested on the 'shaking table test', because they are made out of earth and bamboo lattice. It was tested on movements of the Kobe earthquake, 7.3 [on the] Richter scale. They tested first up to 275% and there was not even a crack, later going on to 670% when the walls buckled but no collapse occurred.

In Sindh, the bamboo structures that survived were built in 2014 and were subjected to a few feet of water standing for 2 months but remained structurally sound".

Training and Sustainable Innovation

Dr. Lari's teams train people to build their own homes. The structures can be adapted to local environments and are inspired by Indigenous construction techniques. Dr. Lari's innovation has been to use bamboo, which has never been done before, as she didn't want to use wood. She explained that "The roof is like an umbrella, so that it folds, so everything can be packed away and sent off anywhere, so that is the ease of construction and no water is being used".

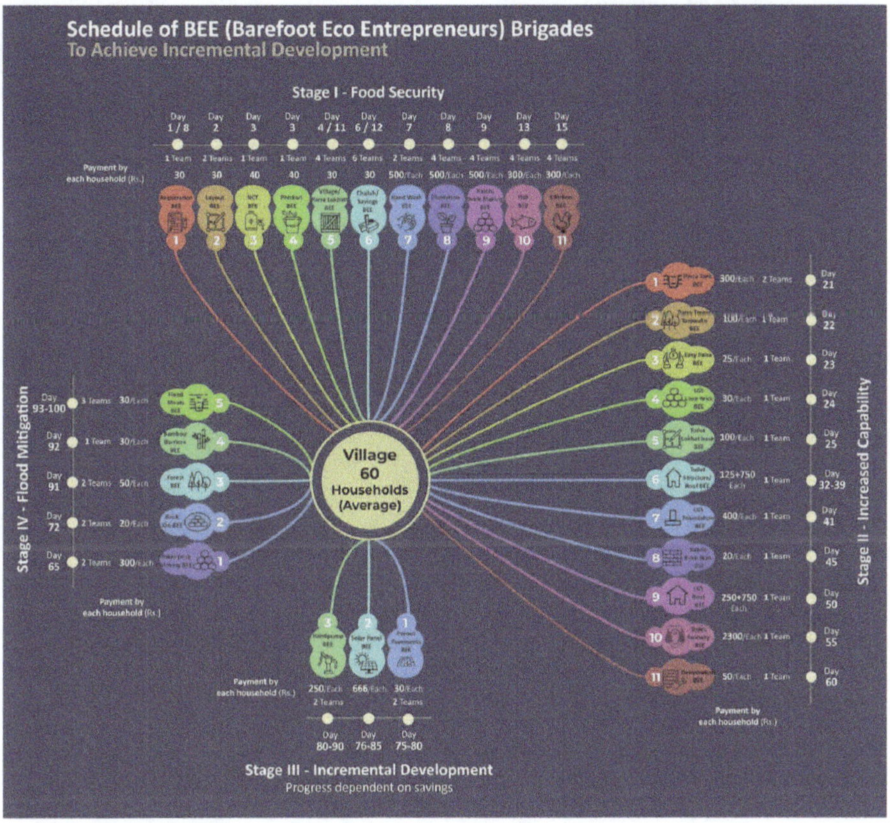
Schedule of BEE (Barefoot Eco Entrepreneurs) Brigades
To Achieve Incremental Development
Stage I - Food Security
Day 1/8
Day 2
Day 3
Day 3
Day 4/11
Day 6/12
Day 7
Day 8
Day 9
Day 13
Day 15
1 Team
2 Teams
1 Team
1 Team
4 Teams
6 Teams
2 Teams
4 Teams
4 Teams
4 Teams
4 Teams
Payment by each household (Rs.)
30
30
40
40
30
30
500/Each
500/Each
500/Each
300/Each
300/Each
1
2
3
4
5
6
7
8
9
10
11
Village
60
Households
(Average)
Stage II - Increased Capability
1
300/Each
2 Teams
Day 21
2
100/Each
1 Team
Day 22
3
25/Each
1 Team
Day 23
4
30/Each
1 Team
Day 24
5
100/Each
1 Team
Day 25
6
125+750 Each
1 Team
Day 32-39
7
400/Each
1 Team
Day 41
8
20/Each
1 Team
Day 45
9
250+750 Each
1 Team
Day 50
10
2300/Each
1 Team
Day 55
11
50/Each
1 Team
Day 60
Payment by each household (Rs.)
Stage IV - Flood Mitigation
Day 93-100
3 Teams
30/Each
5
Day 92
1 Team
30/Each
4
Day 91
2 Teams
50/Each
3
Day 72
2 Teams
20/Each
2
Day 65
2 Teams
300/Each
1
Payment by each household (Rs.)
3
2
1
Payment by each household (Rs.)
250/Each
666/Each
30/Each
2 Teams
2 Teams
Day 80-90
Day 76-85
Day 75-80
Stage III - Incremental Development
Progress dependent on savings

Figure 6.5 Zero donor model.
Source: Image courtesy of ©Heritage Foundation of Pakistan.

Her aim is to transfer skills to people so that they can fend for themselves. Dr. Lari describes how "the holistic model achieves rights-based development in stage 1, in stage 2 they achieve food security, while in stage 3 they begin to implement flood mitigation measures and stage 4 provides them with skills for barefoot livelihoods. In 6 months they start becoming self-sufficient".

Time and Place

In the future, architectural designs for Pakistan: Dr. Lari observed that after the 2022 floods, there was an unprecedented phenomena: the water didn't recede. In her opinion floating houses that rise and subside according to the water level and have already been designed are the best solution. The materials Lari champions are also widespread in time and place: she points out that building in earth was once common and lime was used before the Common Era (BCE). She acts local, in other words, but thinks global.

ETHICAL VALUES Caring, empathy and respect

Dr. Lari commented, "My vision today is to deliver safe structures to anyone in my country at risk of displacement". Her vision means these techniques could have applications in any country or place that has the need for safe shelter (Y. Lari, personal communication, August 30, 2023).

Applications

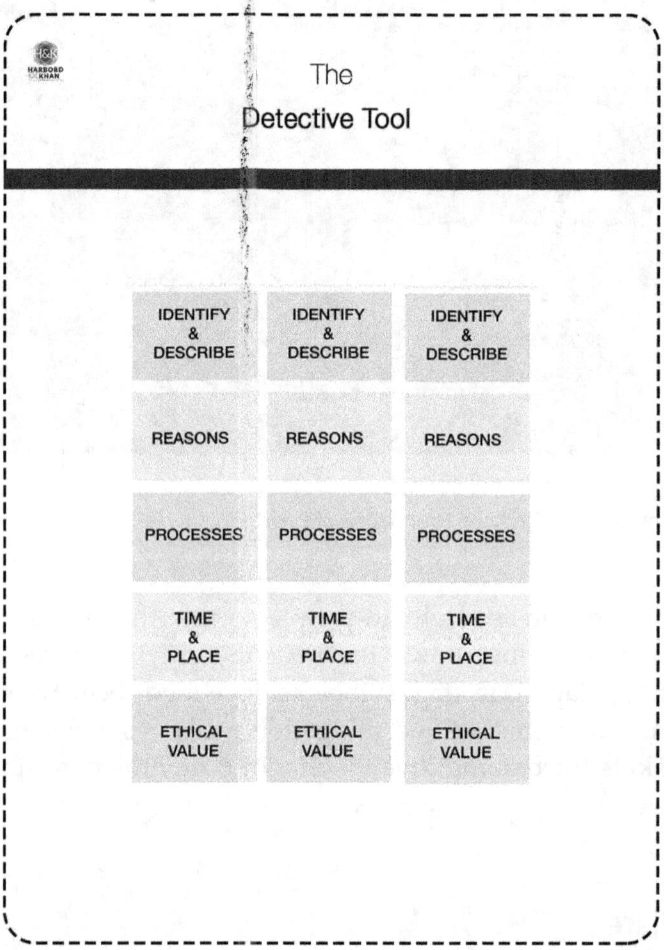
The
Detective Tool
IDENTIFY & DESCRIBE
IDENTIFY & DESCRIBE
IDENTIFY & DESCRIBE
REASONS
REASONS
REASONS
PROCESSES
PROCESSES
PROCESSES
TIME & PLACE
TIME & PLACE
TIME & PLACE
ETHICAL VALUE
ETHICAL VALUE
ETHICAL VALUE

Figure 6.6 The Detective Tool card.

- Students can investigate factors responsible for global warming.
- Drama/theater—Characterization: students can use The Detective Tool to gain insight into the characters they play (WeTeachNYC, 2023).

What if I examined different aspects of the topic to support my understanding?

Figure 6.7 Eagle's-eye view.
Source: Artwork by Linda Weil©.

Suggestions to Align Skills With the Tools

Teachers can share this checklist with students to support them in identifying their higher-order thinking and social emotional skills.

Table 6.1 Suggestions to align higher-order thinking and social emotional learning skills with the tool.

Critical and Creative Thinking Skills for Problem-Solving		Social Emotional Learning Skills
☐ I can analyze and evaluate issues and my ideas. ☐ I can examine different aspects of the topic to support understanding. ☐ I can recognize unstated assumptions and bias. ☐ I can reach conclusions resulting from analysis of the topic. ☐ I can interpret data. ☐ I can evaluate evidence and arguments. ☐ I can break up complicated ideas into different parts and reassemble them to develop new understanding. ☐ I can check the facts and interpretations.	☐ I can use different creative strategies that make thinking visible. ☐ I use brainstorming and visual diagrams to create and develop ideas, connections and inquiries. ☐ I can consider and explore a range of different ideas, including some that may or may not be possible.	☐ I am learning how to make a logical decision after I analyze information. ☐ I can make my conclusions based on my investigations and evidence.

Source: Graphic created by the authors.

Questions for Students to Support Higher–Order Thinking Skills

Table 6.2 Questions for students.

1. Was the tool useful in helping you think about the topic; if so, how?
2. Did you base your conclusions on your investigations and evidence? How did including the ethical value add to your understanding?
3. Can you think of a real-life situation (personal, social, political, etc.) in which you could use the tool to give you more insight?

Source: Graphic created by the authors.

Teacher Reflection

KEY TAKEAWAY Analysis and inquiry generation to promote deeper understanding from multiple perspectives.

- Describe the scenario and classroom context—what was the problem you wanted to address with this tool?
- Did you achieve your goal?
- How did you use the tool to support students' higher-order thinking skills (HOTS)?

Complement With Other Tools

Multiple perspectives: The Building Block Tool and The Points of View Tool.

Chapter Notes

Use this space to plan and write your personal thoughts, ideas and questions here:

Create your mind-map or sketch out your idea

Table 6.3 The Detective Tool blank table

TOPIC:	
IDENTIFY & DESCRIBE	
REASONS	
PROCESSES	
TIME & PLACE	
ETHICAL VALUE	

Source: Graphic created by the authors.

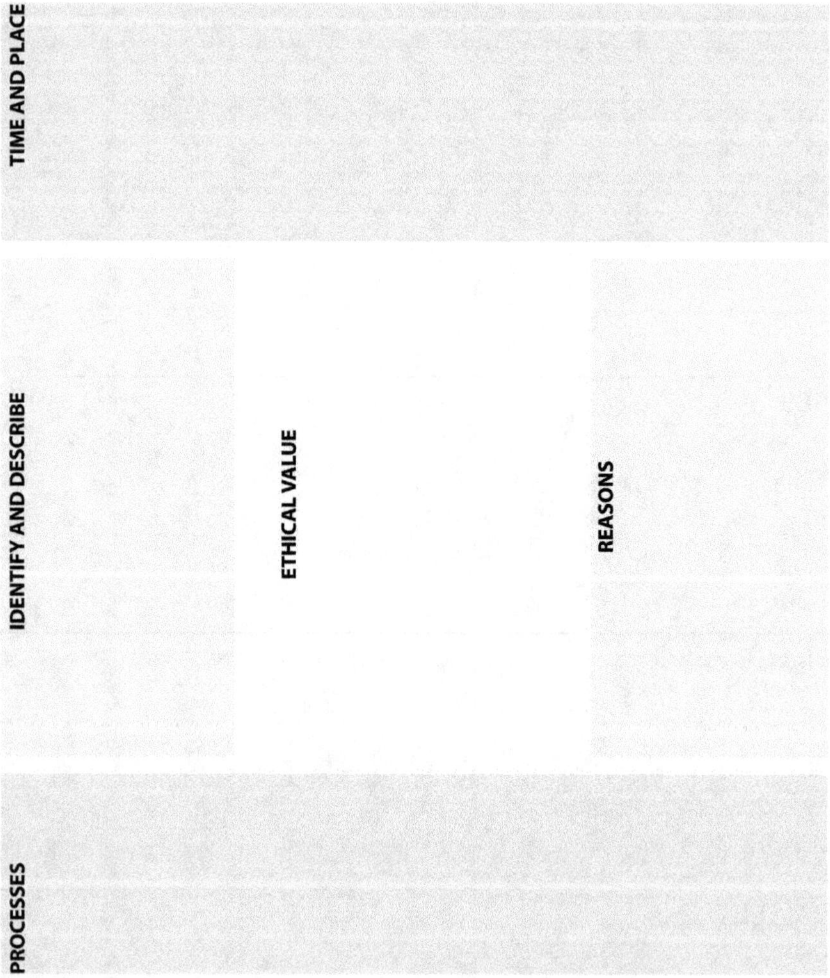
PROCESSES
IDENTIFY AND DESCRIBE
TIME AND PLACE
ETHICAL VALUE
REASONS

Figure 6.8 The Detective Tool template.
Source: Graphic created by the authors.

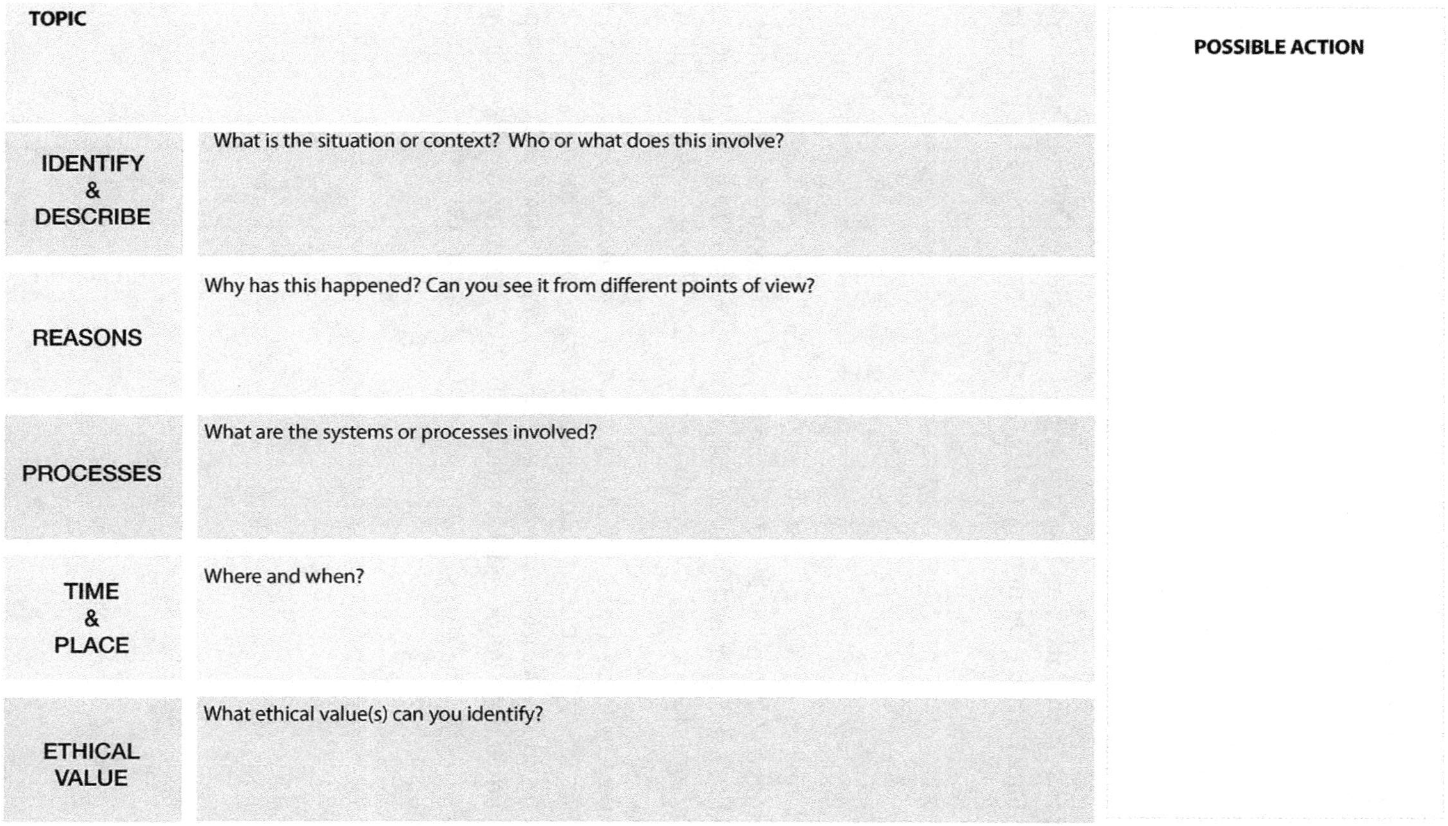
TOPIC
POSSIBLE ACTION
IDENTIFY & DESCRIBE
What is the situation or context? Who or what does this involve?
REASONS
Why has this happened? Can you see it from different points of view?
PROCESSES
What are the systems or processes involved?
TIME & PLACE
Where and when?
ETHICAL VALUE
What ethical value(s) can you identify?

Figure 6.9 The Detective Tool with action.
Source: Graphic created by the authors.

Definitions

Detect: to notice something that is partly hidden or not clear, or to discover something, especially using a particular method.
Ethical values: the beliefs people have, especially about what is right and wrong and what is most important in life, that control their behavior.
Evidence: facts, information, documents, etc., that give reason to believe that something is true.
Fairness: the quality of treating people equally or in a way that is right or reasonable.

The definitions in this list are sourced from Cambridge Online Dictionary (2023), Merriam-Webster Dictionary (2023) and Oxford Learners Dictionaries (2023).

References

Cambridge University Press & Assessment (Ed.). (2023). *Cambridge online dictionary*. Retrieved November 14, 2023, from https://dictionary.cambridge.org/

Merriam-Webster, Incorporated (Ed.). (2023). *Merriam-Webster dictionary*. Merriam-Webster.com. Retrieved November 15, 2023, from www.merriam-webster.com/

Oxford University Press (Ed.). (2023). *Oxford learners dictionaries*. Retrieved November 15, 2023, from www.oxfordlearnersdictionaries.com

WeTeachNYC (Ed.). (2023). *Common core and theater: Improvisation*. NYC Department of Education. Retrieved November 20, 2023, from www.weteachnyc.org/resources/resource/common-core-theater-improvisation/?collection_id=829

7

The Ethical Charter Tool

Package Your Ideas

Suggested Grade Level: 8–10

Key Takeaway—Encourages a consideration of ethical issues when designing/planning a product, project or event.

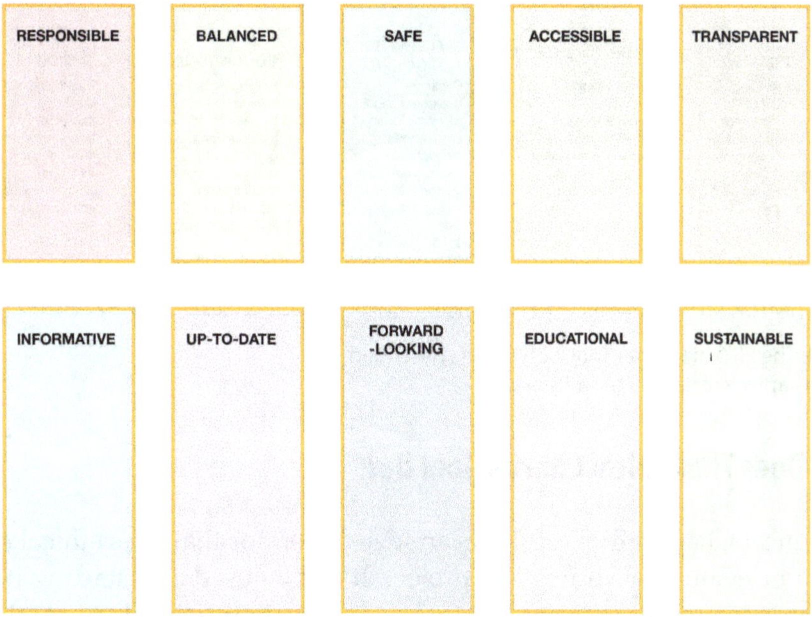
RESPONSIBLE
BALANCED
SAFE
ACCESSIBLE
TRANSPARENT
INFORMATIVE
UP-TO-DATE
FORWARD
-LOOKING
EDUCATIONAL
SUSTAINABLE

Figure 7.1 The Ethical Charter Tool.
Source: Graphic created by the authors.

DOI: 10.4324/9781032664989-8

Global Skills and Key Themes

Skills: Communication, critical thinking, creative thinking, problem-solving and transfer.
Themes: Adaptability, ethical viewpoints, idea generation, inclusion, leadership, real-life issues, service, sustainability and values.

Stories

FROM THE WORLD: Emotional support dog Addi and her owner Jenni Concilia.
DEFINITIONS: Accessible, transparent and sustainable (p 113).

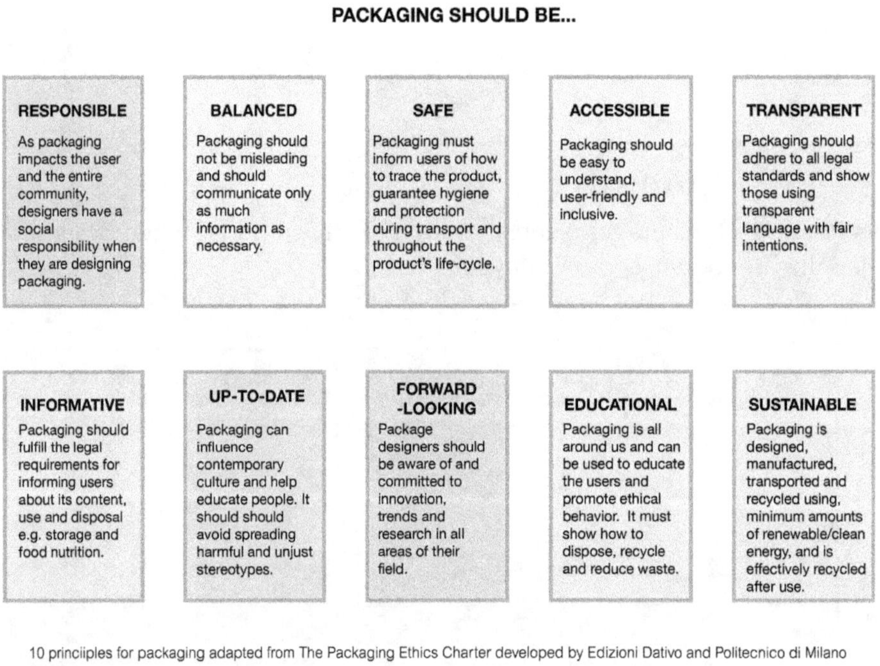
PACKAGING SHOULD BE...
RESPONSIBLE
As packaging impacts the user and the entire community, designers have a social responsibility when they are designing packaging.
BALANCED
Packaging should not be misleading and should communicate only as much information as necessary.
SAFE
Packaging must inform users of how to trace the product, guarantee hygiene and protection during transport and throughout the product's life-cycle.
ACCESSIBLE
Packaging should be easy to understand, user-friendly and inclusive.
TRANSPARENT
Packaging should adhere to all legal standards and show those using transparent language with fair intentions.
INFORMATIVE
Packaging should fulfill the legal requirements for informing users about its content, use and disposal e.g. storage and food nutrition.
UP-TO-DATE
Packaging can influence contemporary culture and help educate people. It should should avoid spreading harmful and unjust stereotypes.
FORWARD -LOOKING
Package designers should be aware of and committed to innovation, trends and research in all areas of their field.
EDUCATIONAL
Packaging is all around us and can be used to educate the users and promote ethical behavior. It must show how to dispose, recycle and reduce waste.
SUSTAINABLE
Packaging is designed, manufactured, transported and recycled using, minimum amounts of renewable/clean energy, and is effectively recycled after use.
10 princiiples for packaging adapted from The Packaging Ethics Charter developed by Edizioni Dativo and Politecnico di Milano

Figure 7.2 The Ethical Charter Tool with criteria described.
Source: Graphic created by the authors.

What Does The Ethical Charter Tool Do?

The Ethical Charter Tool works as an idea generator that uses ethical criteria to plan or evaluate a strategy or project. It can be used as a starting point to generate ideas and make students more aware about ethical values that can then be adapted as required.

This tool was inspired by the ten packaging principles developed by the Ethical Packaging Charter Foundation. The principles originate from a shared reflection between Edizioni Dativo (Italian publisher) and Politecnico di Milano (University in Milan, Italy) and were designed for packaging, but it is fun to take the concepts and use them creatively in a different context (Baule et al., 2023).

How to Use It

1. Choose your topic (idea, strategy or project).
2. Use each of the principles to reflect on how ethical your idea, strategy or project is.

EXAMPLE 1 Planning a New School Club

For example, if students were thinking about creating a new school club, they could think about it through these lenses:

- **RESPONSIBLE:** What would the responsibilities of the club be? How would the club operate in a responsible manner?
- **INFORMATIVE:** How could the club members communicate information in ethical ways?
- **BALANCED:** How would the club advocate a balanced approach to its activities?
  Are they using social media responsibly with an awareness of fake news, greenwashing and biased research?
- **ACCESSIBLE:** This could be through the lens of inclusiveness and physical accessibility.
- **UP-TO-DATE or CONTEMPORARY**: Does the club accommodate changing school communities or gender nomenclature?
- **SAFE**: The club organizers need to ensure that the members meet in a safe space and feel supported.
  Are there any health and safety guidelines they need to be aware of?
- **TRANSPARENT:** The aims of the club are clear, and the manner in which they operate is open and honest.
  If artificial intelligence (AI)–generated technologies are being used, have they been cited?
- **FORWARD-LOOKING:** Has the club planned for growth? Is it a prototype that could be reproduced in other school communities?
- **EDUCATIONAL:** Learning is holistic, so all the experiences at school events in some way lead to educating the whole person.

- **SUSTAINABLE:** The club meets the obligations on the school sustainability guidelines.
  Looking at the project (in this case, starting a new school club) through these different lenses gives you an excellent basis for discussing ethical leadership, ethical behaviors and expectations within the school community or local community.

STORIES FROM THE WORLD

Jenni Concilia, Head of Individual Needs for students from 3 to 12 years old at Wesley College, Melbourne, is responsible for implementing the Therapy Dog program at the school. She used the Ethical Charter Tool criteria to examine her experience

RESPONSIBLE
Training and placing a Therapy dog into the school impacts all stakeholders. The person undertaking this task (handler) needs to ensure the dog is trained by accredited professionals and that the dog will be cared for in an ethical and responsible manner.
BALANCED
The needs of the children and the staff will be balanced against the needs of the therapy dog. We will communicate as much information to parents and staff as necessary and always adhere to the Essential Standards for Therapy Dogs.
INFORMATIVE
The handler will coordinate the implementation of a staff information session and a parent information session, to be delivered by the \ external training body. This will cover topics such as how parents can assist with therapy dog programs, understanding how a therapy dog can support anxious learners; the role of a therapy dog in a school environment.
UP-TO-DATE OR CONTEMPORARY
The latest evidence-based research on Therapy Dogs in schools will be cited and used to educate and help the community as to the benefits of having an onsite school therapy dog.
SAFE
Risk minimization is a priority and the completion of a formal risk-assessment specific for the school will be undertaken prior to the therapy dog coming onsite.
ACCESSIBLE
Our therapy dog will be housed with her trained handler/owner in the Junior School. However she will be accessible to students and staff in other areas of the school through the use of a booking sheet.
24 hours in a week is normally the maximum working hours for a dog. However these hours should be spread across 5 days.
FORWARD-LOOKING
Schools wanting to implement a Therapy Dog should continue to be aware of and committed to innovative use of the dog and ongoing research in all areas.
Ongoing animal re-accreditation every 12 months will be required.
EDUCATIONAL
A therapy dog can be used to educate students, increase motivation and engagement and promote inclusive behaviors. The dog can assist in two key areas - student welfare and connecting to the curriculum e.g. teaching anxious students, engaging students with additional needs, develop core skills in specific curriculum areas.
TRANSPARENT
Placing and integrating a Therapy Dog into a school involves significant planning and training and requires a thorough approach.
We will adhere to all 3 core pillars in the Essential Standards for Therapy Dogs:
1. The Dog's Role
2. Animal Welfare
3. Occupational Health & Safety.
SUSTAINABLE
We comply with the school's sustainability guidelines e.g. zero waste. Our dog has reusable bowls; her kennel was created from existing materials.
Sustainability: The therapy dog's courtyard also serves as an area for sustainable garden with potted plants growing fruit and vegetables safe for dogs to eat.

Figure 7.3 Using The Ethical Charter Tool to explore considerations relating to implementing a therapy dog program.

of implementing the program at her school (J. Concilia, personal communication, October 20, 2023).

Applications

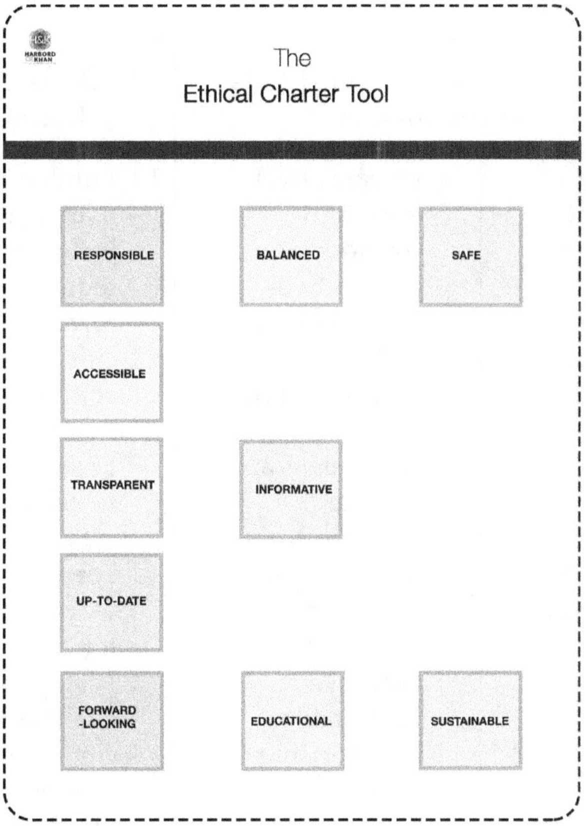
The
Ethical Charter Tool
RESPONSIBLE
BALANCED
SAFE
ACCESSIBLE
TRANSPARENT
INFORMATIVE
UP-TO-DATE
FORWARD -LOOKING
EDUCATIONAL
SUSTAINABLE

Figure 7.4 The Ethical Charter Tool card.

The Ethical Charter Tool has enormous potential to be used in many different situations including subjects such as civics, engineering design, humanities, language arts and visual arts. It could also be used as the focus of an interdisciplinary study.

We had challenged our design students to explore the human-robot dynamic and develop a charter for the rights of robots. The heart of the tool is the ethical issues involved and our human response to them. "Perhaps the key characteristics that defines 'human' is the ability to consider alternative futures and make deliberate choices accordingly, often taking complex and conflicting moral considerations into account. Creatures or technologies without such a capacity cannot be bound into a social contract and take moral responsibility" (Jacofsky, D. Excerpt From: MYP 4. "9781913808693. Apple Books).

Suggestions to Align Skills With the Tools

Teachers can share this checklist with students to support them in identifying their higher-order thinking and social emotional skills.

Table 7.1 Suggestions to align higher-order thinking and social emotional learning skills with the tool.

Critical and Creative Thinking Skills for Problem-Solving		Social Emotional Learning Skills
☐ I can analyze and evaluate issues and my ideas. ☐ I can propose and evaluate a variety of solutions. ☐ I can recognize and evaluate propositions. ☐ I can identify obstacles and challenges. ☐ I can draw reasonable conclusions and generalizations. ☐ I can analyze complex concepts and projects into their constituent parts and synthesize them to create new understanding.	☐ I create novel ideas and consider new perspectives. ☐ I use brainstorming and visual diagrams to create and develop ideas, connections and inquiries. ☐ I can create new solutions to genuine problems. ☐ I can make predictable or surprising connections between objects and/or ideas. ☐ I can use different creative strategies that make thinking visible. ☐ I can describe and make metaphors and analogies.	☐ I understand that making ethical, inclusive decisions requires sensitivity toward all peoples, cultures and communities. ☐ I understand that I have a responsibility to behave in an ethical way. ☐ I can find possible ways to problem-solve for myself and society. ☐ I can plan for and evaluate what the consequences of my actions will be. ☐ I understand what empathy is and can empathize with others. ☐ I can make decisions that are fair and impartial. ☐ I care about others' feelings and the impact of my actions on them. ☐ I take action to support others' well-being.

Source: Graphic created by the authors.

Teacher Reflection

KEY TAKEAWAY—Analysis and inquiry generation to promote deeper understanding from multiple perspectives.

- Describe the scenario and classroom context—what was the problem you wanted to address with this tool?
- Did you achieve your goal?
- How did you use the tool to support students' higher-order thinking skills (HOTS)?

Complement With Other Tools

Multiple perspectives: The Building Block Tool and Points of View Tool.

Chapter Notes

Use this space to plan and write your personal thoughts, ideas and questions here:

Create your mind-map or sketch out your idea

Student Planning

Table 7.2 Student planning.

WHAT AM I WORKING ON?	
RESPONSIBLE	
BALANCED	
SAFE	
ACCESSIBLE	
TRANSPARENT	
INFORMATIVE	
CONTEMPORARY UP-TO-DATE	
FORWARD-LOOKING	
EDUCATIONAL	
SUSTAINABLE	

Source: Graphic created by the authors.

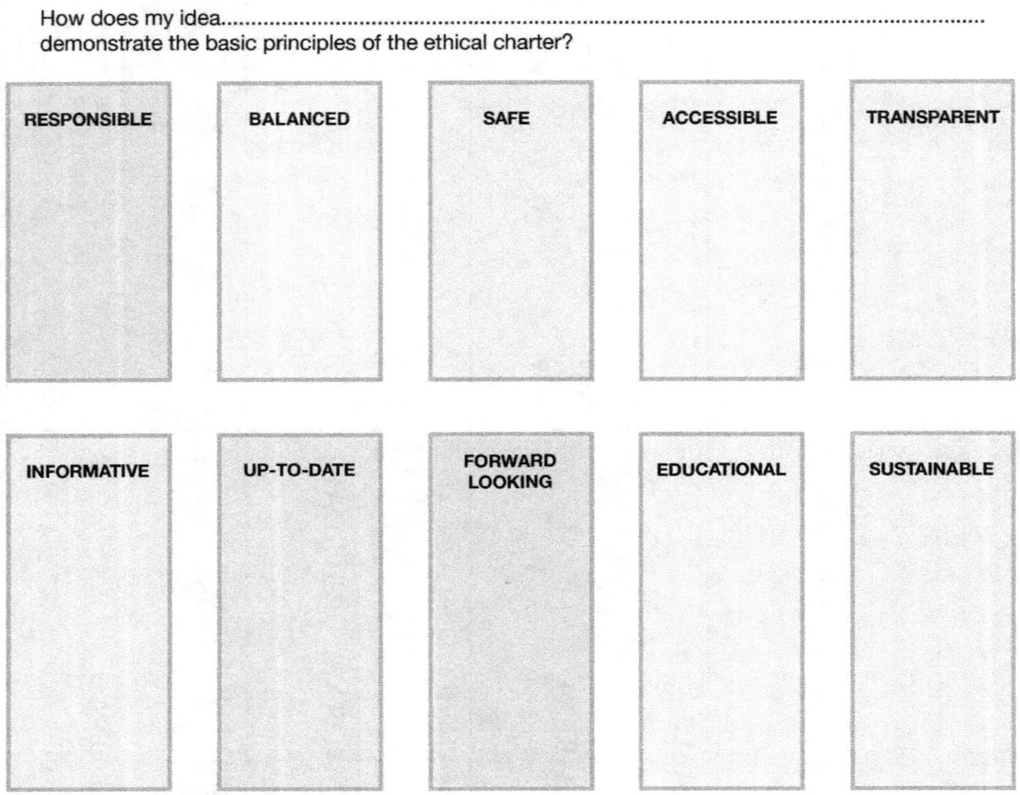
How does my idea..
demonstrate the basic principles of the ethical charter?
RESPONSIBLE
BALANCED
SAFE
ACCESSIBLE
TRANSPARENT
INFORMATIVE
UP-TO-DATE
FORWARD LOOKING
EDUCATIONAL
SUSTAINABLE

Figure 7.5 The Ethical Charter Tool template.
Source: Graphic created by the authors.

Definitions

Accessible: able to be reached or easily obtained.
Transparent: clear and easy to understand or recognize (adjective).
Sustainable: causing, or made in a way that causes, little or no damage to the environment and therefore able to continue for a long time.

The definitions in this list are sourced from Cambridge Online Dictionary (2023) and Merriam-Webster Dictionary (2023).

References

Baule, G., Bucchetti, V., Guidotti, L., & Lavorini, S. (2023). *The ethical packaging charter*. Fondazionecartaeticapackaging.org. November 29, 2023, https://fondazionecartaeticapackaging.org/

Cambridge University Press & Assessment (Ed.). (2023). *Cambridge online dictionary*. Retrieved November 14, 2023, from https://dictionary.cambridge.org/

Merriam-Webster, Incorporated (Ed.). (2023). *Merriam-Webster dictionary*. Merriam-Webster.com. Retrieved November 15, 2023, from www.merriam-webster.com/

8

The Ethical Equation Tool

Find a Solution

Suggested Grade Level: 7–10

Key Takeaway—Constructing and planning ethical inquiry using a math structure/formula.

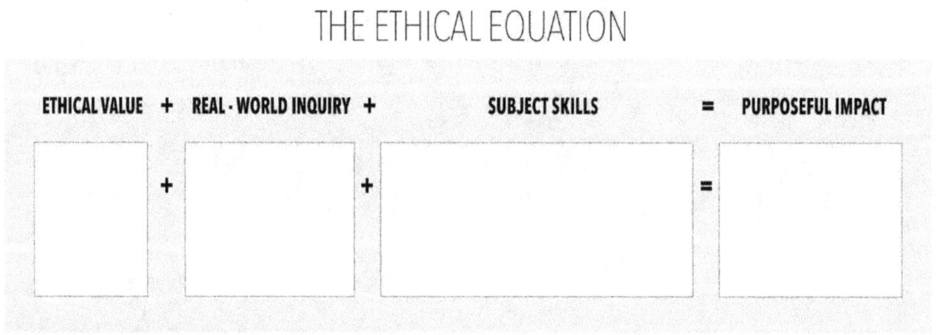

THE ETHICAL EQUATION
ETHICAL VALUE + REAL - WORLD INQUIRY + SUBJECT SKILLS = PURPOSEFUL IMPACT

Figure 8.1 The Ethical Equation Tool.

DOI: 10.4324/9781032664989-9

Global Skills and Key Themes

Skills: Critical thinking, creative thinking, problem-solving and subject or interdisciplinary thinking.
Themes: Change, ethical mindset, ethical values, idea generation, innovation, inquiry generation, real-world issues and service.
DEFINITIONS: Ethical values, real-world inquiry, interdisciplinary and purposeful impact (p 123).

What Does The Ethical Equation Tool Do?

- It encourages student engagement and helps them to connect to their learning and support new understanding.
- The template has different components and breaks down the various aspects of the inquiry through the use of an ethical lens.
- The structure of The Ethical Equation Tool has an ethical value at the beginning and purposeful impact at the end. Students are encouraged to reflect on ethical issues and to be more aware of the consequences of their actions resulting from their inquiry.
- It facilitates planning for teachers to introduce and discuss new units of work or lesson plans and communicate how the inquiry is meaningful, holistic, relevant and purposeful.

The tool is an innovative way to engage learning by showing an inquiry problem using a math structure to break apart and simplify understanding of a word problem using an ethical lens.

The idea of using a math equation to communicate a written problem requires a transfer of understanding, creative thinking and an open mind. This concept also gives students the opportunity to see how through a creative thinking approach, an idea can be flipped or manipulated and given a whole new perspective.

Teachers can also ask students to collaborate in groups to write an equation exploring your chosen topic of inquiry using different math symbols and signs e.g. multiplication or use programming and code.

How to Use It

1. Choose your topic.
2. Choose the ethical value.
3. Identify the real-world issue or problem.
4. Determine the subject and the skills involved.
5. Consider the ethical impact of the scenario.

With its focus on ethical values and real-world inquiry, The Ethical Equation Tool makes planning and designing ethical individual subject or interdisciplinary curriculum easy to accomplish. Teachers not using an interdisciplinary curriculum can use the tool with their individual subject skills. Students could use it to plan their service activities or personal projects.

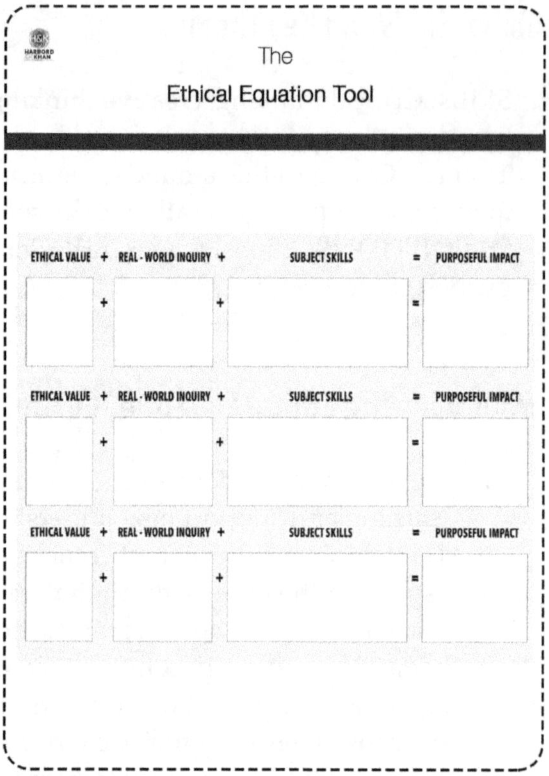
The Ethical Equation Tool

ETHICAL VALUE	+	REAL-WORLD INQUIRY	+	SUBJECT SKILLS	=	PURPOSEFUL IMPACT
	+		+		=	
ETHICAL VALUE	+	REAL-WORLD INQUIRY	+	SUBJECT SKILLS	=	PURPOSEFUL IMPACT
	+		+		=	
ETHICAL VALUE	+	REAL-WORLD INQUIRY	+	SUBJECT SKILLS	=	PURPOSEFUL IMPACT
	+		+		=	

Figure 8.2 The Ethical Equation Tool card.

EXAMPLE 1 An Ethical Equation for Creating Awareness About Homelessness

This example explores homeless children. The purpose of the unit is to sensitize students to the harsh reality of many young people who are forced to live on the streets due to personal, social or economic reasons. The focus of the learning is around an ethical value such as empathy, with the real-world inquiry of homeless children in the United States. The interdisciplinary subjects could be biology, civics or English language arts and with the purposeful impact being an oral presentation in a school assembly to inform students of this growing problem.

Using The Ethical Equation Tool makes planning easier:

1. **Choose your topic:**
   Creating awareness about homelessness.
2. **Choose the ethical value:**
   Empathy.

3. **Identify the real-world issue or problem:**
   The plight of homeless children.
4. **Determine the subject and the skills involved:**
   Biology, civics and English language arts.
5. **Consider the ethical impact of the scenario:**
   Creating student knowledge and awareness about homeless children in the community.

Write the ethical equation:

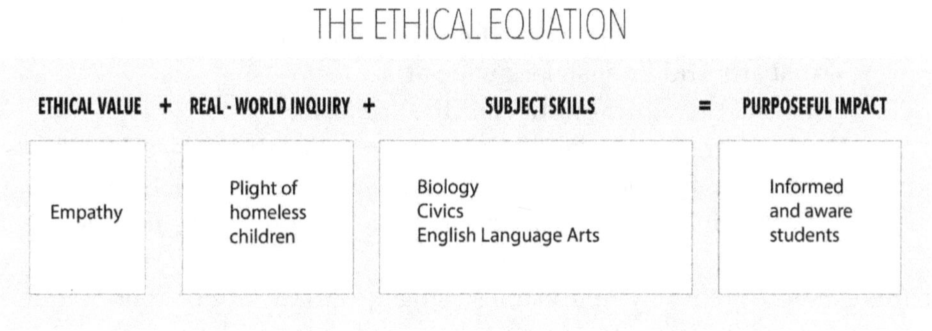
THE ETHICAL EQUATION
ETHICAL VALUE + REAL-WORLD INQUIRY + SUBJECT SKILLS = PURPOSEFUL IMPACT
Empathy
Plight of homeless children
Biology
Civics
English Language Arts
Informed and aware students

Figure 8.3 Using The Ethical Equation Tool to explore homelessness.

Students can replace any of the sections of the equation to explore the topic from different perspectives. For example, what questions would arise if the real-world inquiry was changed to endangered animals and the ethical value was trust?

EXAMPLE 2 Endangered Animals

1. **Choose your topic.**
   Endangered animals.
2. **Choose the ethical value.**
   Trust.
3. **Identify the real-world issue or problem.**
   Endangered animals.
4. **Determine the subject and the skills involved.**
   Biology, civics and English language arts.
5. **Consider the ethical impact of the scenario.**
   Creating student awareness about issues relating to endangered animals and trust e.g. poaching.

Trust + Endangered animals + Biology, civics, English language arts = Student awareness about issues relating to endangered animals.

EXAMPLE 3 Olympic Games

1. **Choose your topic.**
   Exploring honor in the Olympic Games.
2. **Choose the ethical value.**
   Honor.
3. **Identify the real-world issue or problem.**
   Should the Olympic Games continue to be held or be abolished because of scandals?
4. **Determine the subject and the skills involved.**
   Visual arts and English language arts.
5. **Consider the ethical impact of the scenario.**
   Does holding the Olympic Games have a positive impact? Students can explore the topic of the Olympic Games as an athlete or a diplomat or an environmentalist or even through a political lens.

In this example of the Olympic Games using the ethical lens of honor, students can understand the impact to create purposeful change. Through the interdisciplinary connection of English language arts and the visual arts, the teachers have different tasks that address the learning objectives but are specific to their content, and the combination of the two subjects will inspire greater links to the inquiry (Harbord & Khan, 2020, p. 114).

VISUAL ARTS & ENGLISH LANGUAGE ARTS

ETHICAL VALUE + REAL-WORLD INQUIRY + SUBJECT SKILLS

= PURPOSEFUL IMPACT

HONOR + SPORTS + GRAPHIC DESIGN & PRESENTATION OF KNOWLEDGE AND IDEAS

= CAN CREATE CHANGE

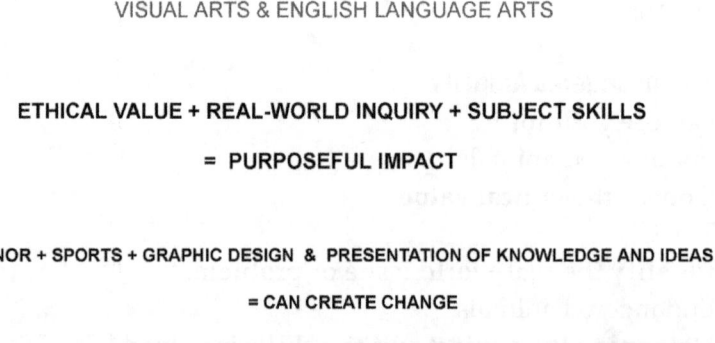

Figure 8.4 Using The Ethical Equation Tool to explore ethical issues in the Olympic Games.

Suggestions to Align Skills With the Tools

Teachers can share this checklist with students to support them in identifying their higher-order thinking and social emotional skills.

Table 8.1 Suggestions to align higher-order thinking and social emotional learning skills with the tool.

Critical Thinking and Creative Thinking Skills for Problem-Solving		**Social Emotional Learning Skills**
☐ I can break up complicated ideas into different parts and reassemble them to develop new understanding. ☐ I can examine different aspects of the topic to support understanding.	☐ I use brainstorming and visual diagrams to create and develop ideas, connections and inquiries. ☐ I can use different creative strategies that make thinking visible.	☐ I understand that I have a responsibility to behave in an ethical way. ☐ I can find possible ways to problem-solve for myself and society. ☐ I can plan for and evaluate what the consequences of my actions will be. ☐ I understand what empathy is and can empathize with others. ☐ I can make decisions that are fair and impartial. ☐ I care about others' feelings and the impact of my actions on them. ☐ I can take action to support others' well-being.

Source: Graphic created by the authors.

Reflecting on their experience of using this tool can help teachers with regard to their professional development, annual reviews and appraisals. The reflection could also be a starting point for an educational article to inspire others.

Teacher Reflection

KEY TAKEAWAY Analysis and inquiry generation to promote deeper understanding from multiple perspectives.

- Describe the scenario and classroom context—what was the problem you wanted to address with this tool?
- Did you achieve your goal?
- How did you use the tool to support students' higher-order thinking skills (HOTS)?

Complement With Other Tools

Ethical mindset: The Ethical Charter Tool and The Thinking Generator Tool.

Chapter Notes

Use this space to plan and write your personal thoughts, ideas and questions here:

Create your mind-map or sketch out your idea

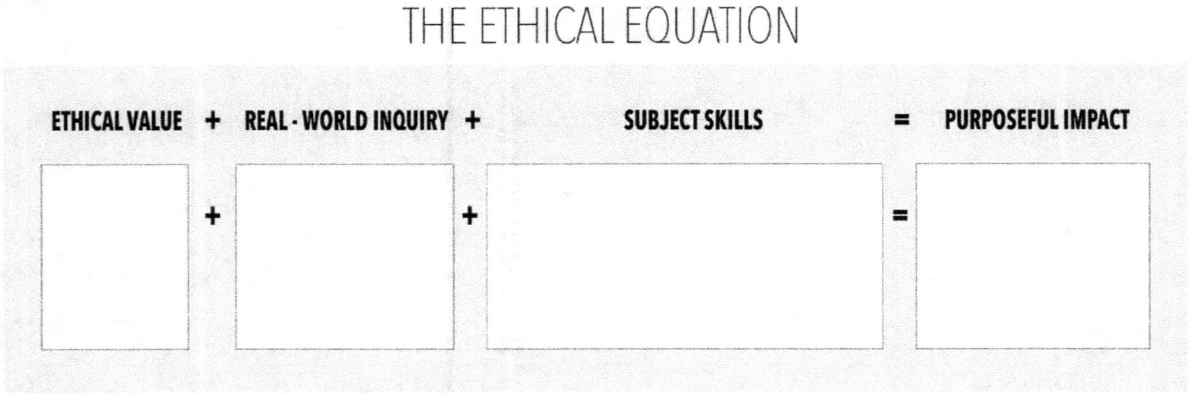
THE ETHICAL EQUATION
ETHICAL VALUE + REAL - WORLD INQUIRY + SUBJECT SKILLS = PURPOSEFUL IMPACT
+
+
=

Figure 8.5 The Ethical Equation Tool template.

Definitions

Ethical values: the beliefs people have, especially about what is right and wrong and what is most important in life, that control their behavior.
Interdisciplinary: involving two or more different subjects or areas of knowledge.
Real-world inquiry: generating questions about and exploring real-life issues as opposed to fictional ones.
Purposeful impact: an intentional action resulting in a powerful positive effect for something or someone.

The definitions in this list are sourced from Cambridge Online Dictionary (2023), Merriam-Webster Dictionary (2023) and Oxford Learners Dictionaries (2023).

References

Cambridge University Press & Assessment (Ed.). (2023). *Cambridge online dictionary*. Retrieved November 14, 2023, from https://dictionary.cambridge.org/

Harbord, M. J., & Khan, S. R. (2020) *Interdisciplinary thinking for schools: Ethical dilemmas*. John Catt.

Merriam-Webster, Incorporated (Ed.). (2023). *Merriam-Webster dictionary*. Merriam-Webster.com. Retrieved November 15, 2023, from www.merriam-webster.com/

Oxford University Press (Ed.). (2023). *Oxford learners dictionaries*. Retrieved November 15, 2023, from https//www.oxfordlearnersdictionairies.com

9

The Go Earth Tool

Which Way Do I Go?

Suggested Grade Level: 8–10

Key Takeaway—Using the Google Earth features through the lens of curiosity, adventure, exploration and discovery, your students can investigate diverse global topics and the world.

Global Skills and Key Themes

Skills: Collaboration, critical thinking, creative thinking and problem-solving.
Themes: Global themes, open-mindedness, multiculturalism, self-awareness and real-world issues.

Stories

FROM THE ROAD: A biking adventure with science teachers Fiona Mason and Marios Mantzoukis.
DEFINITIONS: Curiosity, exploration, migration, monument and wildlife bridge (p 138).

DOI: 10.4324/9781032664989-10

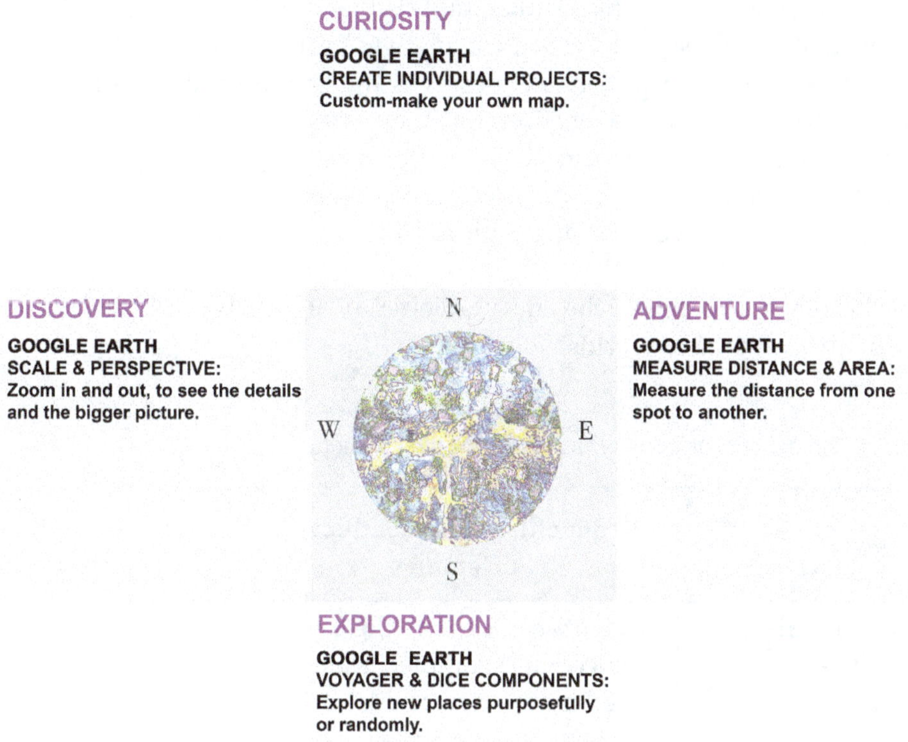
CURIOSITY
GOOGLE EARTH
CREATE INDIVIDUAL PROJECTS:
Custom-make your own map.
DISCOVERY
GOOGLE EARTH
SCALE & PERSPECTIVE:
Zoom in and out, to see the details and the bigger picture.
N
W
E
S
ADVENTURE
GOOGLE EARTH
MEASURE DISTANCE & AREA:
Measure the distance from one spot to another.
EXPLORATION
GOOGLE EARTH
VOYAGER & DICE COMPONENTS:
Explore new places purposefully or randomly.

Figure 9.1 The Go Earth Tool.

What Does The Go Earth Tool Do?

The Go Earth Tool gives students a framework to imagine and feed their curiosity and explore the physical world—to go places they would like to see, visit famous sites or monuments, travel to tropical rainforests or golden beaches. This tool can engage students to grasp distance and measurement through visual transportation.

It is important to let students know that Google Earth uses the Mercator map projection, designed in the 1500s by Gerardus Mercator and useful for sailors. In order to keep the shape and direction accurate, the scale of countries was distorted e.g. the African continent and South American countries are shown smaller than they really are. Europe is placed directly in the middle of the map (Hornish, 2022). This can be a useful starting point for discussions about colonialism and imperialism.

At this point in time the AuthaGraph is the world's most accurate map. The AuthaGraph map was designed in 1999 by Japanese architect Hajime Narukawa. This map projection preserves the shape of all continents and oceans and reduces the distortion, but many find the reality of this visual confronting as they are used to the Mercator map projection (Todd, 2019). Table 9.1 aligns the Google Earth features and application to the individual subject with the power of using ethical dilemmas and explains some of the benefits from this.

This example explores the ethical dilemma, 'Should we stay and save the Earth or travel to new worlds?'

Table 9.1 The benefits of using ethical dilemmas in curriculum.

Google Earth features	Benefits of using ethical dilemmas	Application to my subject
Create individual projects: CURIOSITY	Students can explore the nuanced and complex issues raised by the ethical dilemma that interests them the most.	Offers voice and choice.
Measure distance and area: ADVENTURE	Ethical dilemmas often require adventurous thinking and taking yourself out of your comfort zone. After working through an ethical dilemma, you can reflect on how far you have come and how your viewpoint may have changed. Students may start off believing the future is on other planets but may change their minds.	Opportunities for reflecting on growth and deeper understanding of the topic.
Voyager and Dice: EXPLORATION	The emotional response to ethical dilemmas can harness student attention and motivate students to explore innovative solutions to real-world problems.	Encourage students to consider the purposeful impact of their learning and how it is meaningful to them.

(Continued)

Table 9.1 (Continued)

Google Earth features	Benefits of using ethical dilemmas	Application to my subject
Scale and Perspective: DISCOVERY	Students can explore multiple points of view in the ethical dilemma from the perspectives of astronauts, aerospace engineers, conservation scientists, ordinary people, a 15-year-old teenager, etc.	Develop a more open-minded approach to the topic and consider it in a broader context.

How to Use It

Students can choose their topic and use one or all of the following Google Earth tools to explore it: Scale, Perspective, Create individual projects, Measuring distance and area and the Voyager and Dice (Google, 2023).

Alternatively a problem-based learning unit of work could be based around the four aspects of the tool—curiosity, adventure, exploration and discovery—and would especially be effective for interdisciplinary work.

Create individual projects—curiosity Students can custom-make their own map and explore it with their preferred view. Students can create real or fantasy maps, drawing on inspiration from real places found using Google Earth. **Measure distance and area—adventure** Go on Google Earth and plan your adventure. Students can use measurements to plan a trip, a walk in the jungle or a camping holiday in the desert.	**Voyager and Dice components—exploration** Students can be risk takers and try something different by using these tools to explore new places they want to visit, purposefully or randomly. **Scale and Perspective—discovery** Zoom in and out. Students can see the details and the bigger picture, inspiring them to explore new perspectives.

Ethical Dilemmas and Thinking Tools

Ethical dilemmas require an understanding of the whole situation from multiple points of view. They are always guided by a values-based perspective and encourage students to examine their own values. Ethical dilemmas are one lens teachers can use to engage student interest, and this particular dilemma gives students a wider choice of exploration.

You can use The Go Earth Tool with ethical dilemmas in your curriculum to offer a structured framework for students to use as a context for learning. Students can choose their ethical trajectory and understand how it changes over time as they consider solutions.

For example, if you are studying global warming effects on planet Earth, you could use this ethical dilemma or write your own: *Global warming is a hoax versus sea-level changes prove that global warming exists.*

The four sections, Curiosity, Adventure, Exploration and Discovery, also complement the following International Baccalaureate Learner Profile attributes: knowledgeable, risk-taking, open-minded, inquirers and communicators.

STORIES FROM THE ROAD

How do we plan for an adventure, and can we really plan for the unexpected?

By Marios Mantzoukis and Fiona Mason,
bikepackers and science teachers.

Figure 9.2 Marios and Fiona ready for adventure.
Source: Image credit Marios Mantzoukis & Fiona Mason.

Curiosity

Curiosity has always been a part of our existence and the way in which we engage with the world around us. Having been avid travelers from an early age, we were used to looking both outwards and inwards for inspiration for our travels. It was not until we encountered our first bikepackers in the backwaters of Kyrgyzstan that we started considering exploring the world by bicycle.

Picture this: On a hot summer day, in the village of Bokonbayevo, just off the southern shore of Lake Karakol, two sunburnt, sweaty and hungry looking cyclists, covered in dust, arrive at the doorstep of our homestay. Furthermore, they are not riding regular bicycles. They are riding a tandem bike, best described as a weird adaptation of the classic bike that requires a continuous act of balance paired with perfect synchronization of movements as two riders sit on the long steel frame and pedal their way forward. "Where did you come from?" was our first question. "Marseille, France", they replied.

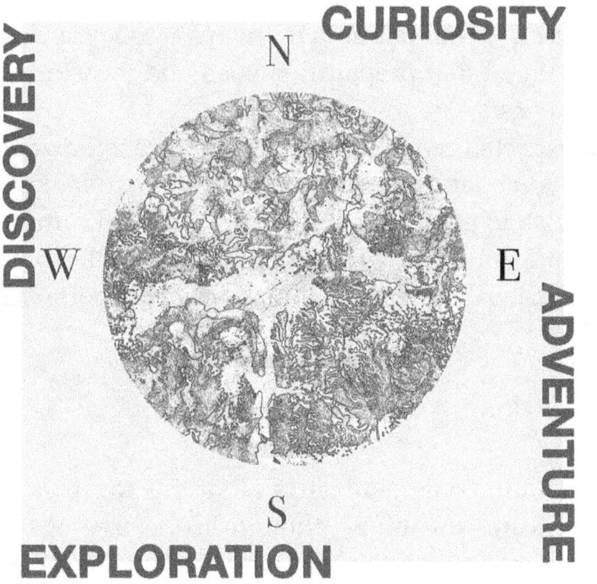
CURIOSITY
N
DISCOVERY
W
E
ADVENTURE
S
EXPLORATION

Figure 9.3 Earth with headings.
Source: Graphic created by the authors.

The acute realization of the enormity of the task behind our new acquaintances, to cycle from France to the center of Asia, contrasted with the simplicity of their answer. Intrigued and in a state of relative disbelief, we moved on to examine the battered tandem bicycle and dusty equipment resting against a wall.

Adventure

Fast-forward five years, we find ourselves sitting on the side of the road, more than 4,200 meters up the eastern slopes of the Bolivian Andes. For two days, we have been cycling and pushing our bicycles up the winding road and into thin air.

The sun's rays are relentless and so are the steep inclines that we are fighting against. The air is poor in oxygen, just 13% instead of the 21% found at sea level, and we can feel it with every breath. Water is running low, our morale even lower. The closest town is decidedly out of reach, the night will soon be falling fast, and with it the wind chill is expected to reach freezing point. Not much has gone as expected during this last segment of our adventure. Our choices are now limited: spend the night next to the exposed road or continue pushing until what looked like a mine entrance surrounded by huts, some 20 kilometers and several hills ahead. We squeeze a bit of energy inside us in the form of Oreo biscuits, gulp some of our remaining water and get on our bikes. We are going to push on!

Exploration

So how do you plan for the unexpected? The quick answer is: You can never fully do so. Poring over Google Maps, zooming in and out of remote parts of the globe, trying to identify land features and to unlock information about distances, inclines, road surfaces and wind patterns is always a great starting point. What also has to come with all that preparation is a good measure of open-mindedness and self-awareness.

Successfully tackling the unexpected can only happen if you are self-aware. Knowing your limits, knowing your partner, knowing what you are looking for and what you are willing to risk to get there, all these are essential components when problem-solving in the wilderness. Honing additional skills, such as collaboration and creative and critical thinking, is also of critical importance.

Discovery

Probably the most important skill, the one that brings all of this together, is open-mindedness. It can take various meanings, though in the case of the adventure cyclist it often means being open to ideas, agreements and disagreements and changes of direction; being open to other peoples' perspectives and to the local cultural norms; being open to the possibility of others not being as open as you might be and vice versa.

Empathy

In our case, nearing the end of our tether, we had to rely on the open-mindedness and kind-heartedness of a local miner. We reached the man's door at dusk and inquired about getting water and a place to build our tent. He promptly took us to the back of his very modest house and showed us a spot against his outer wall where we would be relatively protected from the wind. He gave us water and, most importantly, he gave us his trust. Come to think of it, he was as vulnerable as we were, in the close vicinity of two strangers. We mustered enough strength to prepare our shelter and to cook some warm food before collapsing into our sleeping bags. The next morning, feeling rested, we soaked up the sun and smiled at each other. We were ready once again to face the unexpected (M. Mantzoukis; F. Mason, personal communication, November 23, 2023).

STUDENT REFLECTION IDEAS FROM MARIOS & FIONA

Have you found yourself in an unexpected situation?

How did you feel when that happened?

What skills did you have to employ?

Was there anything new that you discovered about yourself?

Figure 9.4 Student reflection ideas from Marios and Fiona.
Source: Graphic created by the authors.

Applications

This tool can be used by students to:

- Explore migration and the movement of vulnerable populations.
- Use the Voyager Tool to explore complex environmental challenges such as 'Sea Level Rise and the Fate of Coastal Cities' and 'Protecting the Earth's Wild Places'.
- Look for existing wildlife bridges. Can you suggest some other locations where they would be useful?
- Research where your ancestors came from.
- Trade routes and their impact on arts and culture.
- Explore stadiums that were built for the Olympic Games over the years. What happened to them?

- Explore how our cities have changed.
- Follow the route of major rivers over time to see if they are different.
- Look at your school when it was originally built and now. Track the changes.
- Compare Antarctica prior to exploration and now.

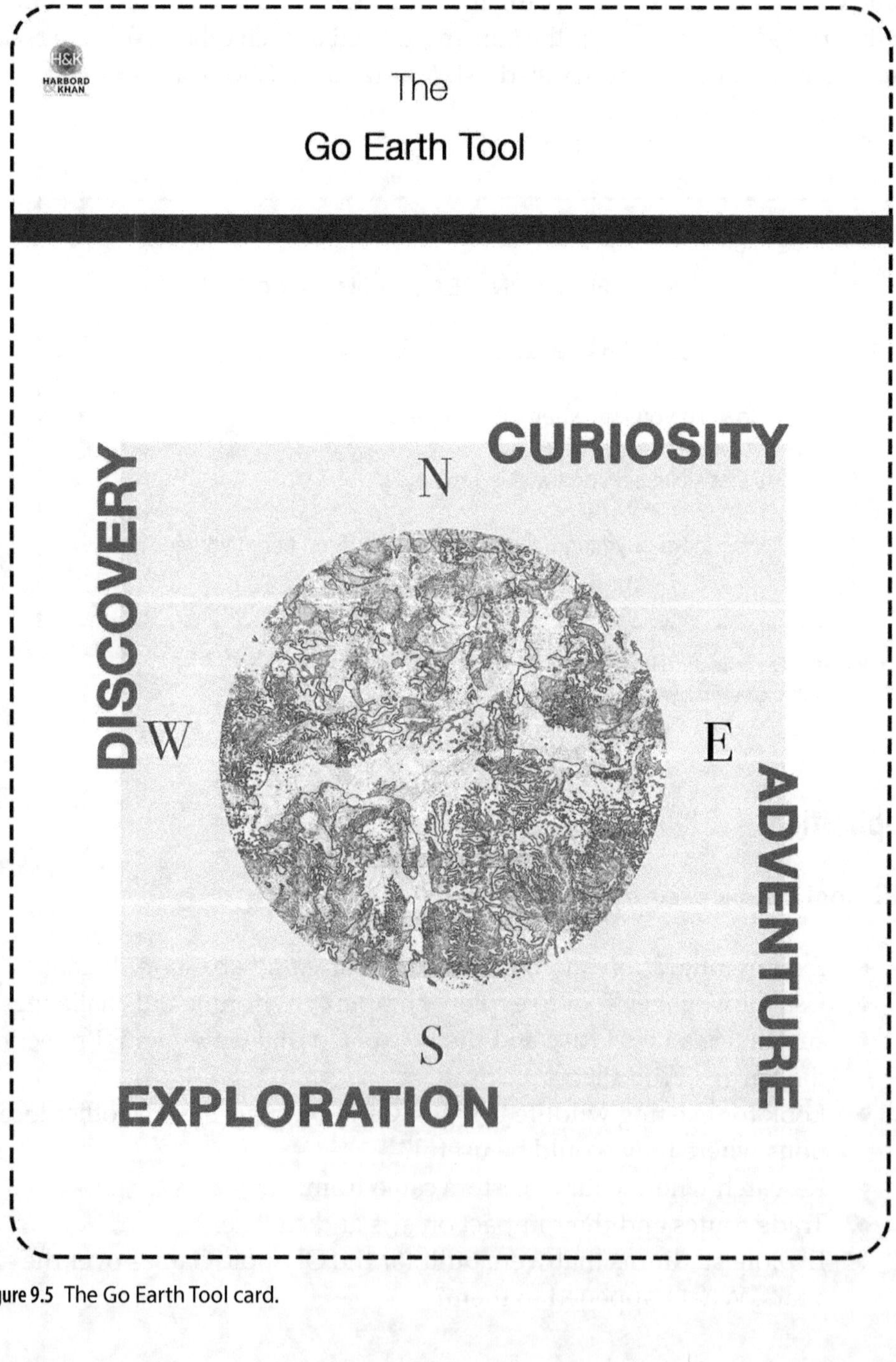
H&K
HARBORD KHAN
The
Go Earth Tool
CURIOSITY
N
DISCOVERY
W
E
ADVENTURE
S
EXPLORATION

Figure 9.5 The Go Earth Tool card.

Suggestions to Align Skills With the Tool

Teachers can share this checklist with students to support them in identifying their higher-order thinking and social emotional skills

Table 9.2 Suggestions to align higher-order thinking and social emotional learning skills with the tool.

Critical and Creative Thinking Skills for Problem-Solving	Social Emotional Learning Skills
Critical Thinking ☐ I can use different creative strategies that make thinking visible. ☐ I can analyze and evaluate issues and my ideas. ☐ I can use models and simulations to explore complex systems and issues. ☐ I can consider ideas from multiple perspectives. **Creative Thinking** ☐ I create novel ideas and consider new perspectives. ☐ I use brainstorming and visual diagrams to create and develop ideas, connections and inquiries. ☐ I can speculate and ask "what if" questions. ☐ I can use my existing knowledge to create novel concepts, products or processes. ☐ I can consider and explore a range of different ideas, including some that may or may not be possible. ☐ I know how to think in flexible ways to develop a range of perspectives and viewpoints. ☐ I create innovative works and ideas. ☐ I transform existing ideas and works and find innovative uses for them. ☐ I can describe and make metaphors and analogies.	☐ I am curious and open-minded.

Source: Graphic created by the authors.

Questions for Students to Support Higher-Order Thinking Skills

Table 9.3 Questions for students.

1. How did you use your critical (e.g. evaluation, analyzing, identifying, comparing and contrasting) and creative thinking using The Go Earth Tool? Please explain how. 2. This tool makes creative connections between features in Google Earth and your learning. Choose one of the following to answer: If you could make up a new feature in Google Earth, what would it be and how would it work? **OR** choose a topic or idea you are interested in and which Google Earth feature would be mostly interesting or useful? **OR** how would you improve the user experience of Google Earth?

Source: Graphic created by the authors.

Teacher Reflection

KEY TAKEAWAY: Using the Google Earth features through the lens of curiosity, adventure, exploration and discovery, your students can investigate diverse global topics and the world.

- Describe the scenario and classroom context—what was the problem you wanted to address with this tool?
- Did you achieve your goal?
- How did you use the tool to support students' higher-order thinking skills (HOTS)?

Complement With Other Tools

Multiculturalism: The Bias and Fairness Tool.

Chapter Notes

Use this space to plan and write your personal thoughts, ideas and questions here:

Create your mind-map or sketch out your ideas

CURIOSITY

GOOGLE EARTH
CREATE INDIVIDUAL PROJECTS:
Custom-make your own map.

ADVENTURE

GOOGLE EARTH
MEASURE DISTANCE & AREA:
Measure the distance from one spot to another.

DISCOVERY

GOOGLE EARTH
SCALE & PERSPECTIVE:
Zoom in and out, to see the details and the bigger picture.

EXPLORATION

GOOGLE EARTH
VOYAGER & DICE COMPONENTS:
Explore new places purposefully or randomly.

Figure 9.6 The Go Earth Tool blank worksheet.

Definitions

Curiosity: an eager wish to know or learn about something.
Exploration: the activity of searching and finding out about something.
Migration: the process of people traveling to a new place to live, usually in large numbers.
Monument: a structure or building that is built to honor a special person or event.
Wildlife bridge (corridor): a narrow area of land that is a habitat (= a suitable living environment) for wild animals and plants and that connects other habitats across an area where they cannot easily live.

The definitions in this list barring the last are sourced from Cambridge Online Dictionary (2023) and Merriam-Webster Dictionary (2023).

References

Cambridge University Press & Assessment (Ed.). (2023). *Cambridge online dictionary*. Retrieved November 14, 2023, from https://dictionary.cambridge.org/

Google. (2023). *Google earth outreach*. google.com. Retrieved November 24, 2023, from www.google.com/earth/outreach/tools/

Hornish, U. (2022, June 14). *Why your view of the world may be completely wrong*. lsa.umich.edu. Retrieved November 24, 2023, from https://sites.lsa.umich.edu/qmss/2022/06/14/why-your-view-of-the-world-may-be-completely-wrong/#:~:text=The%20Mercator%20map%2C%20though%20created,Bias%20and%20its%20withstanding%20implications.

Merriam-Webster, Incorporated (Ed.). (2023). *Merriam-Webster dictionary*. Merriam-Webster.com. Retrieved November 15, 2023, from www.merriam-webster.com/

Todd, A. (2019, August 1). *The AuthaGraph is the world's most accurate map*. Discovery.com. Retrieved November 30, 2023, from www.discovery.com/science/AuthaGraph-World-Accurate-Map

10

The Inquiry Builder Tool

Adding It All Up

Suggested Grade Level: 6–8

Key Takeaway—Developing strategies for inquiry generation.

understand think know imagine believe change
a an the
can could will do does should
+
topic choice
before already now then
ways things habits
new old biased open-minded right wrong
stereotypes bias assumptions prejudice
by with from and or
easy hard
in on
?
learned learn learning
have be
but if because
what why when how which
influenced influence(s) impact(s) impacted
I my me we our
this that
feelings ideas emotions behavior thinking
behave put challenge recognize feel
to for of about
is am are
use want need help make create

Figure 10.1 The Inquiry Builder Tool.
Source: Graphic created by the authors.

DOI: 10.4324/9781032664989-11

Global Skills and Key Themes

Skills: Collaboration, critical thinking, creative thinking, inquiry generation, open-mindedness and problem-solving.
Themes: Emotions, language and stereotypes.

Stories

FROM THE WORLD: Eco-tourism and conflict resolution.
DEFINITIONS: Assumptions, bias, open-minded, prejudice and stereotypes (p 151).

What Does The Inquiry Builder Tool Do?

The Inquiry Builder Tool gives students innovative ways to generate their own questions. As students' questions need to be written using a limited choice of words, this exercise can also encourage students to be more aware of the challenges faced by those learning a new language. Thinking more deeply about the words they use can support students in being more aware of the precise meaning of these words.

How to Use It

1. Choose your topic.
2. Choose relevant words from the boxes in addition to your keywords for the topic. You do not need to use all the boxes.
3. Use the addition/plus (+) symbol to connect the words and make a question.
4. Complete your question with the question mark.

EXAMPLE 1 Bullying in School

1. Choose your topic e.g. bullying in school.
2. Choose relevant words from the boxes in addition to your keywords e.g. **bullies, right** and **wrong.**
3. Use the addition/plus (+) symbol to connect the words and make a question using the question mark:
   Have + ***bullies*** + learned + ***right*** + from + ***wrong*** +?
   Do + ***bullies*** + have + feelings +?

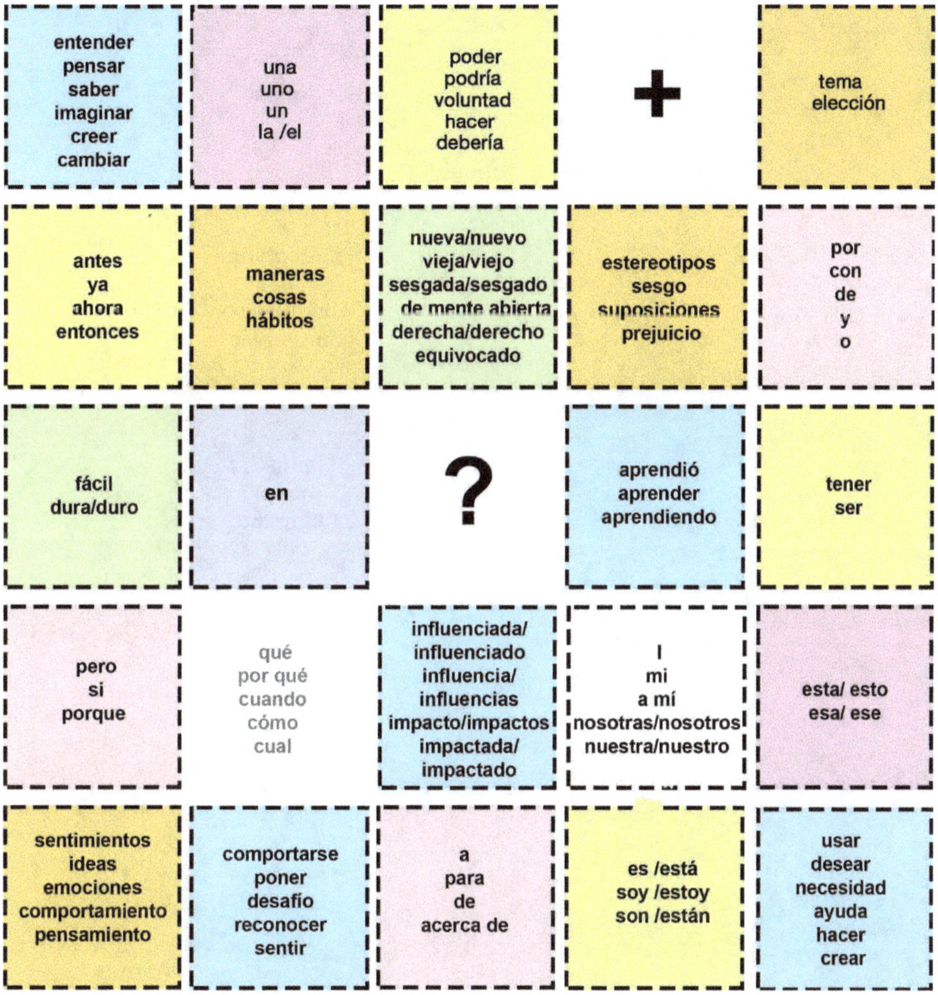
entender pensar saber imaginar creer cambiar
una uno un la /el
poder podría voluntad hacer debería
+
tema elección
antes ya ahora entonces
maneras cosas hábitos
nueva/nuevo vieja/viejo sesgada/sesgado de mente abierta derecha/derecho equivocado
estereotipos sesgo suposiciones prejuicio
por con de y o
fácil dura/duro
en
?
aprendió aprender aprendiendo
tener ser
pero si porque
qué por qué cuando cómo cual
influenciada/ influenciado influencia/ influencias impacto/impactos impactada/ impactado
I mi a mí nosotras/nosotros nuestra/nuestro
esta/ esto esa/ ese
sentimientos ideas emociones comportamiento pensamiento
comportarse poner desafío reconocer sentir
a para de acerca de
es /está soy /estoy son /están
usar desear necesidad ayuda hacer crear

Figure 10.2 The Inquiry Builder Tool Spanish version.
Source: Graphic created by the authors.
Herramienta Para La Creación De Preguntas
Spanish version translated by Manuela López Gil

understand think know imagine believe change
a an the
can could will do does should
+
topic choice
before already now then
ways things habits
new old biased open-minded right wrong
stereotypes bias assumptions prejudice
by with from and or
easy hard
in on
?
learned learn learning
have be
but if because
what why when how which
influenced influence(s) impact(s) impacted
I my me we our
this that
feelings ideas emotions behavior thinking
behave put challenge recognize feel
to for of about
is am are
use want need help make create

Figure 10.3 Example 1—The Inquiry Builder Tool.
Source: Graphic created by the authors.

Teachers should feel free to modify the tool. We have provided a blank template (p 150) for students to use with their own words or when using a language other than English. As more of a challenge, students can use just the words in the box, without keywords.

EXAMPLE 2—Topic: Impact and Prejudice
EXAMPLE 3—Topic: Stereotypes and My Emotions

EXAMPLE 2
Keyword: ***Security guards***
Topic: Impact and Prejudice

When I go into a shopping center I feel like security guards make assumptions about me based on the color of my skin.

Are	**security guards**	biased	?				
Are	**security guards**	influenced	by	bias	and	assumption	?
Can	**security guards**	change	old	ways	?		

EXAMPLE 3
Keyword: None
Topic: Stereotypes and My Emotions

Sometimes I judge people by the way they look. Can I change my attitudes towards stereotypes?

Can	I	challenge	my	ideas	about	stereotypes	?
Are	stereotypes	influenced	by	emotions	?		
Are	emotions	hard	to	recognize	?		

Figure 10.4 Writing questions—examples 2 and 3.
Source: Graphic created by the authors.

STORIES FROM THE WORLD

Eco-tourism and conflict resolution have been the focus for wildlife conservationist, author and former international cricketer, Saad Bin Jung, for many years. His work in South India and East Africa has transformed the lives of many people.

Saad used The Inquiry Builder Tool to generate questions relating to some of the challenges he and his team face as they try and find solutions to complex problems.

Topics: Human-Animal Conflict in Rural Areas and Eco-Tourism

Keywords: Animals, change, conflict, conservation, eco-tourism, human-animal, officials, people, rural, value and villagers.

Generating Inquiry

1. Can + human-animal + conflict + be + influenced + by + learning + about + challenges +?
2. Are villagers open-minded to change? Are officials open-minded to change?
3. Do rural people understand they can challenge stereotypes?
4. How can eco-tourism impact conservation?
5. Does eco-tourism help animals?
6. Do officials understand the value of conservation?
7. Can eco-tourism help villagers learn new ways?

(S. Bin Jung, personal communication, January 23, 2023)

Figure 10.5 Zebras.
Source: Image credit Saad Bin Jung.

Applications

Other ideas for your students to consider:

• Texting and emotions • Friendships and influences • Screen time and habits	• Sports and prejudice • Beliefs and values

What's in the Box?

The words in the boxes have been deliberately chosen e.g. **understand, think, know, imagine, influence, believe, change, behave, challenge, recognize, feel, learn, use, want, need, help, make** and **create** to refer to many of the ways we commonly think and act.

As students generate their questions using the words in the boxes, skills such as understanding, thinking, knowing, imagining, believing, recognizing, learning, making and creating are already embedded into the inquiry.

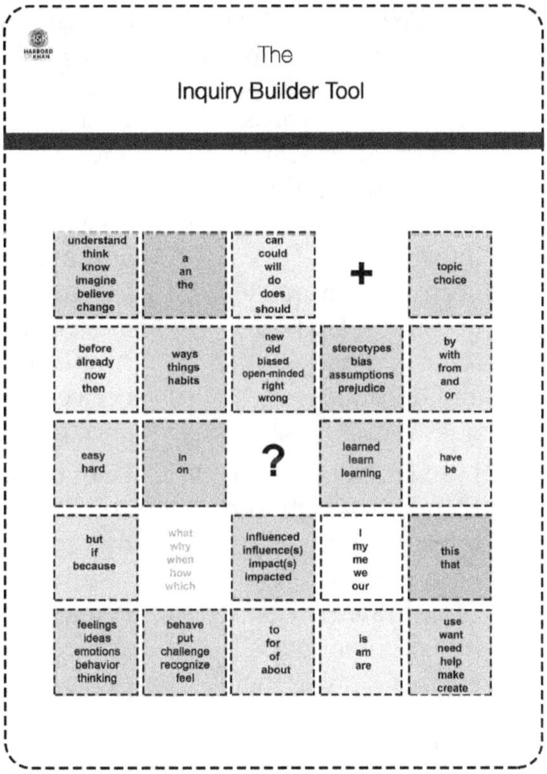
The
Inquiry Builder Tool
understand think know imagine believe change
a an the
can could will do does should
+
topic choice
before already now then
ways things habits
new old biased open-minded right wrong
stereotypes bias assumptions prejudice
by with from and or
easy hard
in on
?
learned learn learning
have be
but if because
what why when how which
influenced influence(s) impact(s) impacted
I my me we our
this that
feelings ideas emotions behavior thinking
behave put challenge recognize feel
to for of about
is am are
use want need help make create

Figure 10.6 The Inquiry Builder Tool card.
Source: Graphic created by the authors.

The choice of the words **stereotypes, bias, assumptions, prejudice, feelings, ideas, emotions, behavior** and **choice** guides students in generating inquiry relating to ethical issues and their own beliefs and values. Using words relating to time, such as **before, now, then** and **change** can give students opportunities to reflect on personal growth in conjunction with the key terms of the topic.

As the focus is on constructing questions with an already limited selection of words, the minus sign has not been used in the tool.

Suggestions to Align Skills With the Tool

Teachers can share this checklist with students to support them in identifying their higher-order thinking and social emotional skills.

Table 10.1 Skills alignment table.

Critical and Creative Thinking Skills for Problem-Solving		Social Emotional Learning Skills
☐ I can use keywords to generate research questions to gather and organize information. ☐ I can create inquiry questions, factual, topical, conceptual and debatable questions. ☐ I can check the accuracy of facts and interpretations. ☐ I can break up complicated ideas into different parts and reassemble them to develop new understanding.	☐ I use brainstorming and visual diagrams to create and develop ideas, connections and inquiries. ☐ I make unpredictable or surprising connections between objects and/or ideas. ☐ I can use different creative strategies that make thinking visible. ☐ I create novel ideas and consider new perspectives.	☐ The tool can be used to generate inquiry about any topic or subject, including social and emotional learning.

Source: Graphic created by the authors.

Questions for Students to Support Higher-Order Thinking Skills

1. Having to choose words from the boxes might limit how you express yourself. How did this make you feel?
2. Write a question using one of the following words: bias, stereotypes, assumptions and prejudice. Did using the tool help you think about these subjects in different ways?

Teacher Reflection

KEY TAKEAWAY Developing strategies for inquiry generation.

- Describe the scenario and classroom context—what was the problem you wanted to address with this tool?
- Did you achieve your goal?
- How did you use the tool to support students' higher-order thinking skills (HOTS)?

Complement With Other Tools

Inquiry generation: The Clock Tool and The Detective Tool.

Chapter Notes

Use this space to plan and write your personal thoughts, ideas and questions here:

Create your mind-map or sketch out your ideas

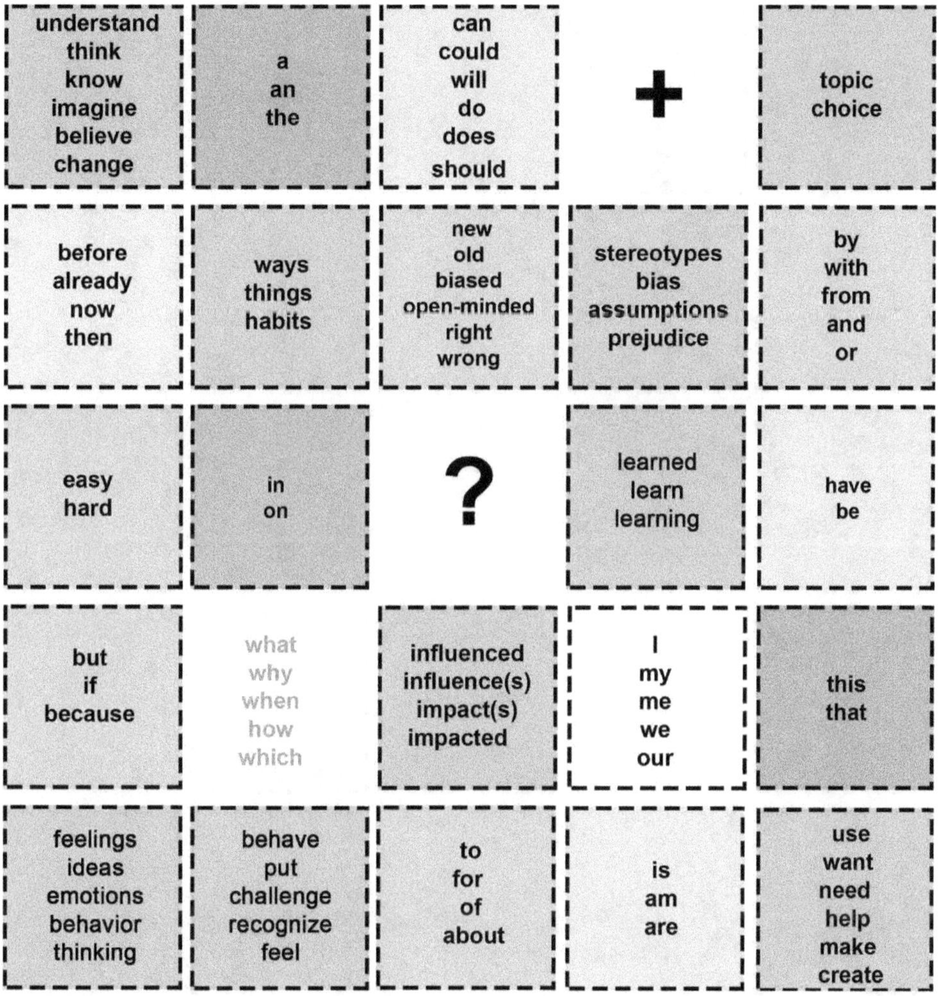
understand think know imagine believe change
a an the
can could will do does should
+
topic choice
before already now then
ways things habits
new old biased open-minded right wrong
stereotypes bias assumptions prejudice
by with from and or
easy hard
in on
?
learned learn learning
have be
but if because
what why when how which
influenced influence(s) impact(s) impacted
I my me we our
this that
feelings ideas emotions behavior thinking
behave put challenge recognize feel
to for of about
is am are
use want need help make create

Figure 10.7 The Inquiry Builder Tool template.
Source: Graphic created by the authors.

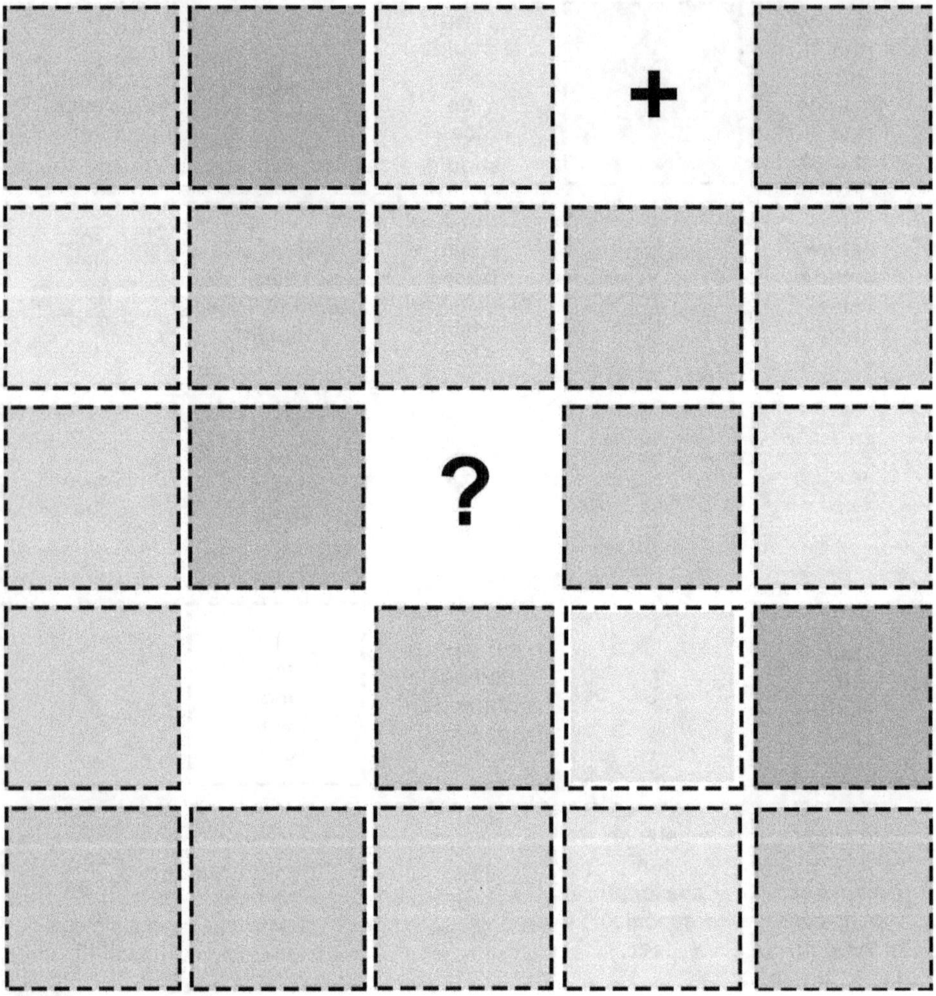
+
?

Figure 10.8 The Inquiry Builder Tool blank template
Source: Graphic created by the authors.

Definitions

Assumption: a belief or feeling that something is true or that something will happen, although there is no proof.
Bias: a strong feeling in favor of or against one group of people or one side in an argument, often not based on fair judgment.
Open-minded: willing to consider ideas and opinions that are new or different from your own.
Prejudice: an unfair and unreasonable opinion or feeling, especially when formed without enough thought or knowledge
Stereotypes: a set idea that people have about what someone or something is like, especially an idea that is wrong.

The definitions in this list are sourced from Cambridge Online Dictionary (2023), Merriam-Webster Dictionary (2023) and Oxford Learners Dictionaries (2023).

References

Cambridge University Press & Assessment (Ed.). (2023). *Cambridge online dictionary*. Retrieved November 14, 2023, from https://dictionary.cambridge.org/

Merriam-Webster, Incorporated (Ed.). (2023). *Merriam-Webster dictionary*. Merriam-Webster.com. Retrieved November 15, 2023, from www.merriam-webster.com/

Oxford University Press (Ed.). (2023). *Oxford learners dictionaries*. Retrieved November 15, 2023, from https//www.oxfordlearnersdictionairies.com

11

The Knowledge Twister Tool

Truth and Lies

Suggested Grade Level: 8–10

Key Takeaway—Understanding that knowledge can be manipulated to create new meaning and the importance of questioning your sources.

Global Skills and Key Themes

Skills: Critical thinking, creative thinking and problem-solving.
Themes: Imagination, flexibility, manipulation of information e.g. fake news and self-awareness.

Stories

FROM THE WORLD: Award-winning author Daniyal Mueenuddin and advertising-creative director and copywriter Kate Lightfoot.
DEFINITIONS: Amend, extrapolate, connect, deepen, distort, erase, imagine, integrate, invert, misunderstand, misremember, predict, saturate, reassemble, revise and translate (p 164).

DOI: 10.4324/9781032664989-12

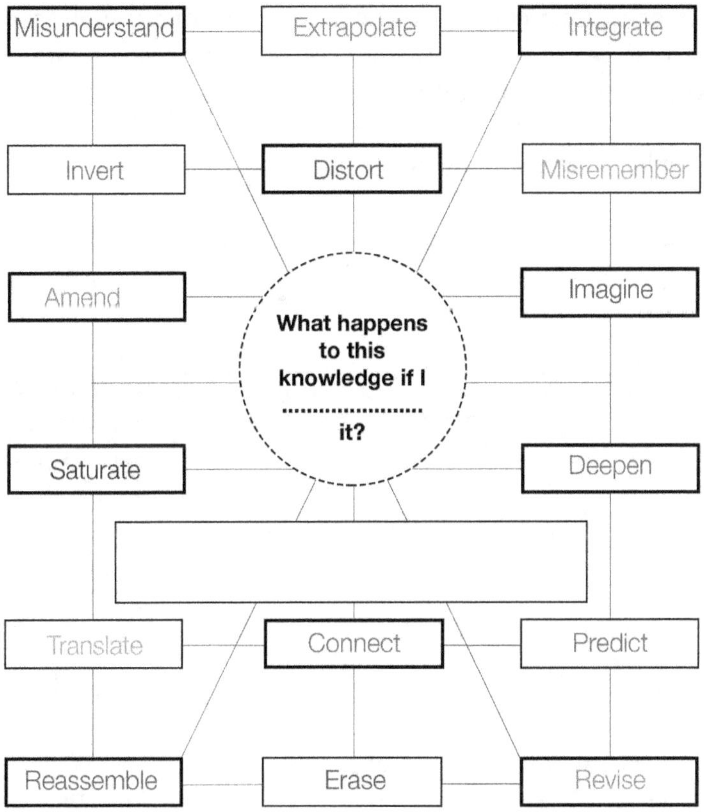
Misunderstand
Extrapolate
Integrate
Invert
Distort
Misremember
Amend
Imagine
What happens to this knowledge if I .... it?
Saturate
Deepen
Translate
Connect
Predict
Reassemble
Erase
Revise

Figure 11.1 The Knowledge Twister Tool.
Source: Graphic created by the authors.

What Does The Knowledge Twister Tool Do?

This tool gives students the opportunity to play with ideas and explore how facts and knowledge can be manipulated in both positive and negative ways.

How to Use It

Before using the tool, teachers can ask students to think about different ways of changing facts. Teachers could also replace 'knowledge' with 'music' or 'drama'.

1. Choose your topic/knowledge and place it in the long rectangle.
2. Select some of the words in the smaller boxes and apply these to your topic/knowledge e.g. what happens to this topic/knowledge if I 'translate' it?

Teachers can make connections between the manipulation of language and images, with reference to how the words invert, distort, saturate and ease are also tools and filters in Photoshop.

EXAMPLE 1 Topic: 'Dinosaurs Sang and Danced'

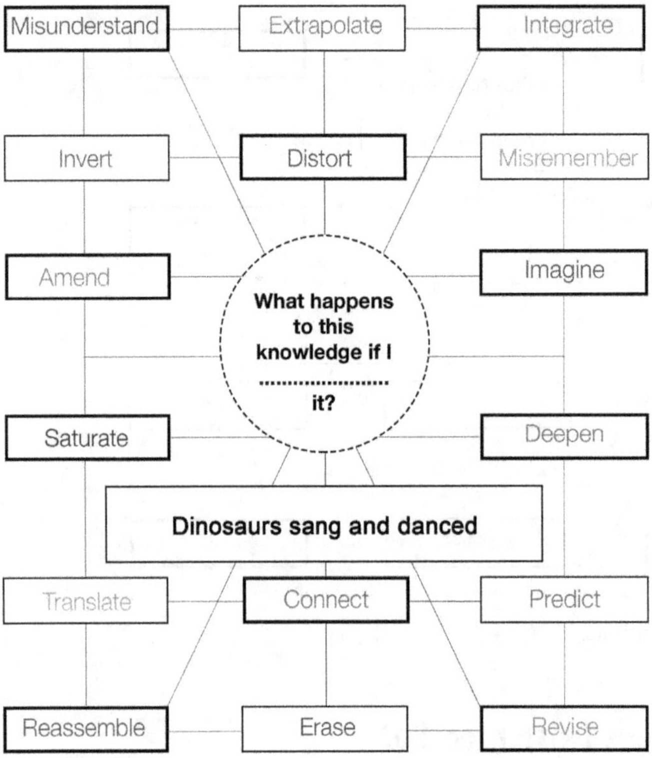

Misunderstand
Extrapolate
Integrate
Invert
Distort
Misremember
Amend
Imagine
What happens to this knowledge if I .... it?
Saturate
Deepen
Dinosaurs sang and danced
Translate
Connect
Predict
Reassemble
Erase
Revise

Figure 11.2 Example of using The Knowledge Twister Tool.
Source: Graphic created by the authors.

Most people would imagine that dinosaurs are reptiles and look like something out of *Jurassic Park*. Jack Horner, an American paleontologist, says that dinosaurs were probably brightly colored and danced and sang and were more like birds than reptiles (Funk & Muscosky, 2022).

What happens if this fact is deepened, inverted or erased?

Deepen

We would look more closely at the research and develop greater understanding.

Invert

We could say that dinosaurs had no voice and were not at all agile. How would this impact them and the world around them?

Erase

If the fact that dinosaurs sang and danced was erased, what would happen to our understanding of how they lived?

I transform existing ideas and works and find innovative uses for them.
POOF!

Figure 11.3 Platypus magician.
Source: Artwork by Linda Weil©.

STORIES FROM THE WORLD

We interviewed award-winning author Daniyal Mueenuddin and Kate Lightfoot, creative director, for some fresh outlooks on The Knowledge Twister Tool and how it could be used for creative inspiration not in a school context.

Author

Daniyal Mueenuddin (Danny) commenting on The Knowledge Twister Tool stated, "When I work I don't so consciously use these techniques of dislocation or disorientation—you must have a vocabulary for it—but to a great extent the process of writing fresh prose requires exactly that, shaking loose of the conventional or predictable associations—writing well is so much about making it new" (D. Mueenuddin, personal communication, August 22, 2023).

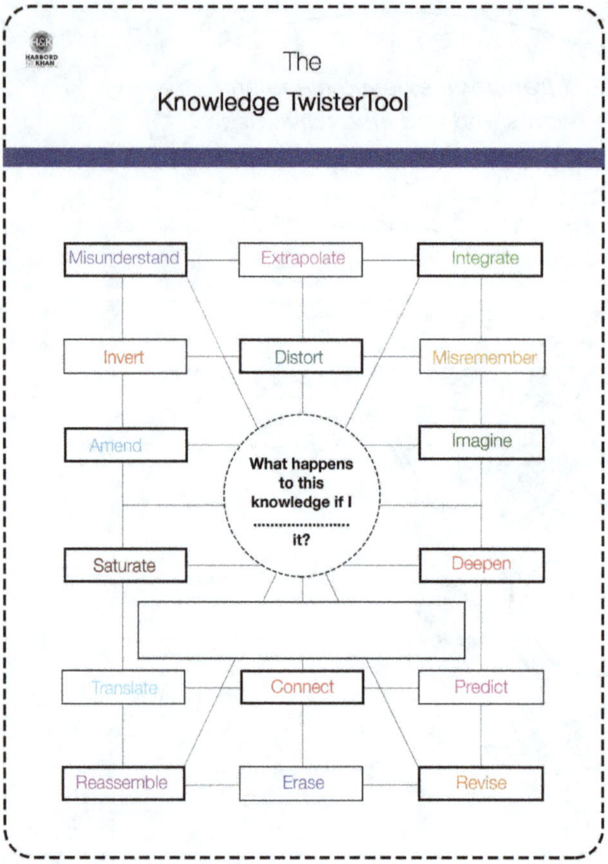
The
Knowledge TwisterTool
Misunderstand
Extrapolate
Integrate
Invert
Distort
Misremember
Amend
Imagine
What happens to this knowledge if I .... it?
Saturate
Deepen
Translate
Connect
Predict
Reassemble
Erase
Revise

Figure 11.4 The Knowledge Twister Tool card.
Source: Graphic created by authors.

Danny used The Knowledge Twister Tool to explore crocodile management!

Topic: Nobody is despised who can manage a crocodile.
Deepen this topic: Managing crocodiles requires special equipment, such as a crocodile-proof suit and a good understanding of emergency medicine, in case the management proves more challenging than anticipated.
Amend this topic: While it is true that no one who can manage a crocodile is despised, it is quite possible that this is not a skill that is of great use to the layman. Crocodile wrangling does not put jam on the table, except for Steve Irwin and his ilk.
Invert the topic: All persons who manage crocodiles are despised. After all, what did the poor croc do to justify your so-called 'management'. The poor croc was 'managing' himself well enough, darn you, until you came along with your rubber boots and your crocodile-noose. Leave the poor crocs alone, get a real job!
Daniyal Mueenuddin's book of connected novellas, titled This Is Where the Serpent Lives, is forthcoming from Knopf.

Creative Director (Advertising)

Kate Lightfoot is a creative director and copywriter who has worked in ad agencies and in-house creative departments since 1996. Her entire career has involved coming up with novel ideas to help clients solve business problems. Kate's job is all about coming up with a broad variety of ideas, which she can refine later. Kate used The Knowledge Twister Tool to think about how she could communicate the idea that 'ABC Energy is one of Australia's greenest power companies' in an interesting way

Topic: ABC Energy is one of Australia's greenest power companies

At this point I'd start sniffing around the topic. At its most basic level, this sentence combines two thoughts (power company + green), so I'd start expanding on those areas e.g. What images/words do I associate with green: polar bears, bees, nature, carbon neutral, dolphins, etc.

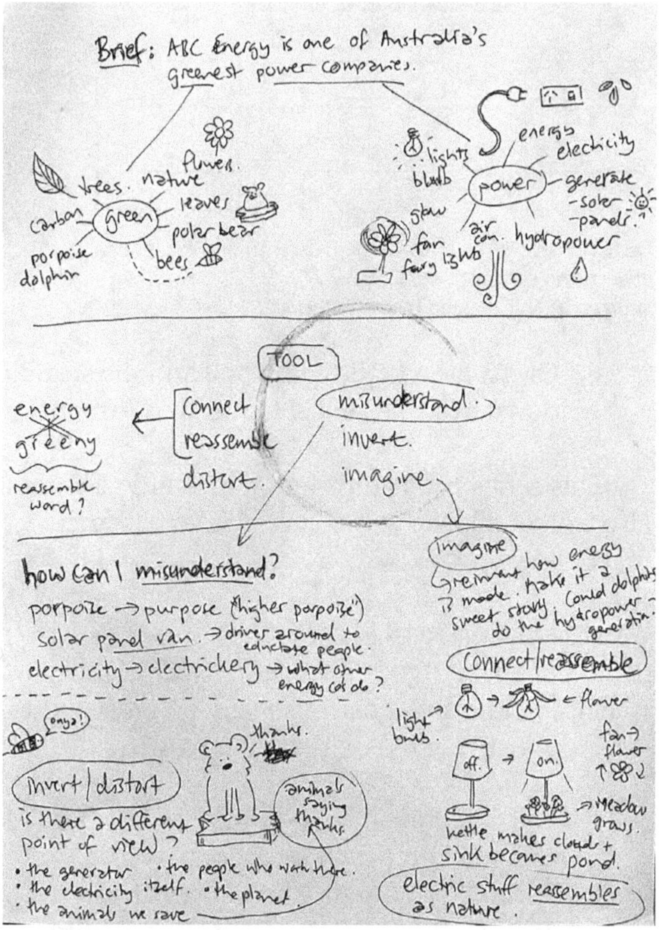
Brief: ABC Energy is one of Australia's greenest power companies.
green
trees. nature
flower.
leaves
polar bear
bees
carbon
porpoise dolphin
power
energy
electricity
generate
-solar
-panels.
light bulb
hydropower
fan
air con.
fairy lights
TOOL
connect
reassemble
distort.
misunderstand.
invert.
imagine
energy
greeny
reassemble word?
how can I misunderstand?
porpoise → purpose (higher porpoise)
solar panel van. → driver around to educate people.
electricity → electrickery → what other energy cd do?
imagine
connect/reassemble
light bulb
flower
off.
on.
meadow grass.
kettle makes clouds + sink becomes pond.
electric stuff reassembles as nature.
invert/distort
is there a different point of view?
• the generator • the people who work there.
• the electricity itself. • the planet
• the animals we save
thanks.
animals saying thanks.

Figure 11.5 Kate's Lightfoot's brainstorm.
Source: Graphic created by Kate Lightfoot.

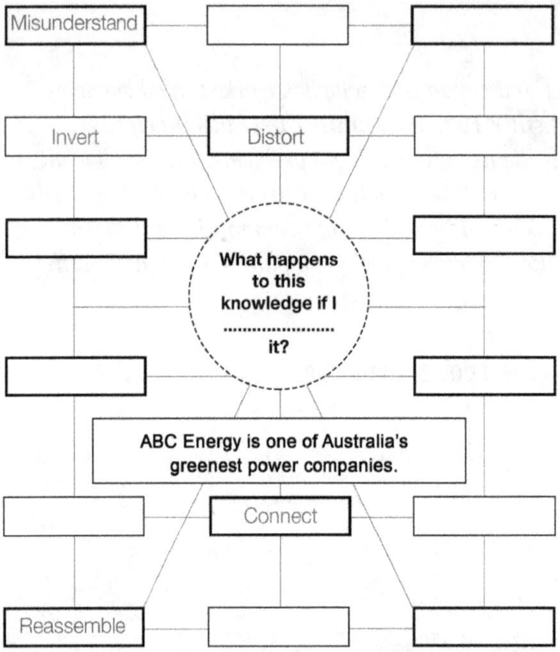
Misunderstand
Invert
Distort
What happens
to this
knowledge if I
....
it?
ABC Energy is one of Australia's
greenest power companies.
Connect
Reassemble

Figure 11.6 Using The Knowledge Twister Tool to explore an advertising concept.
Source: Graphic created by the authors.

What If I Connect or Reassemble the Topic?

Let's try connecting some of those green associations with some energy associations. Could this lead to interesting visuals for a video?

- Maybe I start with a light globe, but it's also a plant—petals could peel away to reveal a globe inside.
- Or maybe there's a desk lamp and when it's turned on, the light makes a little meadow grow underneath it.
- Or maybe a kettle could boil and the steam forms clouds which rain down over the sink. Oh, then it'd turn into a little frog pond.

This series could turn into a nice little TV commercial or video. I could also reassemble the word 'energy' to make 'greeny'. Maybe there's an idea in that too.

What If I Misunderstand the Topic?

Sometimes when you're working with a creative partner, one of you says something and the other mishears it. And you have this great idea nobody came up with! Let me try that on my own.

- You could mishear 'porpoise' as 'purpose'. Maybe using this power company gives you a higher porpoise.
- 'Electricity' sounds a bit like 'electrickery'. Maybe I could talk about greenwashing as electrickery—something our competitors do!
- Solar panel → Solar Panel Van. Maybe we deck out a panel van with solar panels and send our 'Solar Panel Van' to schools or events to explain the benefits of solar power. Might get us some PR.

What If I Invert/Distort the Topic?

What if I look for a distorted point of view? Usually in advertising we'd look at things from the energy company's point of view or the customer's point of view.

But what if we looked at this from the electricity's point of view. (Would electricity be happier if it was renewable? How would it talk?) Or the planet's point of view. (How would it feel about the situation? What would it do?) What about the animal's point of view—maybe I show polar bears and bees and dolphins all thanking people in different ways for choosing ABC Energy (K. Lightfoot, personal communication, November 16, 2023).

Suggestions to Align Skills With the Tool

Teachers can share this checklist with students to support them in identifying their higher-order thinking and social emotional skills.

Table 11.1 Skills alignment table.

Critical and Creative Thinking Skills for Problem-Solving	Social Emotional Learning Skills
Critical Thinking ☐ I can analyze and evaluate issues and my ideas. ☐ I can develop contrary or opposing arguments. ☐ I can break up complicated ideas into different parts and reassemble them to develop new understanding. ☐ I can check the facts and interpretations. **Creative Thinking** ☐ I can consider and explore a range of different ideas, including some that may or may not be possible. ☐ I make unpredictable or surprising connections between objects and/or ideas. ☐ I can use different creative strategies that make thinking visible. ☐ I can describe and make metaphors and analogies.	☐ This tool could be used to explore social emotional learning by replacing: 'What happens to this (knowledge) if I ———it?" with "What happens to me/my relationships if I ———this emotion or feeling?"

Source: Graphic created by the authors.

Questions for Students to Support Higher-Order Thinking Skills

Table 11.2 Questions for students.

1. Do you think it makes a difference if facts are intentionally 'misremembered' or 'misunderstood' in the real world (e.g. fake news in politics and historical documents)?
2. Did the tool make you think more creatively about the topic in different ways?
3. What other boxes such as 'invert' and 'deepen' could you add to the diagram? How would these impact the facts and knowledge?

Source: Graphic created by the authors.

Teacher Reflection

KEY TAKEAWAY: Understanding that knowledge can be manipulated to create new meaning and the importance of questioning your sources.

- Describe the scenario and classroom context—what was the problem you wanted to address with this tool?
- Did you achieve your goal?
- How did you use the tool to support students' higher-order thinking skills (HOTS)?

Complement With Other Tools

Multiple perspectives: The Building Block Tool and The Points of View Tool.

Chapter Notes

Use this space to plan and write your personal thoughts, ideas and questions here:

Create your mind-map or sketch out your ideas

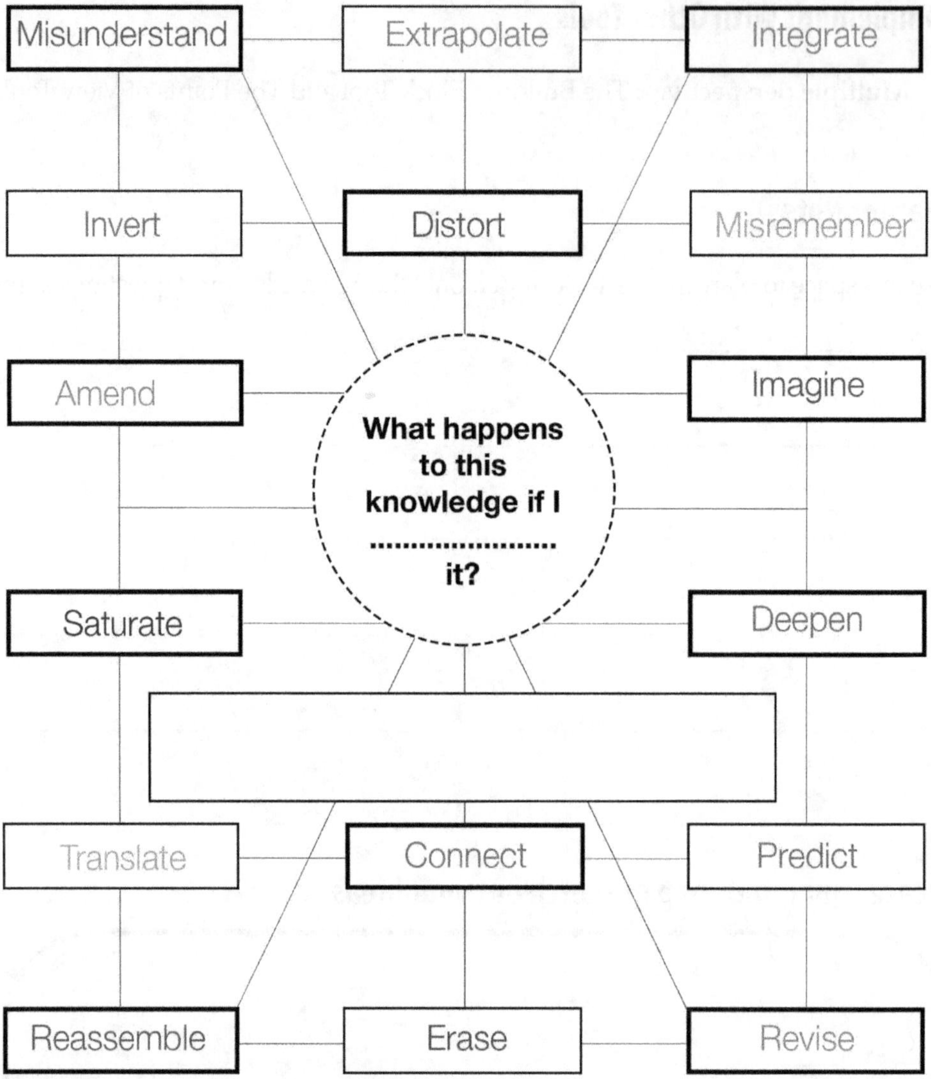
Misunderstand
Extrapolate
Integrate
Invert
Distort
Misremember
Amend
What happens to this knowledge if I .... it?
Imagine
Saturate
Deepen
Translate
Connect
Predict
Reassemble
Erase
Revise

Figure 11.7 The Knowledge Twister Tool template.
Source: Graphic created by the authors.

Definitions

Amend: to change the words of a text.
Connect: to join or be joined with something else.
Deepen: going or being a long way down from the top or surface to make something deeper.
Distort: to change the shape of something so that it looks strange or unnatural.
Extrapolate: to guess or think about what might happen using information that is already known.
Erase: to remove something, especially a pencil mark by rubbing it.
Imagine: to form or have a mental picture or idea of something.
Integrate: to mix with and join society or a group of people, often changing to suit their way of life, habits and customs.
Invert: to turn something upside down or change the order of two things.
Misunderstand: to think you have understood someone or something when you have not.
Misremember: to remember something in the wrong way.
Predict: to say that an event or action will happen in the future, especially as a result of knowledge or experience.
Saturate: to fill a thing or place completely so that no more can be added.
Reassemble: to make something whole again by joining its separate parts together.
Revise: to look at or consider again an idea, piece of writing, etc., in order to correct or improve it.
Translate: to change words into another language.

The definitions in this list are sourced from Cambridge Online Dictionary (2023) and Merriam-Webster Dictionary (2023).

References

Cambridge University Press & Assessment (Ed.). (2023). *Cambridge online dictionary*. Retrieved November 14, 2023, from https://dictionary.cambridge.org/

Funk, M., & Muscosky, L. (Hosts). (2022, August). Highlights, Jack Horner, Renowned dinosaur palaeontologist [Video podcast interview]. In *Oneplanetpodcast.org*. Spotify. https://open.spotify.com/episode/7sL5Mxd78QFwqHlJMvOiL6

Merriam-Webster, Incorporated (Ed.). (2023). *Merriam-Webster dictionary*. Merriam-Webster.com. Retrieved November 15, 2023, from www.merriam-webster.com/

12

The Myself Tool

Same or Different?

Suggested Grade Level: 5–8

Key Takeaway—Gaining a deeper understanding of who we are in different contexts and the factors that influence us.

Global Skills and Key Themes

Skills: Critical thinking, creative thinking, problem-solving and reflection.
Themes: Ethical dilemmas, identity, open-mindedness, peer pressure, relationships, social conformity and self-awareness.

Stories

FROM THE CLASSROOM: Discussions about bullying with Grade 5 - Creativity and identity in Grade Visual Arts.
DEFINITIONS: Ethical dilemmas, harmony and conflict (p 176).

DOI: 10.4324/9781032664989-13

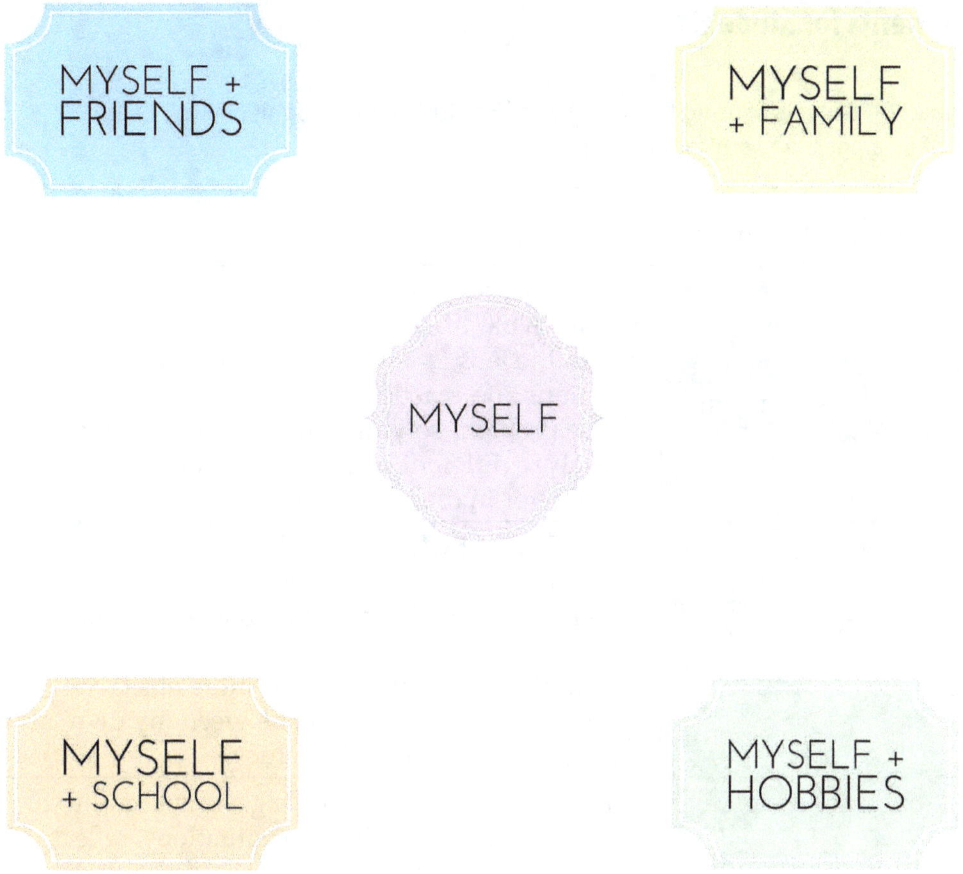
MYSELF +
FRIENDS
MYSELF
+ FAMILY
MYSELF
MYSELF
+ SCHOOL
MYSELF +
HOBBIES

Figure 12.1 The Myself Tool.
Source: Graphic created by the authors.

What Does The Myself Tool Do?

The Myself Tool can support students in analyzing and understanding people and situations that influence them.

Benefits for Students

Table 12.1 Benefits of using the tool to support student metacognition, well-being, self-awareness and ethical thinking.

The Myself Tool can help me:	
Metacognition Can support creative and critical thinking, problem-solving and reflection	• Consider ideas from multiple perspectives. • Ask "what if" questions. • Can the lens I view myself through affect my actions and reactions? • Use problem-solving skills to describe and analyze different solutions to feelings and behavior in different contexts.
Well-being and self-awareness	• Think about who I am and how I can be different in different situations. • Reflect on people and situations that influence me. • Examine stressful situations more objectively e.g. when there is conflict between my own, my family's or my school's values.
Ethical thinking	• Explore ethical dilemmas e.g. How I have to or want to behave in different situations, reflect on what is fair or honest. • Do these different ways I behave with different important people and places create an ethical dilemma?

Source: Graphic created by the authors.

How to Use It

This tool gives you a template to discuss any issue with students and is a starting point for deep discussions. Students can also consider the dynamics between these different relationships.

1. Choose your topic.
2. Use the different shapes to explore your topic and think about who you are and how you act in different situations.

Some questions to discuss with your students:

EXAMPLE 1 Ethical Dilemmas

Do you feel harmony or conflict when you change your point of view? An ethical dilemma can be a way to explore how you feel, think and behave about a sticky situation.

An ethical dilemma is a situation or problem where you have two different perspectives and both points of view have ethical issues. For example, you see a new student who is picking on another student at the same time your friend is being bullied by an older student. What do you want to do? Do you want to take action and, if so, which action, or do you walk away?

MYSELF + FRIENDS	MYSELF + FAMILY	MYSELF + SCHOOL	MYSELF + HOBBIES
How are you with your family and with your friends? Do you change who you are when you are with some of your friends or at school? What influences you to be a different person? Is it culture, your beliefs, your environment, your age, your interests, your own or others' expectations, your peers and your school or other factors?	Why are we often different in different situations and with different people e.g. in the style, tone and choice of language we use with our friends? Would it be the same for a conversation in a more formal setting for example at the principal's office or the doctor's?	How we speak, dress and act can be very different, and why is this? Is it because of social conformity, our fear of consequences if we 'break' the rules of our family, school or peer group? Is it just because we can change who we are and reflect different parts of our character?	Do we get to choose our own hobbies or are they chosen for us? How do our hobbies and other activities give us opportunities to meet different people and groups? Do our hobbies relieve our stress or add to it? Do our hobbies give us a chance to express a side of ourselves that we usually don't show?

Figure 12.2 The Myself Tool with questions.
Source: Image created by the authors.

- What questions do you need to ask?
- Who has been affected and how have they been affected?
- Can you explain how you feel?
- Do you feel like you made the best choice? Can you give reasons why you chose the option that you did?
- If the students are unhappy, what needs to be done to fix their friendship?
- What could be done so this situation doesn't happen again?

Now think about what would your family expect you to do?
What would your friends expect you to do?
What about your school?
What would your teacher or sports coach expect you to do?

EXAMPLE 2 Exploring Personal Identity

Jenny Chen, a Chinese teacher from Wesley College, Melbourne, translated The Myself Tool into Mandarin (Figure 12.3) and explained how she could use it in class:

> *The "Myself Tool©" is a resource that can be utilized in a classroom to promote self-expression, and a deeper understanding of personal identity. This tool encourages students to explore various aspects of themselves by reflecting on different facets such as personal interest, school and family. Students can create a presentation of themselves to share their unique identities with their peers, fostering a sense of community within the classroom.*
>
> (J. Chen, personal communication, November 18, 2023).

The Myself Tool Same or Different? 我自己的工具相同 或 不同？

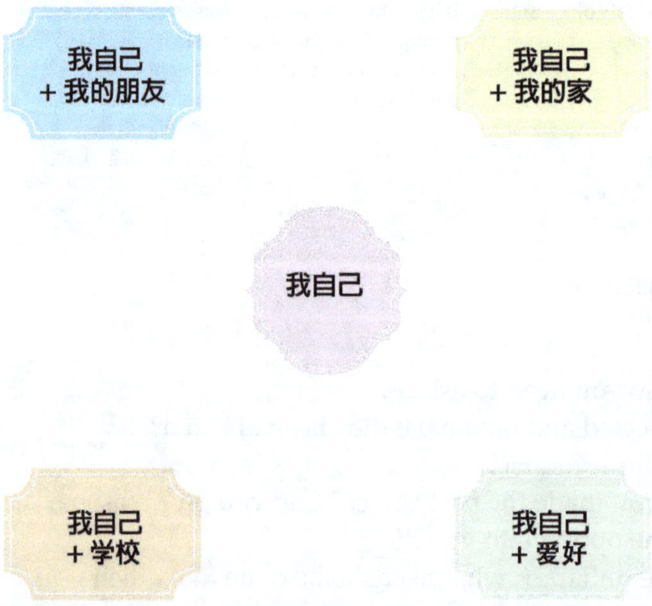
我自己
+ 我的朋友
我自己
+ 我的家
我自己
我自己
+ 学校
我自己
+ 爱好

Myself 我自己

Myself + My Friends 我自己 + 我的朋友

Myself +My Family 我自己 + 我的家

Myself + School 我自己 + 学校

Myself+Hobbies我自己 + 爱好

Figure 12.3 The Myself Tool in Mandarin.
Source: Graphic created by the authors.

STORIES FROM THE CLASSROOM

Bullying and the Impact of the Tool Beyond School

A Grade 5 teacher used The Myself Tool in her classroom to explore ideas about identity and bullying. Students understood how they are often different people at home and at school. They spoke about how and why this happens and shared thoughts on how they could bridge the gap in some ways, but not all. Most students felt it was important to keep aspects of who they are with friends in separate boxes from their relationships with family.

Students discussed their personal or friends' experiences with bullying and how their reactions would be affected by the influence of family, friends and school. They reflected on their parents' response to a situation in which someone was being bullied at school as well as what action they felt prepared or unprepared to take to protect their friends.

Discussion also included the school's response to incidents of bullying which had been reported. Using the tool helped some students to share that they had been bullied by older students. Two of them had found the courage to confront those bullies, encouraged by their peers. They described the fear they felt during the confrontation followed by the relief and sense of empowerment when it worked.

The discussion in the classroom inspired some students to find the courage to address stressful situations in their own homes (conflict with siblings or cousins) and were glad they had taken that step. One girl was being bullied online. She confronted her bully and reported him to her parents. Others talked about how their own reactions during the discussion had surprised them. One student said the discussion on influences had made her think at length about how her innate shyness held her back from facing challenging situations and she felt, going forward, she may be able to take a different approach (Teacher A, personal communication, July 10, 2023).

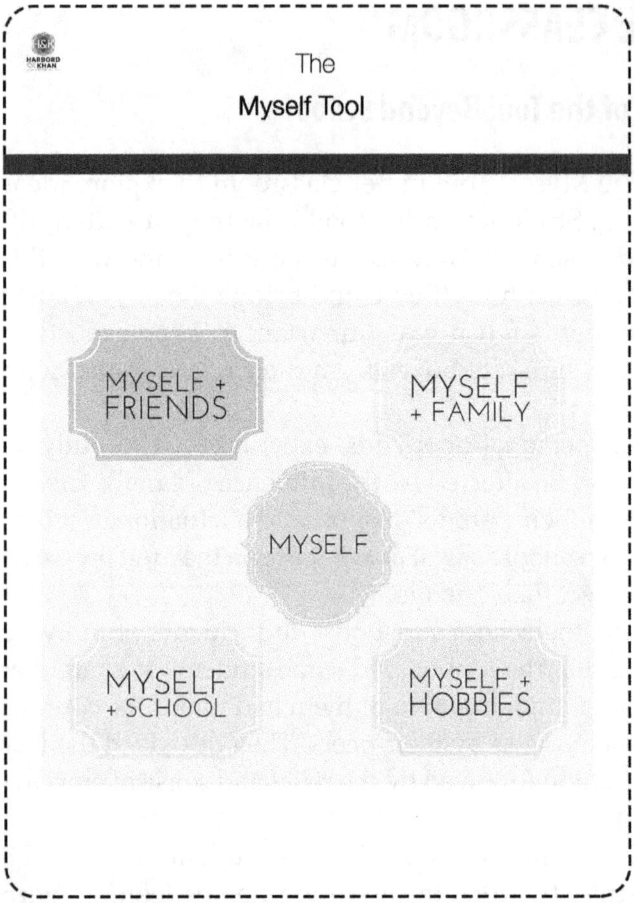
The
Myself Tool
MYSELF + FRIENDS
MYSELF + FAMILY
MYSELF
MYSELF + SCHOOL
MYSELF + HOBBIES

Figure 12.4 The Myself Tool card.
Source: Graphic created by the authors.

Grade 8 students used The Myself Tool to explore identity and creativity in visual arts.

Topic: How do I express my creativity depending on my circumstances?

A Grade 8 student from ABA Oman International School, Dhiaeddine Keskes, reflected on creativity in different situations and ways of behaving with different people.

How did it feel to imagine yourself in different situations?

I feel that it is difficult in school when you have to be creative in Art and English, but when it is about being creative in my hobbies, then I can be really creative. I can play really good football and find a creative way to score.

You have to be a bit different with different people especially when they are from a different place and have different cultures. You can maybe do something that will make them really angry or is really insulting to them, and maybe they can do something that you will find very insulting. That is why you will have to be a bit different, so that you don't insult them even though you mean it in a good way (D. Keskes, personal communication, November 2, 2023).

I can consider ideas from
multiple perspectives.

Figure 12.5 Dragon looking at its reflection in the mirror.
Source: Artwork by Linda Weil©.

Suggestions to Align Skills With the Tool

Teachers can share this checklist with students to support them in identifying their higher-order thinking and social emotional skills.

Table 12.2 Skills alignment table.

Critical and Creative Thinking Skills for Problem-Solving	Social Emotional Learning Skills
Critical Thinking ☐ I can analyze and evaluate issues and my ideas in different situations/scenarios. ☐ I can consider ideas from multiple perspectives. ☐ I can develop contrary or opposing arguments. ☐ I can analyze and evaluate my emotions **Creative Thinking** ☐ I can use different creative strategies that make thinking visible. ☐ I create novel ideas and consider new perspectives. ☐ I can speculate and ask "what if" questions.	☐ I can manage and communicate my emotions in a thoughtful way. ☐ I can reflect on my own, my family's and my community's well-being.

Source: Graphic created by the authors.

Questions for Students to Support Higher-Order Thinking Skills

Table 12.3 Questions for students.

1. Explain how it felt to imagine yourself in different situations.
2. Did the tool get you to think about how and why you can be different with different people? Give reasons for your answer.
3. Explain how the tool impacted or didn't impact your understanding of other people's viewpoints.

Source: Graphic created by the authors

Teacher Reflection

KEY TAKEAWAY: Gaining a deeper understanding of who we are in different contexts and the factors that influence us.

- Describe the scenario and classroom context—what was the problem you wanted to address with this tool?
- Did you achieve your goal?
- How did you use the tool to support students' higher-order thinking skills (HOTS)?

Complement With Other Tools

Self-regulation and identity: The Orange Sun Tool, The Plus-Minus Tool, The Polka Dot Tool and The Points of View Tool.

Chapter Notes

Use this space to plan and write your personal thoughts, ideas and questions here:

Create your mind-map or sketch out your ideas

The Myself Tool© Blank Template (available as online support material)

MYSELF + HOBBIES
MYSELF + SCHOOL
MYSELF + FAMILY
MYSELF + FRIENDS

Figure 12.6 The Myself Tool blank template.

Definitions

Conflict: an active disagreement between people with opposing opinions or principles.
Ethical dilemmas: an ethical dilemma is a situation or problem where you have two different perspectives and both points of view have ethical issues.
Harmony: a situation in which people are peaceful and agree with each other, or when things seem right or suitable together.

The definitions in this list are sourced from Cambridge Online Dictionary (2023) and Merriam-Webster Dictionary (2023).

References

Cambridge University Press & Assessment (Ed.). (2023). *Cambridge online dictionary*. Retrieved November 14, 2023, from https://dictionary.cambridge.org/

Merriam-Webster, Incorporated (Ed.). (2023). *Merriam-Webster dictionary*. Merriam-Webster.com. Retrieved November 15, 2023, from www.merriam-webster.com/

13

The Orange Sun Tool

Shine a Light

Suggested Grade Level: 5–7

Key Takeaway—Developing a deeper understanding of factors e.g. events, beliefs and emotions that can impact us.

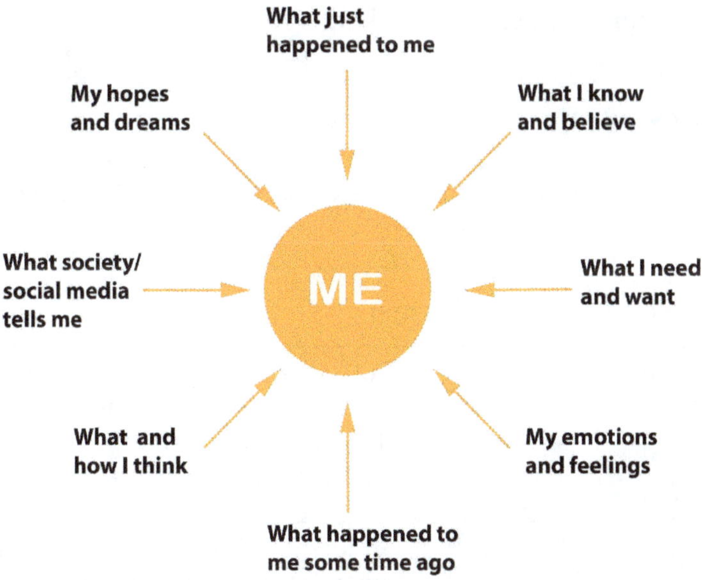
What just happened to me
What I know and believe
What I need and want
My emotions and feelings
What happened to me some time ago
What and how I think
What society/ social media tells me
My hopes and dreams
ME

Figure 13.1 The Orange Sun Tool.
Source: Graphic created by the authors.

DOI: 10.4324/9781032664989-14

Global Skills and Key Themes

Skills: Critical thinking, problem-solving and reflection.
Themes: Conflict resolution, identity, relationships, social and self-awareness.

Stories

FROM THE COUNSELING OFFICE: Rebuilding a friendship in Grade 5.
DEFINITIONS: Beliefs, emotions, feelings, hopes and dreams (p 189).

What Does The Orange Sun Tool Do?

Illuminates student understanding of experiences, events, thinking, knowledge, beliefs, emotions, influences, aspirations and wants and needs. This tool is flexible in that it can be used in different situations and it can support students in taking stock of and reflecting on something that has happened recently or some time ago.

Teachers can use the tool at their discretion, to guide students when discussing a range of social emotional issues. Only teachers know their students and their emotional well-being, so bear this in mind, as this tool needs to be used with sensitivity in certain situations. Teachers could also apply it in relation to their own thinking.

Benefits for Students

Table 13.1 Benefits of using the tool to support student metacognition, well-being, self-awareness and ethical thinking.

The Orange Sun Tool can help me:	
Metacognition Can support critical thinking, problem-solving and reflection.	• Problem-solve by breaking up all the factors so I can think about other perspectives. • Think about what happened and how I could think about solutions.
Well-being Support self-management and regulation.	• Understand how I can self-regulate my behavior and grow my resilience.

(Continued)

Table 13.1 (Continued)

The Orange Sun Tool can help me:	
Self-awareness Reflect critically on my emotions and behavior. Be aware of the influence of society and media on me. Move toward an understanding of what I know and believe. Move toward an understanding of what I need and want.	• Understand my emotions better. • Think about how my emotions can have an effect on both myself and my classmates. • Realize how social media can change my opinions or sometimes my actions. • Realize what I know as opposed to what I think. • Think about what I need and what I want. Also, with class discussions, it can help me understand the differences between needs and wants.
Ethical thinking Think about ethical issues and values e.g. empathy, fairness, caring, integrity, open-mindedness	• Think about looking at a problem using an ethical lens, such as empathy or fairness. • If I have an ethical problem, does looking at it through caring, for example, change my opinions or actions?

How to Use It

Read The Orange Sun Tool clockwise or in any order the teacher chooses to use it and answer the questions.

What just happened to me?	Students can describe what their emotions are and how they feel.
What happened to me some time ago? Students can identify the event that took place recently or some time ago. This could be connected to content from the curriculum or it could be used for social and emotional situations.	**What and how I think** (about the situation) What do students think about the situation and how are they thinking? Are they reflecting calmly? Are they worrying or anxious? Do students want to be on their own when thinking or prefer to be in a group?

What I know and believe (about the event) Students can communicate what they know and believe about what happened. If more than one student is involved, it can help students and teachers understand the bigger picture using multiple perspectives. **What I need and want** (at this moment or in the future) What do students need and want to bring some kind of resolution to the situation? **My emotions and feelings**	**What society/social media tells me** This can be used if and when necessary. What do the people around students and social media have to say about the situation? **My hopes and dreams** This can be used if and when necessary. What do students hope for in this situation? What do they dream of? We understand that hopes and dreams are relative; some students may take them for granted, but for others these may seem like a reach. The scale of students' hopes and dreams doesn't need to be huge and most likely will change with their life experience.

STORIES FROM THE COUNSELING OFFICE

Counselor

Shawn Edwards, an Elementary School counselor from Saigon South International School, used The Orange Sun Tool with a Grade 5 student who was working through an internal conflict she was having with some past behaviors toward a classmate.

I met with a Grade 5 student who has lots of thoughts, and they are often scattered, so this was a helpful tool to allow her the time and space to sort through some of these thoughts and feelings. She has been working through a situation between her and another student last year. She has some guilt around her actions of not being kind toward this person, but she was unsure what to do about something that had happened in the past. We used this tool to create a plan to bring some closure to this situation she was struggling with.

She shared that she is not very organized both in her physical world (her room and locker at school) as well as with her thoughts and feelings sometimes. She said she often does not organize things because if you do, you might get lost trying to find something! Because of this, she will often just speak her thoughts all at once and jumbled up and doesn't always seem to find her way out of them. I asked her if we could use this tool together to see if it might help her organize her thoughts about this specific situation that she was still having some big feelings about and she agreed to see if it would help.

Though the questions are given in present tense, I adjusted them to meet her needs of sorting through a previous situation.

Through the leading questions, she was able to move past just the actions toward herself and a classmate and begin to identify some of the feelings this brought up in her. She used the 'What I need and want' to give direction to how she could move forward with solving this past conflict, which was creating large feelings of remorse in her. She was caught up in reiterating the situation again and again but had been unable to move out of that into recognizing her feelings and the feelings of the other person.

When we moved to the 'What happened to me some time ago' prompt, she was able to make a connection between the actions of her siblings toward her and how she felt and then compare this to how her actions might have made her classmate feel. It was definitely an 'aha!' moment for her when she was able to have that connection of emotions.

In the end, her 'Hopes and dreams' were to apologize to this student. Once she was able to find herself in a similar situation with her siblings and realize how it felt for her and then possibly how it felt for her classmate, she made the choice to ask them for their forgiveness for her previous behavior.

It took a lot of bravery on her side, but the end result was a great relief for her and a rekindled friendship between the two students (S. Edwards, personal communication, November 21, 2023).

Applications

Here are a few ideas that could be used at the teacher's discretion to inspire discussions, thoughtful reflections and build student resilience.

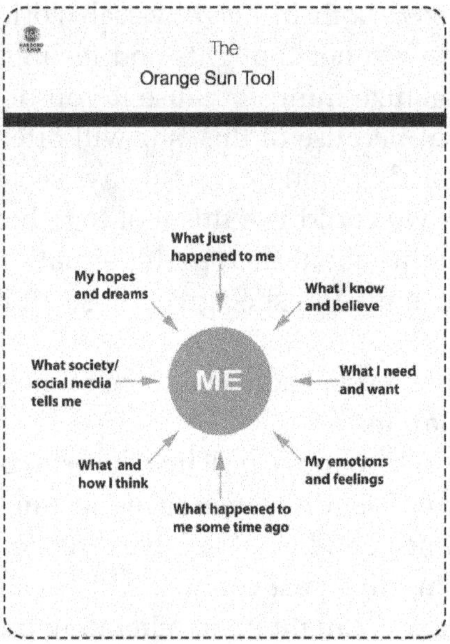
The
Orange Sun Tool
What just happened to me
What I know and believe
What I need and want
My emotions and feelings
What happened to me some time ago
What and how I think
What society/ social media tells me
My hopes and dreams
ME

Figure 13.2 The Orange Sun Tool card.
Source: Graphic created by the authors.

- Bullying situations.
- A new student in the class.
- Students not included in groups or activities.
- Not being asked to the prom.
- Students who are isolated during lunch breaks.
- Students who come from a different socioeconomic or cultural background from others in school.
- Being the student who is always chosen last for sports teams.
- Not being asked to answer questions in class.

I can recognize and examine my emotions and understand how they impact other people.

Figure 13.3 Meerkat standing in the spotlight smiling.
Source: Artwork by Linda Weil©.

Suggestions to Align Skills With the Tool

Teachers can share this checklist with students to support them in identifying their higher-order thinking and social emotional skills.

Growing empathy: Students can reflect on the questions from another person's perspective and imagine what they might say and feel about their problem, together with generating some solutions.

Table 13.2 Suggestions to align higher-order thinking and social emotional learning skills with the tool.

Critical and Creative Thinking Skills for Problem-Solving	Social Emotional Learning Skills
Critical Thinking Skills ☐ I can explain what happened to me and identify my obstacles and my challenges. ☐ I can be open-minded to consider ideas from many different perspectives. ☐ I can analyze and evaluate my emotions. **Creative Thinking Skills** ☐ I can use different creative strategies that make thinking visible. ☐ I use brainstorming or visual diagrams to generate new ideas, connections and inquiries.	☐ I can recognize and examine my emotions and understand how they impact other people. ☐ I can manage and communicate my emotions in a thoughtful way. ☐ I can reflect on my own, my family's and my community's well-being. ☐ I can find possible ways to problem-solve for myself and society. ☐ I care about others' feelings and the impact of my actions on them. ☐ I take action to support others' well-being.

Source: Graphic created by the authors.

Questions for Students to Support Higher-Order Thinking Skills

Table 13.3 Questions for students.

Grade 5–6

1. Did The Orange Sun Tool help you to communicate your emotions in a thoughtful way? Give reasons for your answer.
2. Did the tool help you think about ideas from different perspectives? Give reasons for your answer.

Grade 7

1. Did The Orange Sun Tool help you to communicate your emotions in a thoughtful way? If so, can you explain how?
2. Did the tool help you to be more open-minded and to think about ideas from different perspectives? Can you think of another situation in which you can use the tool?
3. Did The Orange Sun Tool help you to think about your own OR your family's OR your community's well-being?

Source: Graphic created by the authors.

Teacher Reflection

KEY TAKEAWAY: Developing a deeper understanding of factors e.g. events, beliefs and emotions that can impact us.

- Describe the scenario and classroom context—what was the problem you wanted to address with this tool?
- Did you achieve your goal?
- How did you use the tool to support students' higher-order thinking skills (HOTS)?

Complement With Other Tools

Self-regulation and identity: The Myself Tool, The Plus-Minus Tool, The Polka Dot Tool, The Points of View Tool and The Snowman Tool.

Chapter Notes

Use this space to plan and write your personal thoughts, ideas and questions here:

Create your mind-map or sketch out your ideas

Table 13.4 The Orange Sun Tool student table.

What just happened to me? **Or** **What happened to me sometime ago?**	
What I know and believe about the event	
What I need and want at this moment or in the future	
My emotions and feelings	
What and how I think about the situation	
What society/social **media tells me**	
My hopes and dreams	
Other student thoughts . . .	

Source: Graphic created by the authors.

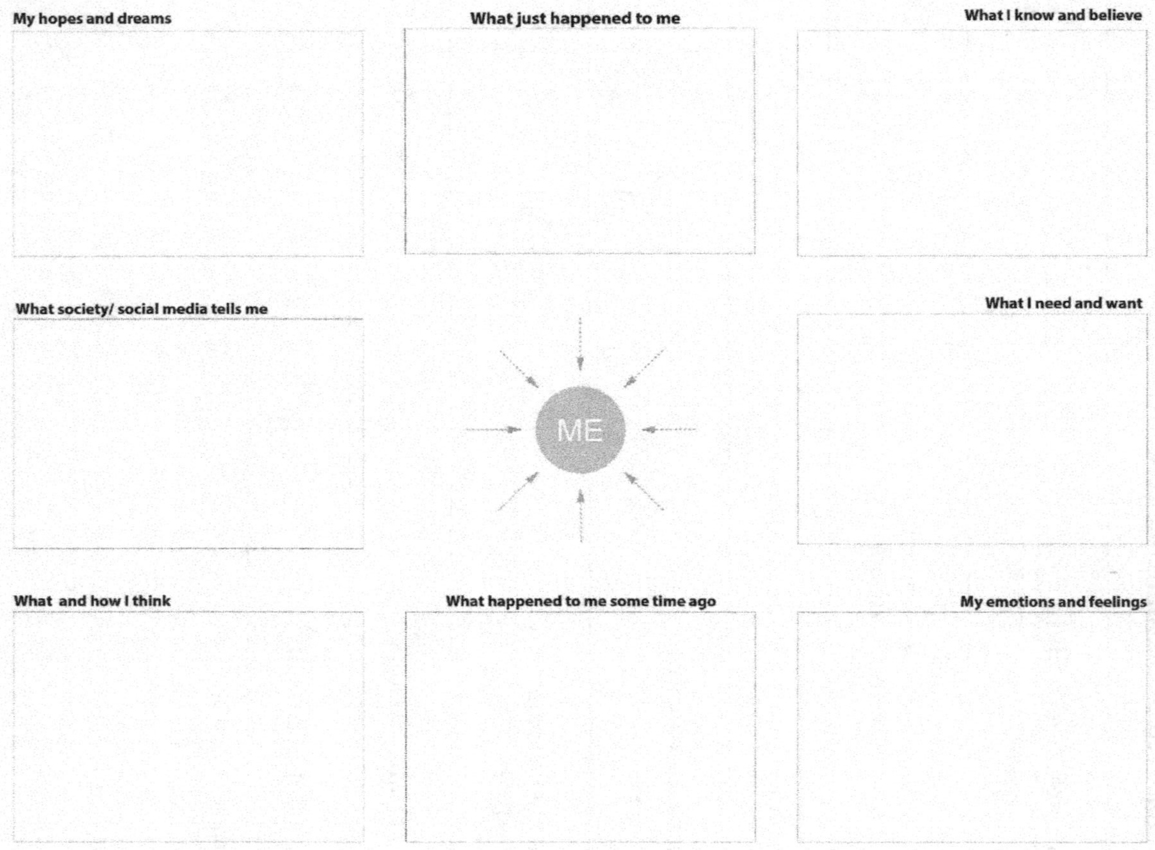
My hopes and dreams
What just happened to me
What I know and believe
What society/ social media tells me
ME
What I need and want
What and how I think
What happened to me some time ago
My emotions and feelings

Figure 13.4 Student reflection template.
Source: Graphic created by the authors.

Definitions

Emotion: a strong feeling, such as love, anger, fear, etc.
Feelings: emotions, especially those influenced by other people.
Hope: to want something to happen or to be true, and usually have a good reason to think that it might.
Dream: something that you want to happen very much but that is not very likely.

The definitions in this list are sourced from Cambridge Online Dictionary (2023) and Merriam-Webster Dictionary (2023).

References

Cambridge University Press & Assessment (Ed.). (2023). *Cambridge online dictionary*. Retrieved November 14, 2023, from https://dictionary.cambridge.org/

Merriam-Webster, Incorporated (Ed.). (2023). *Merriam-Webster dictionary*. Merriam-Webster.com. Retrieved November 15, 2023, from www.merriam-webster.com/

14

The Plus-Minus Tool

Game of Numbers

Suggested Grade Level: 5–8
Key Takeaway—Helping students to reflect on a situation or problem and monitor emotional reactions.

Global Skills and Key Themes

Skills: Critical thinking, creative thinking, problem-solving and reflection.
Themes: Emotional regulation, empathy, identity, open-mindedness, curiosity and self-awareness.

Stories

FROM THE CLASSROOM: Mandarin language classroom with Grade 5 students.
DEFINITIONS: Open-minded, curious, confident and empathic (p 201).

DOI: 10.4324/9781032664989-15

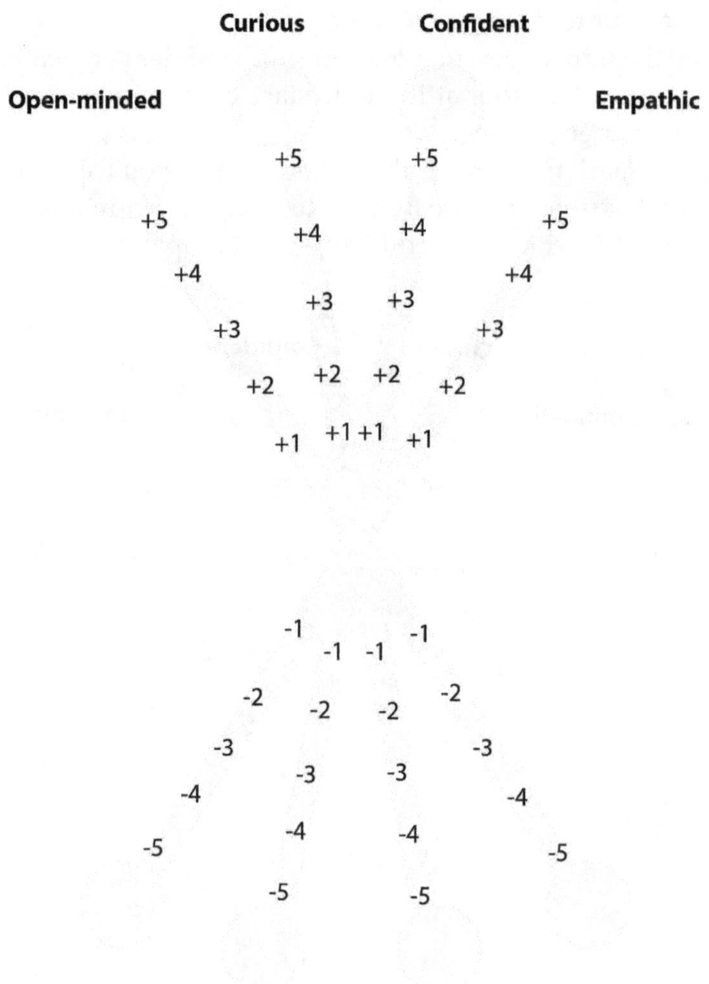
Curious
Confident
Open-minded
Empathic
+5 +5 +5 +5
+4 +4 +4 +4
+3 +3 +3 +3
+2 +2 +2 +2
+1 +1 +1 +1
-1 -1 -1 -1
-2 -2 -2 -2
-3 -3 -3 -3
-4 -4 -4 -4
-5 -5 -5 -5

Figure 14.1 The Plus-Minus Tool.
Source: Graphic created by the authors.

What Does The Plus-Minus Tool Do?

The Plus-Minus Tool offers students opportunities to reflect on and be more aware of how open-minded, curious, confident and empathic they are in a given scenario.

How to Use It

1. Choose your topic or problem.
2. Define the terms open-minded, curious, confident and empathic.
3. Choose one of the four attitudes to start: open-minded, curious, confident or empathic.
4. Circle or mark the number that reflects where you feel on the scale.
4. Give each attitude a score from +5 to –5 e.g. Open-minded has a score of +2, Curious –3, Confident –2 and Empathic +1

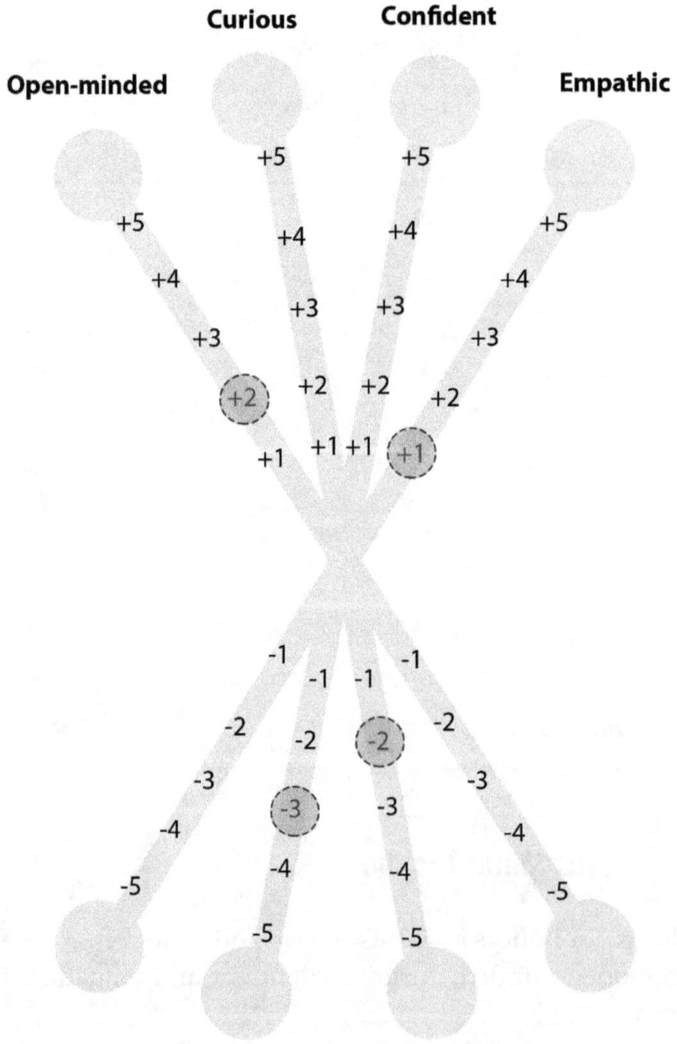
Curious
Confident
Open-minded
Empathic
+5 +4 +3 +2 +1
-1 -2 -3 -4 -5

Figure 14.2 How to use The Plus-Minus Tool.
Source: Graphic created by the authors.

Marking how you feel on a line may seem like a simple task, but assessing your level of open-mindedness, ethical values, confidence and empathy actually requires careful thought. Students may find that some of their responses overlap. Some responses could be quite different on the sliding scale, while others may be very similar.

EXAMPLE 1 Alien Encounter: How Would I Feel If I Met an Alien?

Person 1

Open-minded: +2
Curiosity: –3
Confident: –3
Empathic: +1
How open-minded would I actually be if I were to meet an alien?
"I would be curious but also terrified, so that would affect where I would score myself. I would like to say I would be **+5** because I feel I am very open minded but really I would probably be **+2**."

Person 2

Open-minded: +5
Curiosity: +5
Confident: +4
Empathic: +4

Hello
Figure 14.3 Alien saying hello.
Source: Artwork by Linda Weil©.

"I would love to travel to new worlds as I am a very confident (+4) and curious person, (+5) I am open-minded (+5) and seek adventure. I am very interested in meeting an alien and exploring our similarities and differences. I understand how I feel when I am different so I would be sensitive when I meet the alien +4 (empathy)."

EXAMPLE 2 Community Service: Feeding the Homeless

Each winter our school helps out at a homeless shelter serving meals to homeless people.

Open-minded: +2
Curiosity: +4
Confident: +1
Empathic: +4

"I was quite nervous about helping at the shelter (Confident: +1) I have seen homeless people hanging around the entrance to the mall but I haven't ever spoken to them.

I wonder if I will get to talk to them and learn their stories as to how they became homeless (Curiosity: +4).

I wonder how open-minded I really am (Open-minded: +2).

Do I feel sorry for them and do I have empathy for them or are they homeless due their own mistakes? Did they lose their job or are they sick, maybe both? I will try to be kind and caring."

EXAMPLE 3 Field Trip to the Zoo: Should Animals Be Kept in Zoos?

Figure 14.4 Sea lion at Edinburgh Zoo.
Source: Image credit Aalia Khan.

Open-minded: +2
Curiosity: +5
Confident: +3
Empathic: +2

"When I went to the zoo with my class it was a lot of fun and I found watching the animals sometimes really funny (Curiosity: +5) but then the zookeeper explained how zoos play a really important role in helping save endangered species (Empathic: +2).

I was confident exploring the different animals until I entered the reptile house. I am scared of snakes so I didn't feel very [brave] (Confident: +3) but the keeper said I should be open-minded, because the snakes really don't want to get in the way of humans and will usually move away when they hear feet approaching (Confident: +3).

STORIES FROM THE CLASSROOM

Grade 5 Mandarin Composition (International School China)

In a Mandarin composition class the teacher asked the students to describe Dumbledore. The students burst into laughter when they heard the teacher read the name 'Dumbledore' in Mandarin. For a while the students kept saying Dumbledore's name repeatedly in Mandarin with strange accents and kept laughing (T. Zhang, personal communication, April 12, 2023).

Table 14.1 Describing 'Dumbledore' in Mandarin class.

Grade 5	Open-minded	Curiosity	Confident	Empathic
Student 1	+4	+1	+2	+3
Student 2	–2	–1	–1	–5
Student 3	+3	+3	–3	+1
Student 4	+4	+5	+3	+4
Student 5	+3	+3	–1	+1

Source: Graphic created by the authors.

STUDENT 1

Open-minded: +4 I felt like I wasn't like everyone else because at first I thought it was weird but I didn't laugh.
Curiosity: +1 I wasn't too curious about it, for me it was normal.
Confident: +2 I felt confident about it because I was like 'I'm not gonna laugh because [it's] mean to the language".
Empathic: +3 I felt empathy for Ms. Doria because it might be rude.

STUDENT 2

Open-minded: –2 Because I was not that open to the name.
Curiosity: –1 I wasn't curious because I didn't think that the name was funny.
Confident: –1 Because I was a little unconfident about the name.
Empathic: –5 Because I wasn't empathetic towards teacher's feelings.

STUDENT 3

Open-minded: I put +3 because I was just trying to learn how to say it in Chinese.

Curiosity: I put +3 also because I was wondering why they say Dumbledore that way.

Confident: I put –3 because I was not confident saying Dumbledore that way.

Empathic: I put +1 because it was not nice to say it that way.

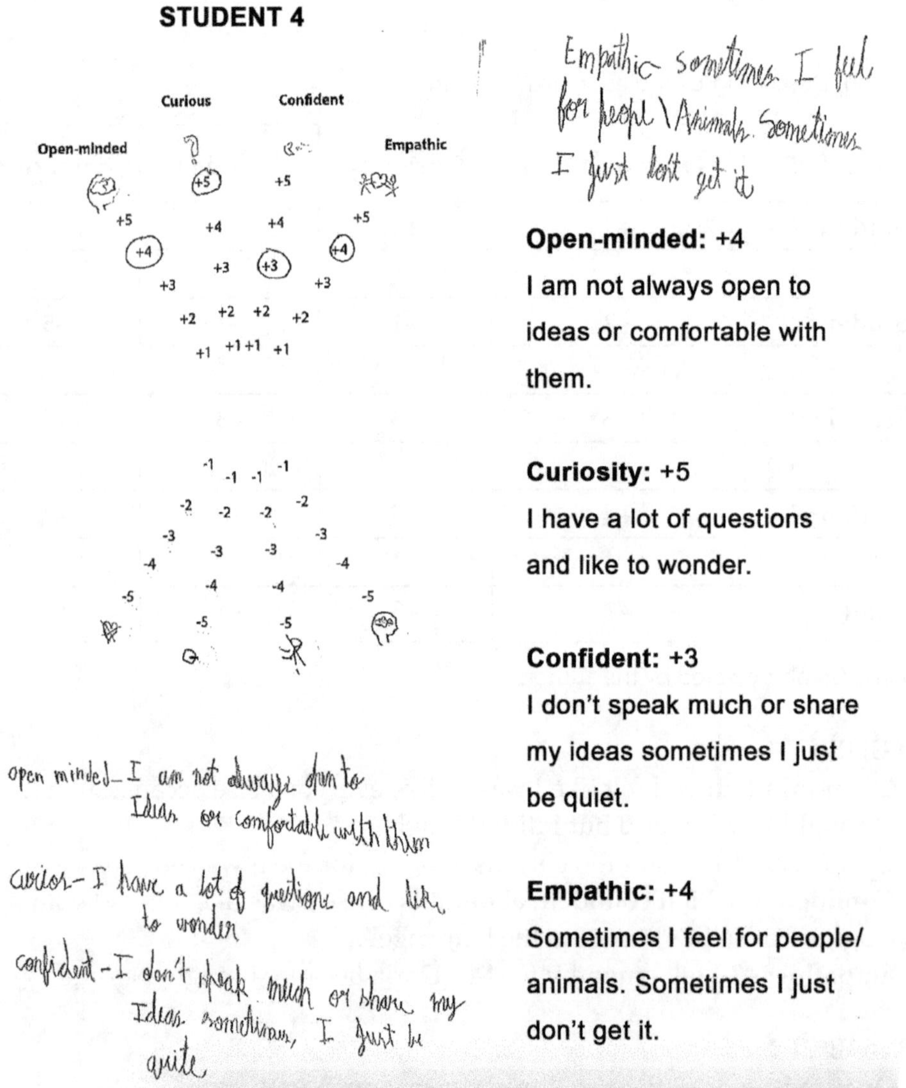
STUDENT 4
Curious
Confident
Open-minded
Empathic
Open-minded: +4
I am not always open to ideas or comfortable with them.
Curiosity: +5
I have a lot of questions and like to wonder.
Confident: +3
I don't speak much or share my ideas sometimes I just be quiet.
Empathic: +4
Sometimes I feel for people/ animals. Sometimes I just don't get it.

Figure 14.5 Student 4 using The Plus-Minus Tool.
Source: Image credit Ting.

STUDENT 5

Open-minded: I chose +3 for open-minded because I wanted to try something new.

Curiosity: I chose +3 for curious because I wanted to know what to do and what to write.

Confident: For confident I chose –1 because I was not confident about my behavior.

Empathic: For empathic I chose +1 because it was not funny.

Zhang, T. (2023, April 12). [Personal interview by the author].

Suggestions to Align Skills With the Tool

Teachers can share this checklist with students to support them in identifying their higher-order thinking and social emotional skills.

Table 14.2 Suggestions to align higher-order thinking and social emotional learning skills with the tool.

Critical and Creative Thinking Skills for Problem-Solving		Social Emotional Learning Skills
☐ I can analyze and evaluate issues and my ideas. ☐ I can identify obstacles and challenges. ☐ I can analyze and evaluate my emotions.	☐ I can use different creative strategies that make thinking visible. ☐ I can consider and explore a range of different ideas, including some that may or may not be possible.	☐ I can recognize and examine my emotions and understand how they impact other people. ☐ I can manage and communicate my emotions in a thoughtful way. ☐ I am curious and open-minded.

Source: Graphic created by the authors.

Questions for Students to Support Higher-Order Thinking Skills

Table 14.3 Questions for students.

Grade 5–8

1. Was the tool useful in helping you think about how open-minded you were about the topic; if so, how?
2. Did using the tool show you a different side to yourself?

Only for Grade 7–8

3. Are there any other factors you think are important and would like to add to the tool? Give reasons for your answer.

Source: Graphic created by the authors.

Teacher Reflection

KEY TAKEAWAY: Helping students to reflect on a situation or problem and monitor emotional reactions.

- Describe the scenario and classroom context—what was the problem you wanted to address with this tool?
- Did you achieve your goal?
- How did you use the tool to support students' higher-order thinking skills (HOTS)?

Complement With Other Tools

Self-regulation and identity: The Myself Tool, The Orange Sun Tool, The Polka Dot Tool and The Points of View Tool.

Chapter Notes

Use this space to plan and write your personal thoughts, ideas and questions here:

Create your mind-map or sketch out your ideas

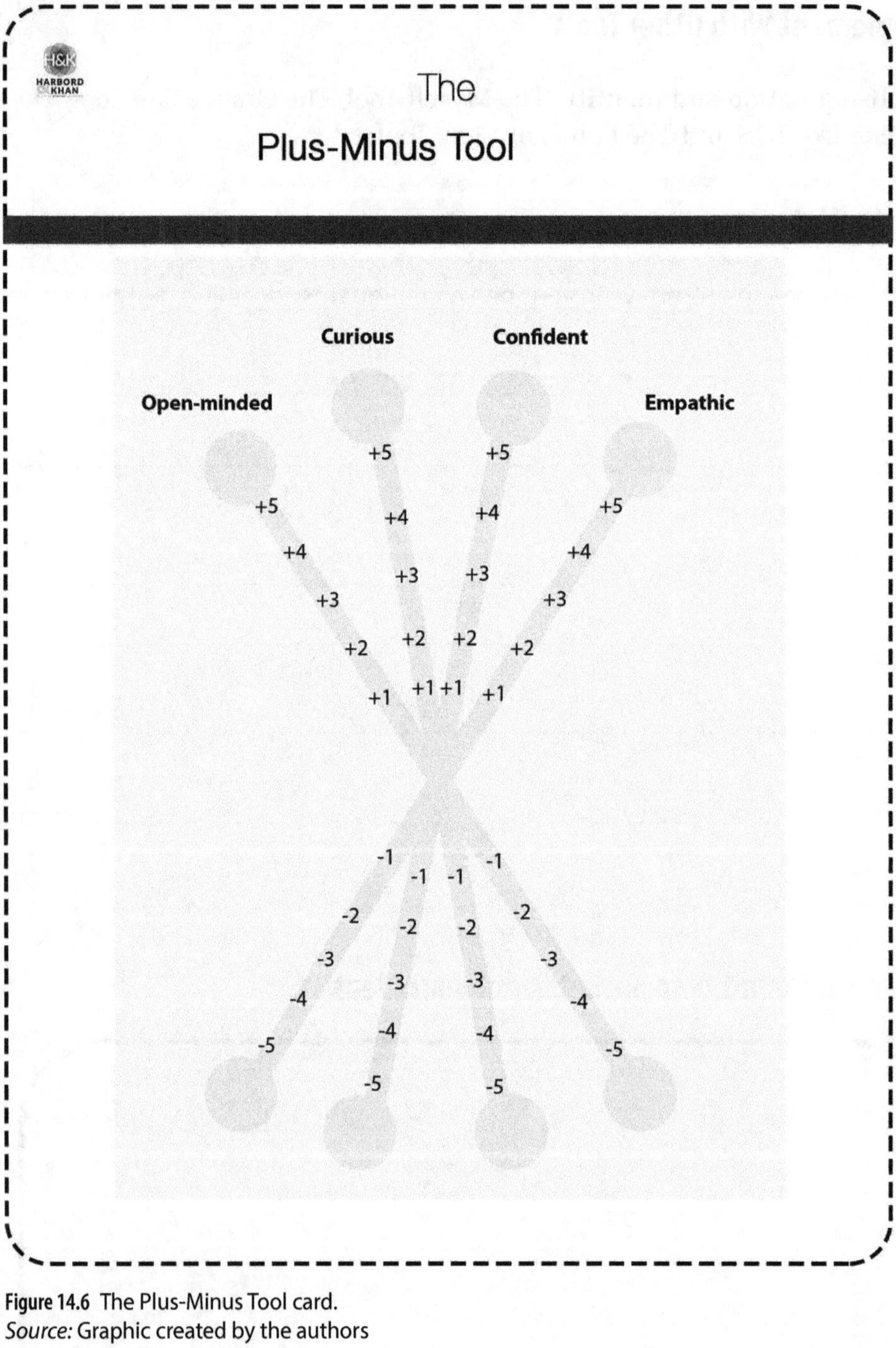
The
Plus-Minus Tool
Curious
Confident
Open-minded
Empathic

Figure 14.6 The Plus-Minus Tool card.
Source: Graphic created by the authors

Definitions

Curious: interested in learning about people or things around you.
Confident: being certain of your abilities.
Empathic: having the ability to imagine how someone else feels.
Open-minded: willing to consider ideas and opinions that are new or different from your own.

The definitions in this list are sourced from Cambridge Online Dictionary (2023) and Merriam-Webster Dictionary (2023).

References

Cambridge University Press & Assessment (Ed.). (2023). *Cambridge online dictionary*. Retrieved November 14, 2023, from https://dictionary.cambridge.org/

Merriam-Webster, Incorporated (Ed.). (2023). *Merriam-Webster dictionary*. Merriam-Webster.com. Retrieved November 15, 2023, from www.merriam-webster.com/

15

The Points of View Tool

No Judgment

Suggested Grade Level: 5–7

Key Takeaway—Comparing and contrasting my personal values and those of different people in my life.

Global Skills and Key Themes

Skills: Critical thinking, creative thinking, open-mindedness and reflection.
Themes: Beliefs, communication, empathy, ethical values, identity, multiple perspectives, relationships and self-awareness.

Stories

FROM THE CLASSROOM: Grade 8 teacher Semantha Springett uses The Points of View Tool in a collaborative creative thinking session.
DEFINITIONS: Empathy, judgment and values (p 215).

DOI: 10.4324/9781032664989-16

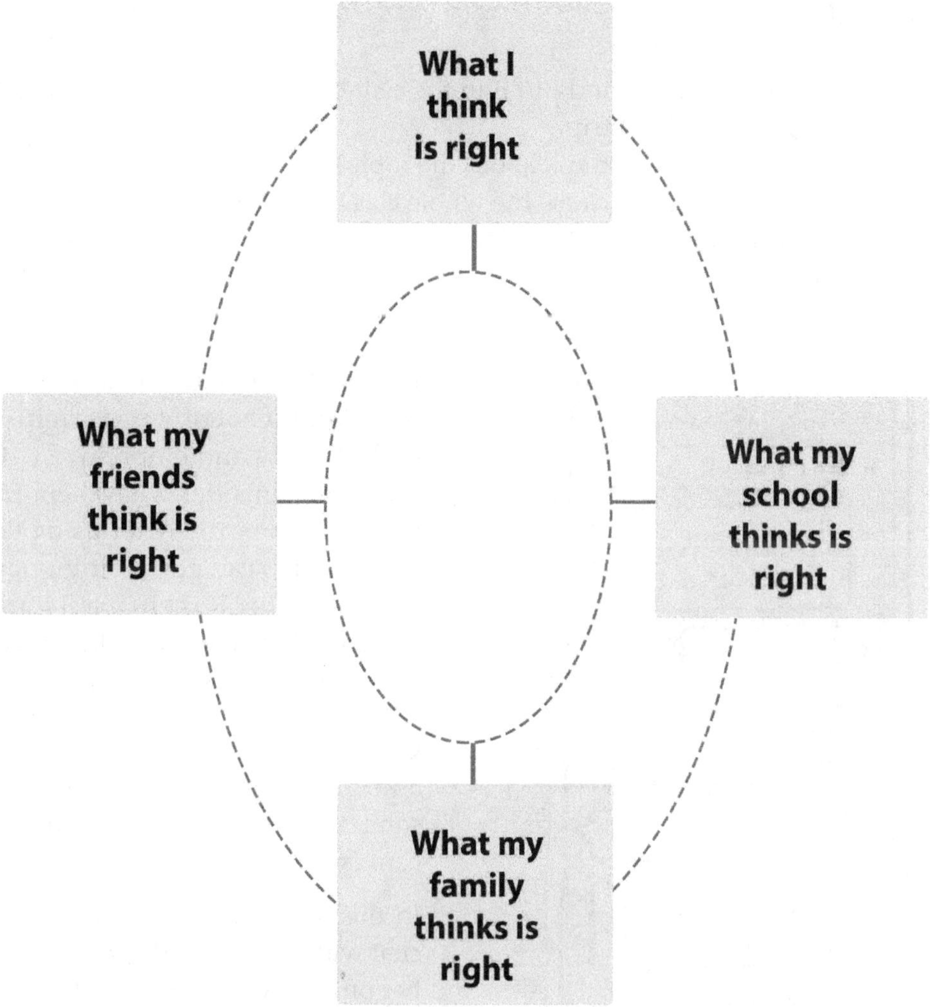
What I think is right
What my friends think is right
What my school thinks is right
What my family thinks is right

Figure 15.1 The Points of View Tool.
Source: Graphic created by the authors.

What Does The Points of View Tool Do?

- Encourages students to reflect on their own beliefs and values in relation to important people in their lives.
- Can be used to examine and compare different viewpoints and also reflect on students' own. These may complement or be in conflict with one another.
- Support students in identifying multiple perspectives that impact their lives, sometimes in a positive way and sometimes negatively.

How to Use It

1. Choose your topic and put it in the center e.g. your parents won't let you go on a school trip.
2. Describe what you think about the topic e.g. you think you should be allowed to go because the whole class is going.
3. Think about the topic from the point of view of your school, your family and your friends.

9:30am
ParrotsR'Us
Polly want a cracker?
Sqwak!
Pieces of eight! Pieces of eight!
Polly??
Pieces of eight! Pieces of eight!
Text

Figure 15.2 Screenshot of Polly Parrot's conversation.
Source: Artwork by Linda Weil©.

The point is not to make a judgment about what or who is right or not, but to try and empathize with others and consider what their different opinions are. After using the tool, students can go and interview people at school, their family and their friends to compare their ideas and the responses they get.

Communicating with each other and understanding the other person's point of view requires a conversation.

In this screenshot of Polly Parrot's chat with the pirate, Polly is making her point of view clear!

Applications

ChatGPT and Empathy

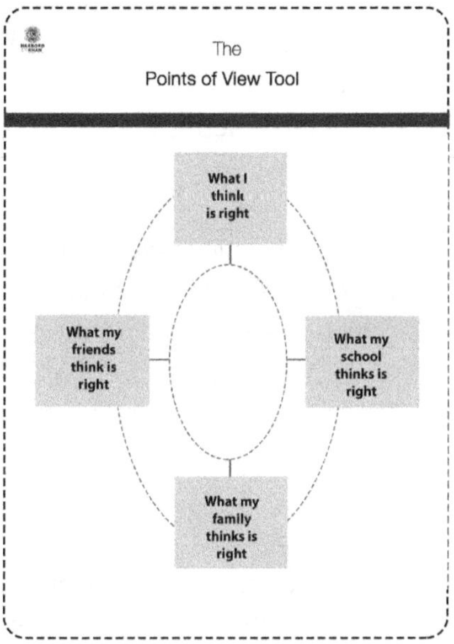
The
Points of View Tool
What I think is right
What my friends think is right
What my school thinks is right
What my family thinks is right

Figure 15.3 The Points of View Tool card.
Source: Graphic created by the authors.

Your friend boasted they had used ChatGPT for their school assignment but didn't cite they had, as they were sure the teacher wouldn't be able to tell it wasn't their own work. Choose an ethical lens to think about how you would deal with this situation, e.g. Empathy—Do you understand why your friend would do this? How would the other important people in your life feel? OR perhaps think of the problem using fairness or honesty. What about trust? Any of these would give you ways to think about the problem you are facing.

Swim Team and Trust

You are captain of the swim team and through circumstances outside of your control you are late to the meet. Your coach says the reasons don't matter, it is your responsibility to make sure you are there. The team lost due to your no-show. The consequence is you are demoted as captain.

Trust—Did you break the trust of your coach or did the coach break your trust? Is it fair? Does kindness come into the situation? OR is it a case that circumstances are irrelevant? Is there a time when the result of your actions means there is no way to avoid consequences?

STORIES FROM THE CLASSROOM

Semantha Springett, a New Zealand Grade 8 teacher, explained how she used The Points of View Tool to explore some real-life situations that had arisen in the class during her absence.

Planning

This work was completed in one session and the students aged 12–13, NZ year 8, were divided into mixed groups of four. Students were asked to score between 1 and 4, with 1 being low/disagree and 4 being high/totally agree. Groups were able to choose which scenario they wanted to unpack. Semantha introduced the different scenarios to each group with the following comment:

> *"This is a way to think about others' points of view, without judgment. At the end you do not decide who or what is 'right', this is for you to reflect on your beliefs and values in relation to others, to consider multiple perspectives and have empathy/awareness. Critical thinking, open mindedness and reflection."*

Topics and Prompts

We used some real-life situations as the prompts for the students to discuss in their groups. They enjoyed it and it provoked some really good discussions. I think they liked how they didn't have to say who was 'right' at the end of it, just consider what each point of view was, to help understand how people see things differently and in situations they will do things differently, for example, the motivation behind the behavior.

Students' and Teachers' Reflections

The students did enjoy the process—they found it helpful (see their 4/4 rating) and recognized it as a way of thinking about situations that maintained mana for all involved. Mana is a Māori belief around personal essence, strength, self-esteem and self-belief. The word *manaakitanga* means respect, holding the mana of the other person as sacred, preserving it. They understand that in discussions there is a responsibility to respect the mana of people who hold different opinions. This thinking tool helped them to see/imagine the perspective of the other people and that act preserved the mana of that person (S. Springett, 2023).

Points of View Tool Student Examples

GROUP 1 SCENARIO: Your friend boasts about using Google to answer their math questions rather than work out the answers or ask for help.

Table 15.1 Group 1 responses to the scenario.

What I think	What my school thinks
I think it's better to ask for help or work it out because then you can actually learn how to answer questions like this in the future.	They would think it's not right to do that because if you keep googling answers they might think you've gotten smarter and you might go up a class then not know anything.
What my friend thinks	**What family thinks**
They're either lazy or they are stuck, and they are worried they will seem dumb if they ask for help.	They might not see why using Google is bad or they might think it's bad because they want their children to learn.

Source: Graphic created by the authors.

Thoughts on character that this scenario provoked:

- If it was my friend I would need empathy to understand how they are feeling, but integrity to inform a teacher that they are stuck so they can get help.
- Other character words that come to mind: integrity, resilience, respect, trust.
- Some key character traits this scenario raised for me was understanding how other people's point of view can affect the outcome and [affect] how someone thinks during a situation.

About The Points of View Tool:
It helped me consider things from different perspectives: 4/4
It made me think about my own perspective: 3/4
Seeing things from different points of view is useful in life: 4/4
The perspectives we found hardest were the school/home.

GROUP 2 SCENARIO: You want to do well so you ask ChatGPT to do some writing for you.

Table 15.2 Group 2 responses to the scenario.

What I think is right	What my school thinks is right
Doing it properly and not cheating was to write it yourself to use your thinking. The teacher will talk to you about your writing so you need to understand it all.	The school needs to see your thinking so you can get a grade, not a computer getting a grade.
What my friend thinks is right	**What my family thinks is right**
Doing it this way I have something to hand in. I told chat what ideas I wanted, and chat made it into the writing I needed. The teacher might not notice?	They might be disappointed and think their child must do it again but by themself.

Source: Graphic created by the authors.

(One of the group members had actually done this—they opted to discuss this scenario.)

Thoughts on character this scenario provoked:

- He tried to do something he shouldn't have without being detected and [has] regret, as he now realizes his mistakes.
- Trust, critical thinking.

About The Points of View Tool:

It helped me consider things from different perspectives/Yes 4/4.
It made me think about my own perspective/Yes 3/4.
Seeing things from different points of view is useful in life/Yes 4/4.
The point of view I found hardest was the home (all students agreed on this).

GROUP 3 SCENARIO: You can't think of an idea so you Google a poem, copy and paste it, then tell the teacher you made it up yourself.

Table 15.3 Group 3 responses to the scenario.

What I think is right	What my school thinks is right
The task was set for us to develop our own creative thinking, even if it is difficult.	It's not ok to copy. You should use your initiative.
What my friend thinks is right	**What my family thinks is right**
If you are struggling and you can find ideas, it's ok to do this. This might help me get an idea.	You can't get a good future if you don't work properly.

Source: Graphic created by the authors.

Thoughts on character that this scenario provoked:

Trust, creativity, just because you can copy doesn't mean you should.
Critical thinking and integrity to decide what to do.

About The Points of View Tool:

It helped me consider things from different perspectives: 3/4.
It made me think about my own perspective: 3/4.
Seeing things from different points of view is useful in life: 4/4.
The perspective that we found hardest was home and friends because it was hard to think why they would do it and what they would think.

GROUP 4 SCENARIO: Your friend does not want to go to the math class they are supposed to be at.

Table 15.4 Group 4 responses to the scenario.

What I think is right	What my school thinks is right
I think they should go to that class and do the work. If they [don't] go back they will need to catch up.	They need to go to that class because it is the right level, it won't be too easy or too hard but they need the education.
What my friend thinks is right	**What my family thinks is right**
Why do they do this? They want to stay with their friends instead of going to a different class. Their friends are more important than learning.	You need to go to the right class to learn what you need to know, so when you are older you can get a job and earn money.

Source: Graphic created by the authors.

Thoughts on character this scenario provokes:

The friend needs resilience to go even though they don't want to.
Trust that there is a reason why you have to do these things and that your friends are your friends even if you go to a different class.
It made me think we can have different perspectives.

About The Points of View Tool:

It helped me consider things from different perspectives: 3/4.
It made me think about my own perspective: 4/4.
Seeing things from different points of view is useful in life: 4/4.
The perspective we found hardest was: friend, school and whānau (Māori language word for the basic extended family group) but we think we could work it out (Springett, 2023).

Suggestions to Align Skills With the Tool

Teachers can share this checklist with students to support them in identifying their higher-order thinking and social emotional skills.

Table 15.5 Suggestions to align higher-order thinking and social emotional learning skills with the tool.

Critical and Creative Thinking Skills for Problem-Solving		Social Emotional Learning Skills
☐ I can consider ideas from multiple perspectives. ☐ I can check the accuracy of facts and recognize different perspectives. ☐ I can check the interpretations of what I research. ☐ I reflect on my own possible bias and compare that to the bias of others.	☐ I can use different creative strategies that make thinking visible. ☐ I can make unpredictable or surprising connections between objects and/or ideas.	☐ I can understand and explore bias and prejudice. ☐ I can manage and communicate my emotions in a thoughtful way. ☐ I understand what empathy is and can empathize with others.

Source: Graphic created by the authors.

Questions for Students to Support Higher-Order Thinking Skills

Table 15.6 Questions for students.

Grade 5–6

1. Is there anyone else whose point of view matters to you?
2. What do you think affects someone's point of view?

Grade 7

1. How did you use your critical and creative thinking to reflect on different people's points of view? Please explain. You can look at the skills table for ideas.
2. How could this tool help you develop empathy toward other people?
3. What do you think affects someone's point of view?

Source: Graphic created by the authors.

Teacher Reflection

KEY TAKEAWAY: Comparing and contrasting my personal values and those of different people in my life.

- Describe the scenario and classroom context—what was the problem you wanted to address with this tool?
- Did you achieve your goal?
- How did you use the tool to support students' higher-order thinking skills (HOTS)?

Complement With Other Tools

Self-regulation and identity—The Myself Tool and The Orange Sun Tool.

Chapter Notes

Use this space to plan and write your personal thoughts, ideas and questions here:

Create your mind-map or sketch out your ideas

The Points of View Tool© Template (Available as online support material)

My topic or scenario..

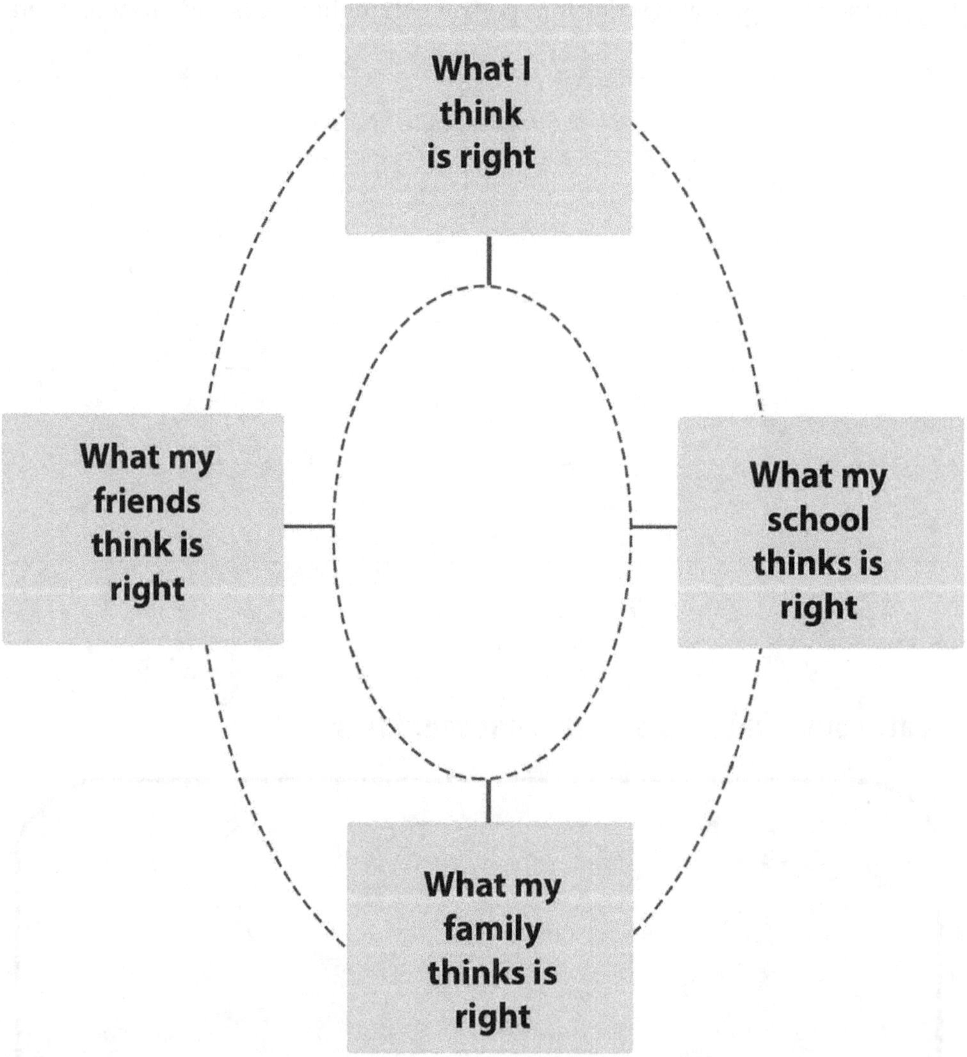
What I think is right
What my friends think is right
What my school thinks is right
What my family thinks is right

Figure 15.4 The Points of View Tool template.
Source: Graphic created by the authors.

Definitions

Empathy: the ability to share someone else's feelings or experiences by imagining what it would be like to be in that person's situation.
Judgment: the ability to form valuable opinions and make good decisions.
Values: the beliefs people have, especially about what is right and wrong and what is most important in life, that control their behavior.
Whānau (Māori pronunciation: [ˈfaːnau]): The Māori language word for the basic extended family group.

The definitions in this list are sourced from Cambridge Online Dictionary (2023), Merriam-Webster Dictionary (2023), Oxford Learners Dictionaries (2023) and Wikipedia (2023).

References

Cambridge University Press & Assessment (Ed.). (2023). *Cambridge online dictionary*. Retrieved November 14, 2023, from https://dictionary.cambridge.org/

Merriam-Webster, Incorporated (Ed.). (2023). *Merriam-Webster dictionary*. Merriam-Webster.com. Retrieved November 15, 2023, from www.merriam-webster.com/

Oxford University Press (Ed.). (2023). *Oxford learners dictionaries*. Retrieved November 15, 2023, from www.oxfordlearnersdictionaries.com

Wikipedia (Ed.). (2023, September 16). *Whānau*. Wikipedia. Retrieved November 27, 2023, from https://en.wikipedia.org/wiki/Wh%C4%81nau#:~:text=Article%20Talk,and%20waka%20(migration%20canoe).au#:~:text=Article%20Talk,and%20waka%20(migration%20canoe).

16

The Polka Dot Tool

Spots Before My Eyes

Suggested Grade Level: 8–10

Key Takeaway—Understanding the difference between wants and needs to inform students' self-awareness of factors that drive behavior.

Global Skills and Key Themes

Skills: Critical thinking, problem-solving, emotional regulation and reflection.
Themes: Emotions, identity, motivation, self-awareness, wants and needs.

Stories

FROM THE CLASSROOM: Grade 8 student reflection on understanding wants and needs.
DEFINITIONS: Want, need, habit, addiction, motivation and incentive (p 227).

Wants and needs can be differentiated on the basis of their level of importance. A *want* is what is desired, while a *need* refers to what is required. It is important that students understand the different meanings between wants and needs in order to be able to problem-solve and analyze the topic they are exploring.

DOI: 10.4324/9781032664989-17

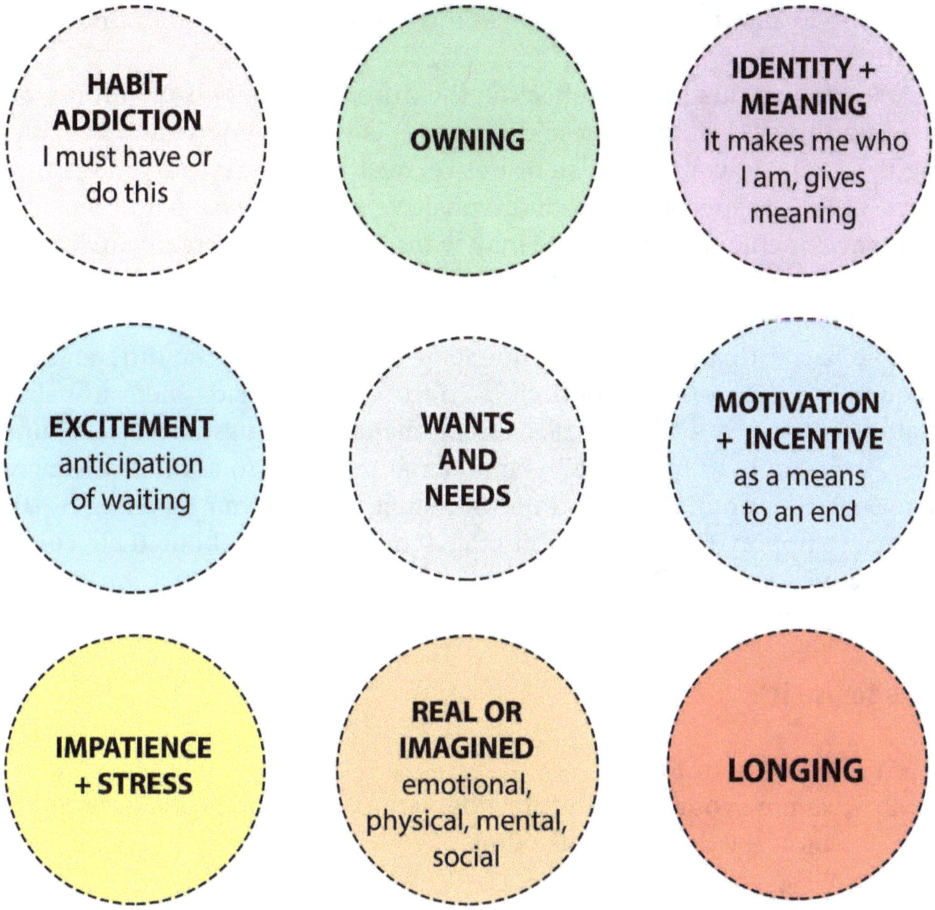
HABIT
ADDICTION
I must have or do this
OWNING
IDENTITY +
MEANING
it makes me who I am, gives meaning
EXCITEMENT
anticipation of waiting
WANTS
AND
NEEDS
MOTIVATION
+ INCENTIVE
as a means to an end
IMPATIENCE
+ STRESS
REAL OR
IMAGINED
emotional, physical, mental, social
LONGING

Figure 16.1 The Polka Dot Tool.
Source: Graphic created by the authors.

Table 16.1 Word ladder from want to need.

WANT	WAND	SAND	SEND	SEED	HEED	NEED

Source: Graphic created by the authors

What Does The Polka Dot Tool Do?

Identifying our emotions can be complex and confusing. The Polka Dot Tool can support students in being more self-aware and reflecting more critically on the differences between wanting and needing things. These emotions can relate to situations that are sometimes stressful and at other times more positive.

We can use this tool to reflect on the differences between wanting and needing things. Defining these differences is often a good start to exploring this tool e.g. want, to wish or desire, need, necessary duty, obligation. Some of these aspects may be more positive e.g. motivation and incentive as a way of achieving things we may want, or they may create anxiety e.g. perceived as impatience and stress. We can ask our students whether most of the things we want and need are for ourselves or for others.

The hardest part for many students is to understand the differences, as frequently the emotional connection to the *want* misleads them to believe that it is a *need*. By systematically asking themselves questions as explained later, they can help to isolate the emotional response to a more considered one. Sometimes our wants and needs change without our realizing it—this tool can support students in thinking more critically about their current perspective.

How to Use It

1. Choose your topic.
2. Examine your topic and consider your wants and needs through the lens of the different polka dots.

Students don't have to use all of the polka dots, just the ones that work best. The different polka dots can be examined individually, although students might make connections between them.

Topic + Wants and Needs → Questions

Topic: My use of social media + Habit or addiction → Questions
e.g. Do I always need to be on social media?
How do I feel if I can't access social media?

Explaining the Polka Dots

Habit or Addiction

Is the want/need something that students do regularly? Is it something that students must have, that they cannot do without? Would further examination of this be useful?

Owning

Is the want/need related to having something or ownership? Why do they want to own it? Do students feel this is something they want/need themselves or is it related to peer pressure?

Identity

Does the want/need serve a purpose of defining who students are? Does it give them insights about what they believe and what they value? How would they feel about their identity if they didn't have this want or need?

Motivation and Incentive

Is the want/need a motivating factor or incentive to achieve something? Is it something being given to them by someone else or to do with self-motivation? Students can reflect on how their wants/needs are driving factors in their lives.

Longing

Is the want/need something students long for? Why do they want it so badly? What are students prepared to do to get it? Does this have ethical implications?

Real or Imagined

How sure are students that their need is real or perceived to be real? Out of a scale of 1–10, how would they rate it? Is it emotional, physical, mental, social, etc.?

Impatience and Stress

Does the want/need make students impatient or generate stress? How much of this is because of their own feelings or due to what others think? What strategies do students have in place to help them deal with their feelings?

Excitement

Is this something that students are looking forward to getting or having, e.g. a special event, a family celebration or new sneakers? Do students feel excited when they give someone a present or plan a surprise?

The Polka Dot Tool doesn't include all aspects of wanting and needing but can be used as a starting point for discussions.

EXAMPLE 1 Topic: Student Mobile Phone Use

Here is an example of just one way you could use this to give your students a topic to explore and develop:

Table 16.2 Example 1 mobile phone use.

Topic	Want/need	Questions
Mobile phone use.	**REAL OR IMAGINED**	Is this a need or a want? Is it real or imagined? Do our needs change depending on the situation?
I am on a screen for most of the day and night.	I *want* to use it when I *want* to.	Do I have to do this or do I *want* to do this?
I get agitated if I don't have my phone on me.	I need it.	How much do I need my phone? Is it an addiction or a habit?
My parents want to be able to contact me and know I am safe.	My parents' need me to have a phone.	Was it my choice to have a phone or my parents'?
I am on many different social media platforms.	**IDENTITY**	Is there a difference between my offline and online identity?

Source: Graphic created by the authors.

Note to Teacher

Self-regulation is such an important part of our learning experience and can be a major challenge for many of us. It can raise complex questions and would be used in a trusting and safe learning environment. The teacher can decide if it is more appropriate to use it as self-reflection or class discussion.

STORIES FROM THE CLASSROOM

A Grade 8 student, Farokh Patel, used The Polka Dot Tool to reflect on the difference between wants and needs. Using the tool gave him insights about the impact of his emotions on his needs and wants. It also helped him reflect on how using critical thinking could support him in developing his self-regulation.

The tool was helpful in helping me think about the difference between wants and needs. Using this tool I was able to understand that needs are something required for completing a task, whereas wants are something that the mind thinks is needed but it really is not necessary. The tool helped me identify and think about my personal needs and wants as well.

It helped me think about how my emotions affect my needs and wants. For example, this tool helped me realize that when I know I am about to get something I want, I feel excited about it and cannot wait; this was something I had not realized before.

Using the tool gave me a clearer understanding about the meaning of self-regulation. As a fact, I was completely unaware that self-regulation existed and played a significant role in thinking and asking questions. I was able to learn this with help from The Polka Dot Tool. It also helped me remember my past reactions when something I wanted or wanted to do was denied towards me, and using critical thinking will most likely help me take more control of my emotions.

In my opinion, there is a difference between real and imagined needs. Real needs are something that is required to perform a task for a fact. However, imagined needs are what the body thinks is required for the task, but it actually is not. For example, when I want to play video games, my mind thinks I absolutely have to or something will happen, but a real need is something like having water and food, which are highly important to live (F. Patel, personal communication, October 25, 2023).

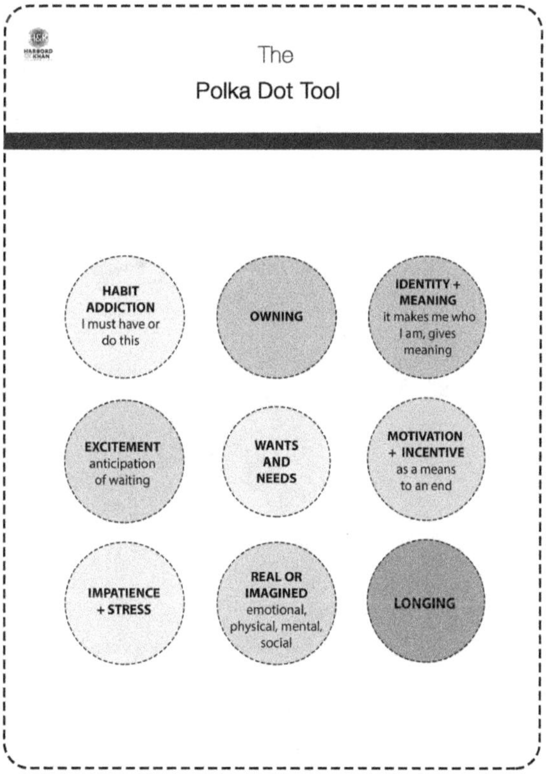
The
Polka Dot Tool
HABIT ADDICTION I must have or do this
OWNING
IDENTITY + MEANING it makes me who I am, gives meaning
EXCITEMENT anticipation of waiting
WANTS AND NEEDS
MOTIVATION + INCENTIVE as a means to an end
IMPATIENCE + STRESS
REAL OR IMAGINED emotional, physical, mental, social
LONGING

Figure 16.2 The Polka Dot Tool card.
Source: Graphic created by the authors.

Applications

This tool can be used to:

- Examine our goals, motivation and lack of motivation.
- Do we want or need to achieve for ourselves, for our families or both?
- What kind of activities and interactions are meaningful and support the development of our sense of self?
- Reflect on some of our habits; can we control these or are these beyond our control?
- Support discussions relating to identity, gender and multiculturalism.

I can manage and communicate my emotions in a thoughtful way.

Figure 16.3 The Polka Dot cat.
Source: Artwork by Linda Weil©.

Suggestions to Align Skills With the Tool

Teachers can share this checklist with students to support them in identifying their higher-order thinking and social emotional skills.

Table 16.3 Suggestions to align higher-order thinking and social emotional learning skills with the tool.

Critical Thinking and Creative Thinking for Problem-Solving		Social Emotional Learning Skills
☐ I can analyze and evaluate issues and my ideas. ☐ I can identify obstacles and challenges. ☐ I can recognize unstated assumptions and bias. ☐ I can examine different aspects of the topic to support understanding. ☐ I can analyze and evaluate my emotions.	☐ I can use different creative strategies that make thinking visible. ☐ I create novel ideas and consider new perspectives. ☐ I use brainstorming and visual diagrams to create and develop ideas, connections and inquiries.	☐ I can recognize and examine my emotions and understand how they impact other people. ☐ I can manage and communicate my emotions in a thoughtful way.

Source: Graphic created by the authors.

Questions for Students to Support Higher-Order Thinking Skills

Table 16.4 Questions for students.

1. Was the tool useful in helping you think about the difference between wants and needs, and if so how?
2. Did the tool help you think about how your emotions affect your needs and wants?
3. Did it give you a clearer understanding of the meaning of self-regulation and how you can take more control of your emotions by using critical thinking?
4. Is there a difference between a real and imagined need? If so, how can you tell between the two, and does understanding this change your behavior?

Source: Graphic created by the authors.

Teacher Reflection

KEY TAKEAWAY: Understanding the difference between wants and needs to inform students' self-awareness of factors that drive behavior.

- Describe the scenario and classroom context—what was the problem you wanted to address with this tool?
- Did you achieve your goal?
- How did you use the tool to support students' higher-order thinking skills (HOTS)?

Complement With Other Tools

Self-regulation and identity: The Myself Tool, The Orange Sun Tool and The Points of View Tool.

Chapter Notes

Use this space to plan and write your personal thoughts, ideas and questions here:

Create your mind-map or sketch out your ideas

The Polka Dot Tool© Worksheet (available as online support material)

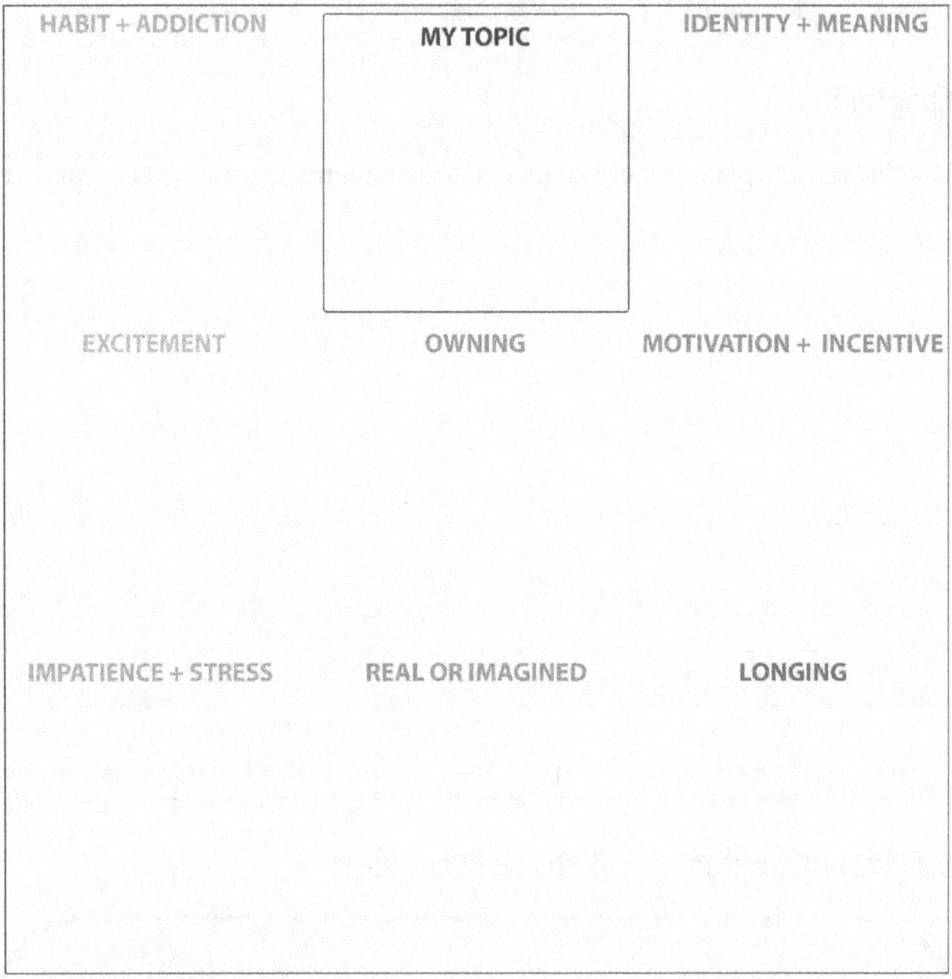
HABIT + ADDICTION
MY TOPIC
IDENTITY + MEANING
EXCITEMENT
OWNING
MOTIVATION + INCENTIVE
IMPATIENCE + STRESS
REAL OR IMAGINED
LONGING

Figure 16.4 The Polka Dot Tool worksheet.
Source: Graphic created by the authors.

Definitions

Want: something that is optional, not necessary for survival.
Need: something that is necessary for human survival.
Habit: a behavioral pattern you can develop by constant repetition of a particular task.
Addiction: when you cannot stop a habit or a behavior in spite of negative consequences.
Motivation: an internal process that drives behavior.
Incentive: an external reward that drives behavior.

The definitions in this list are sourced from Cambridge Online Dictionary (2023).

Reference

Cambridge University Press & Assessment (Ed.). (2023). *Cambridge online dictionary*. Retrieved November 14, 2023, from https://dictionary.cambridge.org/

17

The Snowman Tool

An Emotional Scale

Suggested Grade Level: 5–7
Key Takeaway—Identifying and understanding emotions.

Global Skills and Key Themes

Skills: Critical thinking, creative thinking, problem-solving and reflection.
Themes: Emotion and identity.

Stories

FROM OUR HOMES: A Grade 6 student and her cat.
DEFINITIONS: Emotion, feelings and identity (p 240).

What Does The Snowman Tool Do?

The Snowman Tool gives students an opportunity to think about their emotions and feelings toward a particular situation or event. They can discuss their feelings and what these could look like if they were stronger or weaker.

DOI: 10.4324/9781032664989-18

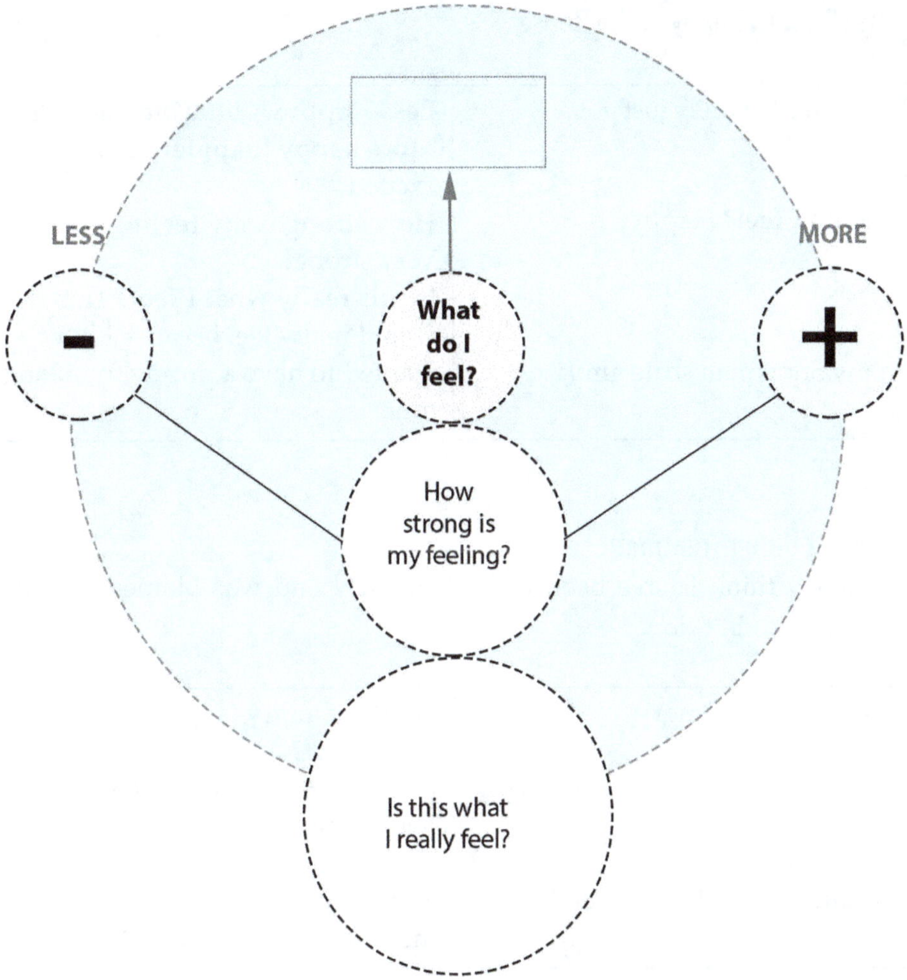
LESS
MORE
-
What do I feel?
+
How strong is my feeling?
Is this what I really feel?

Figure 17.1 The Snowman Tool.
Source: Graphic created by the authors.

The tool supports students in reflecting on the strength of their feelings and thinking more deeply about them and how these feelings affect what they think and how they respond.

How to Use It

1. Choose your topic—this will be an emotion or feeling.
2. Place the emotion or feeling in the box above the head of the Snowman.
3. How can you describe the emotion as
   a. Less strong?
   b. Stronger?

EXAMPLE 1 New Puppy in the House

Situation My family just got a puppy. **What do I feel?** Happy. On my Snowman scale am I:	**Less Happy**: A little bit glad? Or **More happy (happier)**: Super excited? **How strong is my feeling?** Very strong. **Is this really what I feel?** This is what I really feel because I have wanted to have a puppy for a long time.

EXAMPLE 2 Unfair Treatment

Situation: I think I have been treated unfairly and was blamed for doing something I didn't do.

What do I feel? Angry On my Snowman scale am I: **Less angry**: A little bothered?	Or **More angry (angrier)**: Very upset? **How strong is my feeling?** Very strong. **Is this really what I feel?** I feel hurt and sad because no one believes me.

EXAMPLE 3 Being Interested in Something

What would the different stages of 'being interested in something' look like?

- A little curious
- ....
- ....
- Interested in something—what I feel
- ....
- ....
- Can't wait to know more

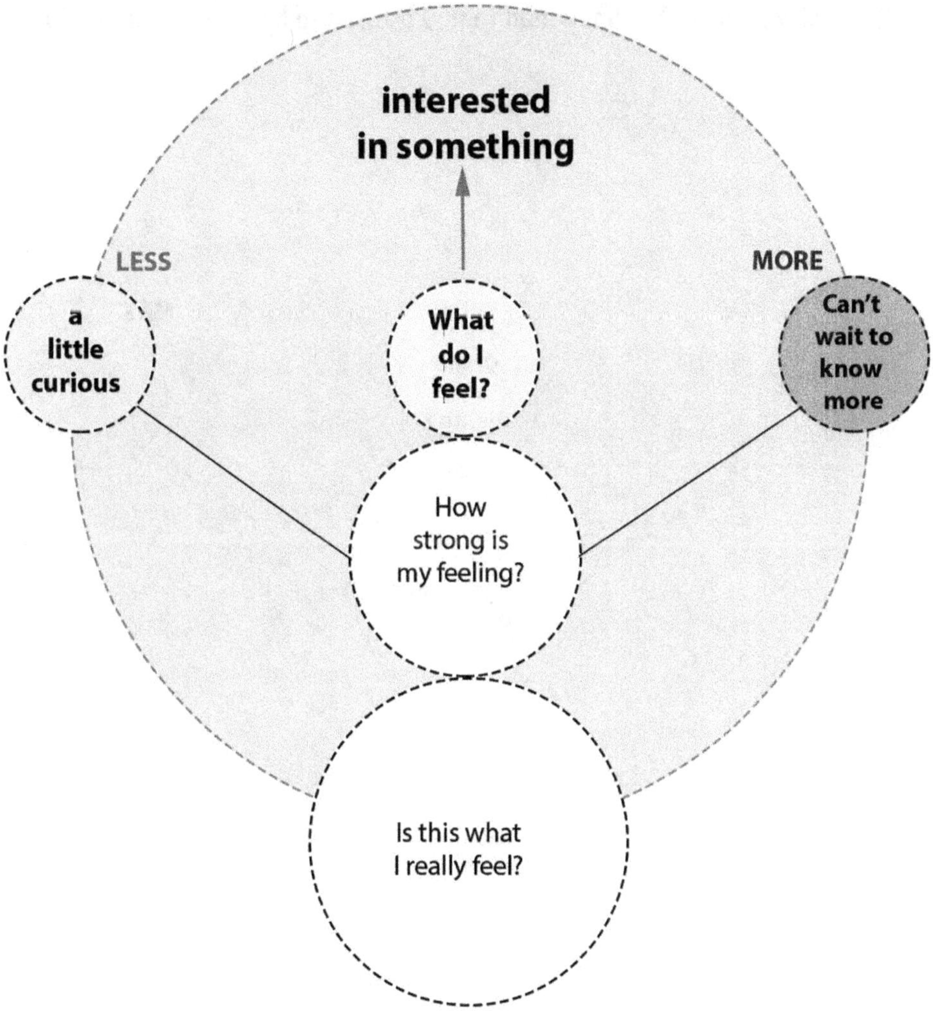
interested
in something
LESS
MORE
a
little
curious
What
do I
feel?
Can't
wait to
know
more
How
strong is
my feeling?
Is this what
I really feel?

Figure 17.2 Using The Snowman Tool to explore 'being interested'.
Source: Graphic created by the authors.

Spanish version of The Snowman Tool© translated by Manuela López Gil

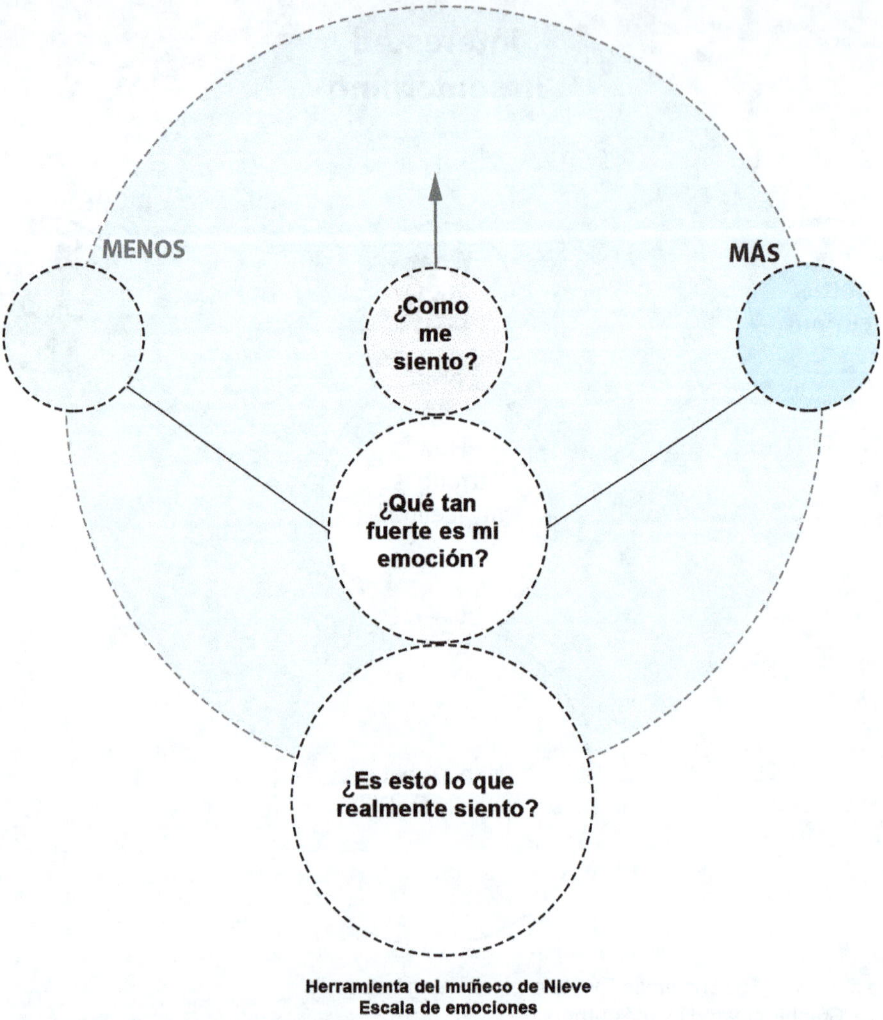
MENOS
MÁS
¿Como me siento?
¿Qué tan fuerte es mi emoción?
¿Es esto lo que realmente siento?
Herramienta del muñeco de Nieve
Escala de emociones

Figure 17.3 The Snowman Tool© in Spanish.
Source: Graphic created by the authors.

STORIES FROM OUR HOMES

A Grade 5 student, Nuria Elahi, used The Snowman Tool to explore something she had been thinking about at home. She had mixed feelings about her cat sleeping in her sister's bed, and using the tool helped her evaluate the situation and have more clarity.

"So initially when the cat chose my sister over me by choosing her bed to sleep on, I was upset and disappointed, but when I used The Snowman Tool, I realized that actually it had both good and bad points. Now I know that I didn't feel very strongly about the cat choosing my sister's bed, I actually felt happy. Happy that she would not disturb me when I slept and I wouldn't hurt the cat at night" (N. Elahi, personal communication, November 25, 2023).

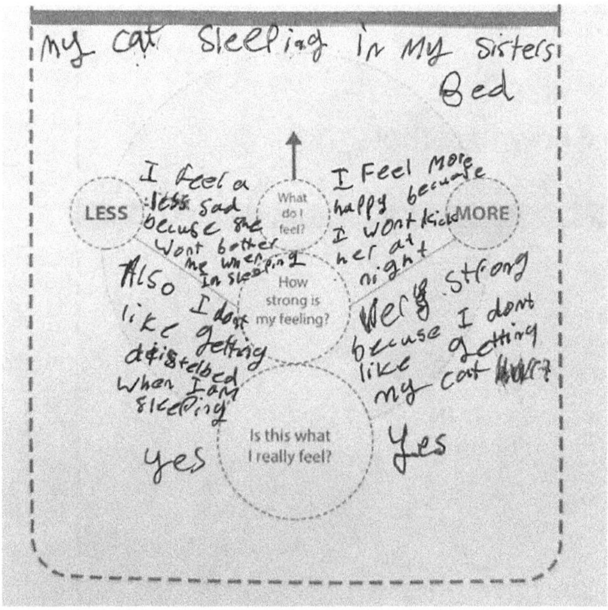
LESS
MORE
What do I feel?
How strong is my feeling?
Is this what I really feel?

Figure 17.4 Student sample of using the tool.
Source: Graphic created by the authors.

Situation: My feelings about my cat sleeping in my sister's bed.

What do I feel? I am okay with it.

On my Snowman scale my feeling was:

Less: I would feel less sad because she won't bother me when I am sleeping. Also I don't like getting disturbed when I am sleeping.
More: I would feel more happy because I won't kick her at night.

How strong is my feeling? Very strong because I don't like my cat getting hurt.
Is this really what I feel? Yes.
Nuria felt the tool helped her recognize her feelings because "It made me find what I really felt". She reflected that the tool helped her understand her feelings because "It made me dig deep". In response to whether the tool helped her think about how one emotion can be felt in different ways, Nuria stated, "Yes. It helped me think about the good things and the bad things" (N. Elahi, personal communication, November 25, 2023).

Teacher tip: This tool is to help students understand their feelings and the strength of these, but it does not give them any course of action to pursue. We can start to self-regulate our feelings by understanding the power of our emotions and recognizing how often our first response to a situation isn't always an accurate reflection of how we feel. Obviously the next stage would be for the teacher to help the student consider if they can take action and suggest solutions to addressing their feelings.

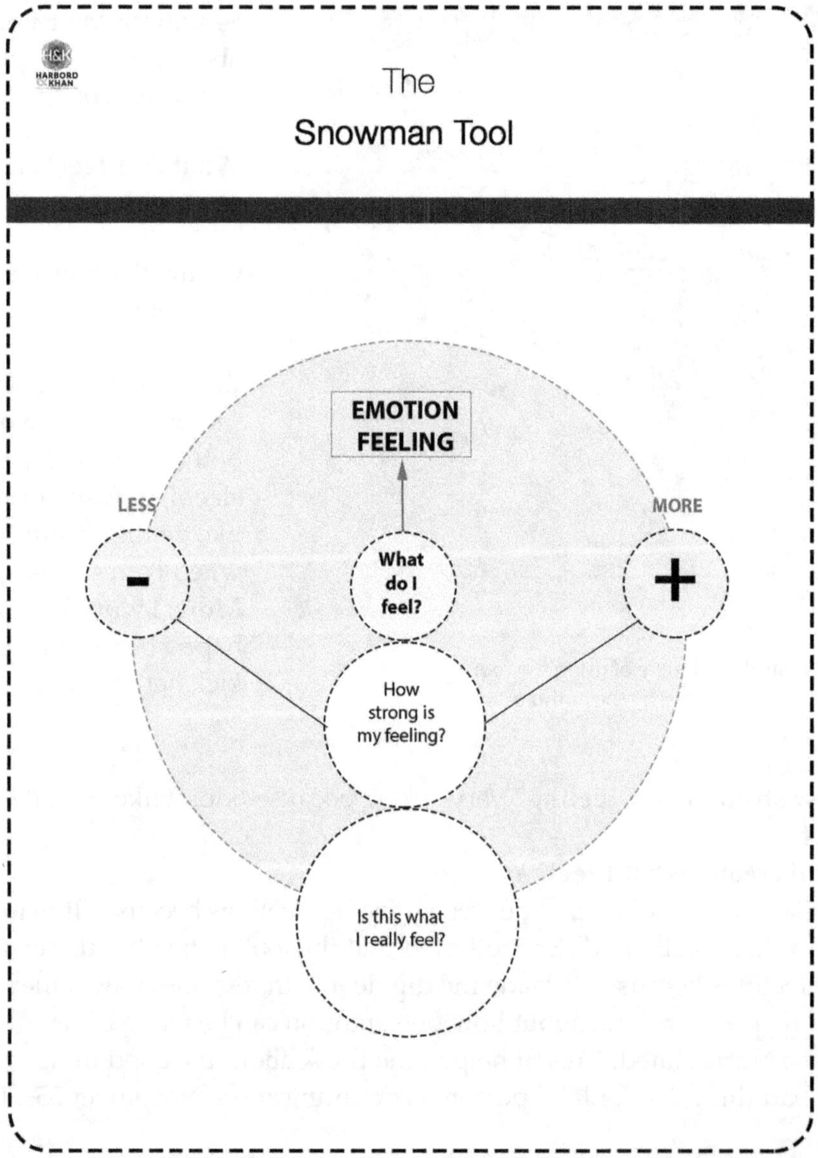
The
Snowman Tool
EMOTION
FEELING
LESS
MORE
-
What do I feel?
+
How strong is my feeling?
Is this what I really feel?

Figure 17.5 The Snowman Tool card.
Source: Graphic created by the authors.

What would happen if I
cared about others'
feelings and the impact
of my actions on them?

Figure 17.6 Sharing feelings.
Source: Artwork by Linda Weil©.

Suggestions to Align Skills With the Tool

Teachers can share this checklist with students to support them in identifying their higher-order thinking and social emotional skills.

Table 17.1 Suggestions to align higher-order thinking and social emotional learning skills with the tool.

Critical and Creative Thinking Skills for Problem-Solving		Social Emotional Learning Skills
☐ I can analyze and evaluate issues and my ideas. ☐ I can analyze and evaluate my emotions. ☐ I can be open-minded to explore my emotions.	☐ I can make unpredictable or surprising connections between objects and/or ideas. ☐ I can use different creative strategies that make thinking visible.	☐ I can recognize and examine my emotions and understand how they impact other people. ☐ I can manage and communicate my emotions in a thoughtful way. ☐ I care about others' feelings and the impact of my actions on them.

Source: Graphic created by the authors.

Questions for Students to Support Higher-Order Thinking Skills

Table 17.2 Questions for students.

1. Did the tool help me recognize my feelings?
2. Did the tool help me understand my feelings?
3. Did the tool help me think about how one emotion can be felt in different ways:
   e.g. happiness could be—a little excited or very happy? anger could be—a little annoyed or very angry?

Source: Graphic created by the authors.

Teacher Reflection

KEY TAKEAWAY—Identifying and understanding emotions.

- Describe the scenario and classroom context—what was the problem you wanted to address with this tool?
- Did you achieve your goal?
- How did you use the tool to support students' higher-order thinking skills (HOTS)?

Complement With Other Tools

Self-regulation and identity: The Myself Tool, The Orange Sun Tool and The Plus-Minus Tool.

Chapter Notes

Use this space to plan and write your personal thoughts, ideas and questions here:

Create your mind-map or sketch out your ideas

The Snowman Tool© Worksheet (available as online support material)

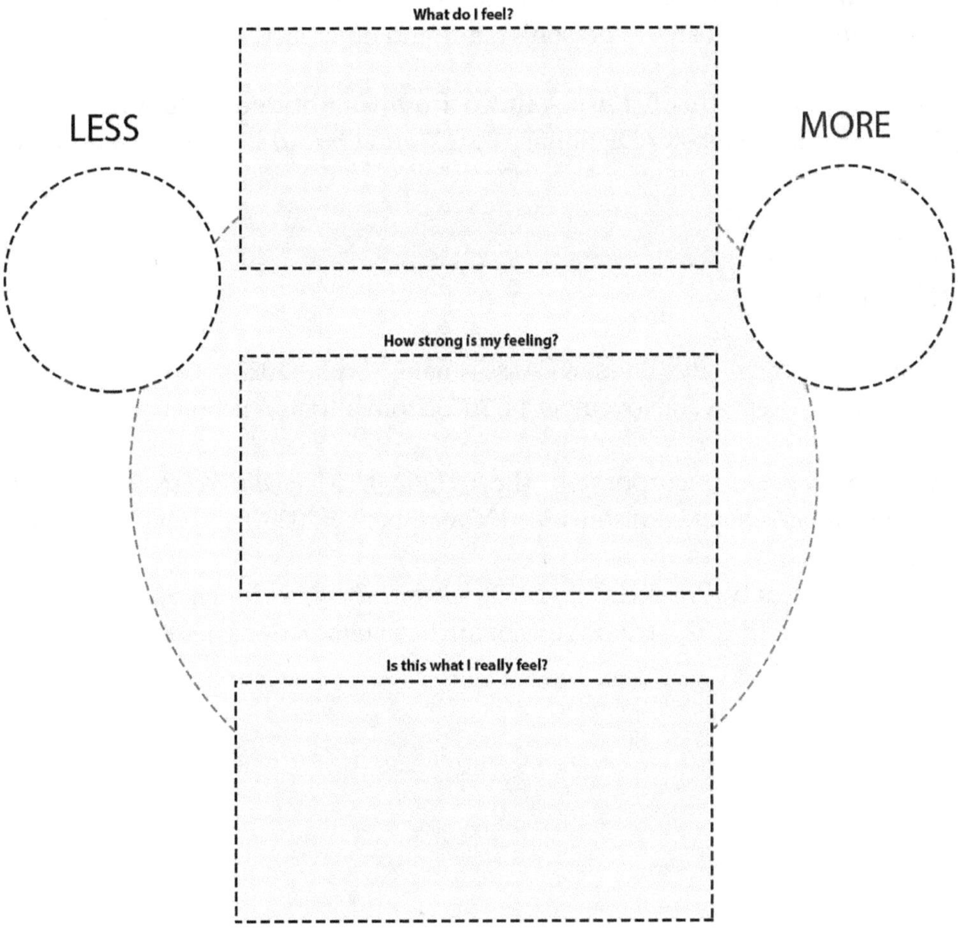
What do I feel?
LESS
MORE
How strong is my feeling?
Is this what I really feel?

Figure 17.7 The Snowman Tool worksheet.
Source: Graphic created by the authors.

Definitions

Emotion: a strong feeling, such as love, anger, fear, etc.
Feelings: how we interpret an emotional state or reaction.
Identity: who you are—a person's name and other facts about who they are.

The definitions in this list are sourced from Cambridge Online Dictionary (2023), Merriam-Webster Dictionary (2023) and Oxford Learners Dictionaries (2023).

References

Cambridge University Press & Assessment (Ed.). (2023). *Cambridge online dictionary*. Retrieved November 14, 2023, from https://dictionary.cambridge.org/

Merriam-Webster, Incorporated (Ed.). (2023). *Merriam-Webster dictionary*. Merriam-Webster.com. Retrieved November 15, 2023, from www.merriam-webster.com/

Oxford University Press (Ed.). (2023). *Oxford learners dictionaries*. Retrieved November 15, 2023, from www.oxfordlearnersdictionaries.com

18

The Thinking Generator Tool

Problem-Solver

Suggested Grade Level: 6–10

Key Takeaway—Reflecting critically on your beliefs, bias, ideas and behavior.

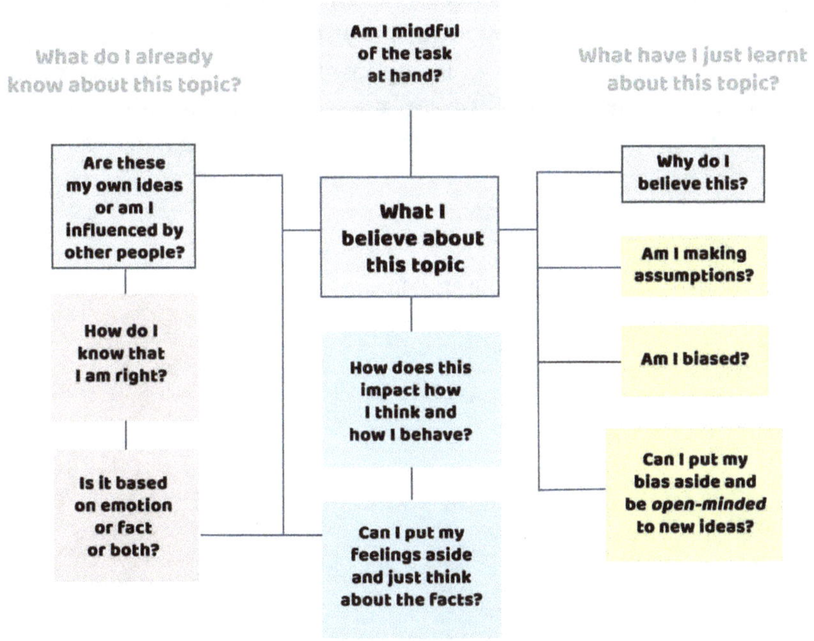

What do I already know about this topic?
Am I mindful of the task at hand?
What have I just learnt about this topic?
Are these my own ideas or am I influenced by other people?
What I believe about this topic
Why do I believe this?
Am I making assumptions?
How do I know that I am right?
Am I biased?
How does this impact how I think and how I behave?
Can I put my bias aside and be *open-minded* to new ideas?
Is it based on emotion or fact or both?
Can I put my feelings aside and just think about the facts?

Figure 18.1 The Thinking Generator Tool.
Source: Graphic created by the authors.

DOI: 10.4324/9781032664989-19

Global Skills and Key Themes

Skills: Collaboration, critical thinking, open-mindedness, problem-solving, resilience and self-management.
Themes: Assumption, bias, empathy, ethical perspectives, mindfulness, open-mindedness, self-awareness and stereotypes.

Stories

FROM OUR SCHOOLS: Student use of social media, bias and assumption (poetry analysis), stressed teachers, bias and miscommunication and adult student revision method.
DEFINITIONS: Assumption, behavior, bias, emotions, feelings, identity and open-minded (p 254).

What Does The Thinking Generator Tool Do?

The Thinking Generator Tool identifies and evaluates students' knowledge and beliefs and encourages reflection on their bias and assumptions. The tool can be used with any topic or subject to help us reflect critically on what we believe, why we believe it, how accurate our beliefs might be, our bias and assumptions and our capacity to be open-minded. This tool is very versatile and can be used in many different ways. You can use all of it or just one section.

Benefits for Students

Table 18.1 Benefits of using the tool to support student metacognition, well-being, self-awareness and ethical thinking.

The Thinking Generator Tool can help me:	
Metacognition Support critical thinking, open-mindedness and problem-solving	• Reflect on prior (What do I already know about this topic) and new knowledge (What have I just learned about this topic) together with what I believe and know about the topic. • Reflect on how I know. • Be more aware of the complex issues that impact the learning process and my own development.
Well being Support self-management	• Be aware of how my emotions can influence my reactions and actions. • Guide me in how to self-regulate and grow my resilience.
Self-awareness Reflect critically on what we believe, why we believe it and how accurate our beliefs might be	• See connections between what I believe and how I act. • Understand how easy or difficult it is to put bias aside and be open-minded to new ideas. I am already taking a step to be more self-aware.
Ethical thinking Support thinking about ethical issues and values e.g. empathy, fairness, caring, integrity, open-mindedness, etc.	• It can encourage me to be more aware of my bias. • It can also help me see how easy or difficult it is for me to rethink and review my beliefs. • Think about how I can be more empathetic to others.

How to Use It

1 Choose your topic.

2 **Am I mindful of the task at hand?**

Are you focused on what you are doing?

3 **What I believe about this topic**

Do your beliefs affect your thinking and behavior?
Can you think about just the facts and not your feelings?

4 **Are these my own ideas or am I influenced by other people?**

Go either left or right.

Why do I believe this?

Left
How do you know you are right? Is this based on your emotions, your facts or both?

Right
Are you biased in your thinking?
Are you open-minded to new ideas?

Figure 18.2 How to use The Thinking Generator Tool.
Source: Graphic created by the authors.

EXAMPLE 1 Posting on Social Media

People only post on social media when they are unhappy.

Am I mindful of the task?
Yes
Are these my own ideas or am I influenced by other people?
Influenced
What I believe about this topic
People only post frequently when they are deeply unhappy.
Why do I believe this?
Articles I've read, general thoughts and views on social media and posts read on social media.
How do I know that I am right?
I know the thought process behind when I post - looking at how I act when I am unhappy or insecure, I can see I don't post.
How does this impact how I think and how I behave?
I stopped posting because I thought it meant I was deeply unhappy even though I didn't feel it. I was also concerned other people would perceive it as me being unhappy.
Am I making assumptions?
Yes
Am I biased?
Yes
Can I put bias aside and be open-minded to new ideas?
Yes, but when beliefs are deeply rooted they are hard to challenge. On a rational level yes, it's harder on an emotional level.
Is it based on emotion or fact, or both?
Both. Looking at my emotional pattern helps to see the facts.
Can I put my feelings aside and just think about the facts?
Yes
I know I don't post to overcompensate or create a certain image - in fact when I am unhappy, I'm more likely to withdraw and go into myself and not post.

Figure 18.3 Using The Thinking Generator Tool to explore social media use.
Source: Graphic created by the authors.

EXAMPLE 2 Using One Section Only of The Thinking Generator Tool in Design/Science/Engineering Design

TOPIC: 'I choose to use sustainable materials in my model'

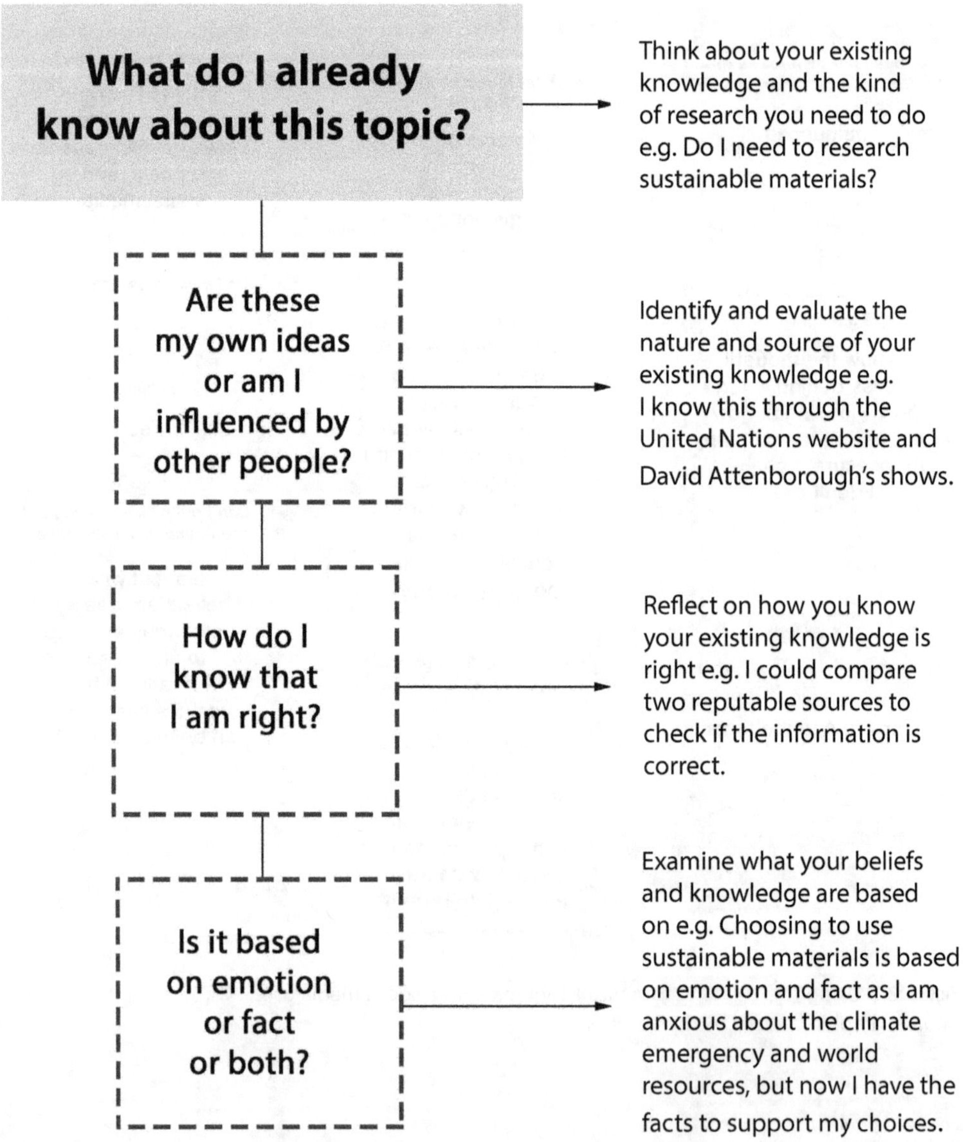
What do I already know about this topic?
Think about your existing knowledge and the kind of research you need to do e.g. Do I need to research sustainable materials?
Are these my own ideas or am I influenced by other people?
Identify and evaluate the nature and source of your existing knowledge e.g. I know this through the United Nations website and David Attenborough's shows.
How do I know that I am right?
Reflect on how you know your existing knowledge is right e.g. I could compare two reputable sources to check if the information is correct.
Is it based on emotion or fact or both?
Examine what your beliefs and knowledge are based on e.g. Choosing to use sustainable materials is based on emotion and fact as I am anxious about the climate emergency and world resources, but now I have the facts to support my choices.

Figure 18.4 Using one section of The Thinking Generator Tool.
Source: Graphic created by the authors.

STORIES FROM OUR SCHOOLS

Social Media

A middle school homeroom teacher has been concerned about the discussions students are having about social media. The teacher wants the students to use The Thinking Generator Tool to check the impact on others and themselves when posting on social media and to explore their beliefs, influences and assumptions. The goal would be for the student to be reflective and more responsible about the use and frequency of postings and emotions.

Year 10 Poetry Analysis of an Examination Poem

Student Bias and Assumption

A high school English teacher, Judith Shannon, wanted to test how The Thinking Generator Tool could support her students to reflect on issues of bias and assumption.

Discussion About Principles, Ethics and Beliefs

I provided my students with the bias and assumption section of the diagram to discuss in relation to capitalism and the commodification of the individual in modern society. It worked very well as a framework for discussion and focused the students in checking their assumptions and biases, making them police the parameters of the discussion and the critical thinking demonstrated. I noticed that it led to much more metacognition and students making the conscious effort to think about thinking, both their own and that of others. It also suited that lesson, which was discussion based and focused on refining ideas, understanding and challenging beliefs. In a nutshell it led to deeper, more meaningful thinking and articulation of complex ideas (J. Shannon, personal communication, April 3, 2023).

Stressed Teachers

Middle School Principal and Faculty Issues

Maria is a middle school principal who was struggling with a faculty issue regarding stressed and overwhelmed teachers. She realized The Thinking Generator Tool offered her opportunities to rethink ways to support teachers through a stressful situation. Maria held a faculty meeting and asked the teachers to use The Thinking Generator Tool to work through all facets and see if they could isolate the issues.

By using the tool, teachers were able to pinpoint the issue as being one of a lack of time. The main problem was that teachers were under time pressure to write responses and mark student work necessary for both student feedback and for grading requirements. Consequently, Maria timetabled additional student free time for teachers to focus on their marking (M. Nemat, personal communication, January 23, 2023).

Bias and Miscommunication Grade 5 Teacher and Faculty Issues

When the Mandarin department held the Chinese Temple Fair, they needed support from all the faculty. But due to a lack of communication and some misunderstandings between the foreign teachers and Mandarin teachers, there was some discontent about the fair. The Grade 5 teacher used The Thinking Generator Tool to reflect on the process with the department after the event.

Working through the questions and expressing their feelings, it became apparent that biases on both sides had impacted the situation. All the faculty agreed that putting their bias aside and being open-minded to new ideas could improve communication issues (T. Zhang, personal communication, April 12, 2023).

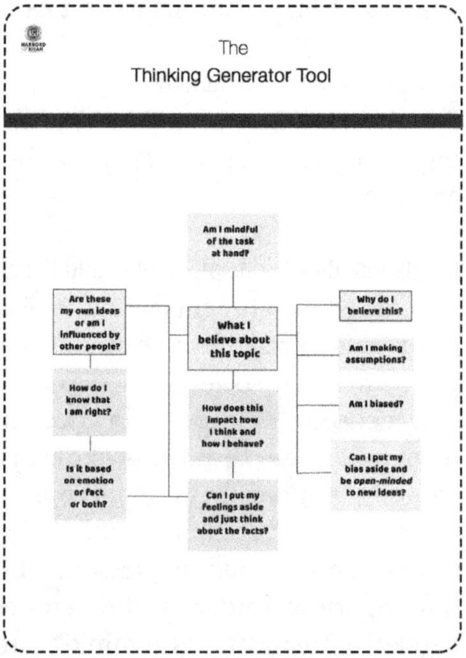
The
Thinking Generator Tool
Am I mindful of the task at hand?
Are these my own ideas or am I influenced by other people?
What I believe about this topic
Why do I believe this?
Am I making assumptions?
How do I know that I am right?
How does this impact how I think and how I behave?
Am I biased?
Is it based on emotion or fact or both?
Can I put my feelings aside and just think about the facts?
Can I put my bias aside and be *open-minded* to new ideas?

Figure 18.5 The Thinking Generator Tool card.
Source: Graphic created by the authors.

Adult Student's Revision Method

Ali Humayun wanted to gain clarity on the usefulness of the 'Active Recall' revision method. This involves reading about a topic, attempting to make notes of the key points from memory and then re-reading the material and filling in any gaps. He found The Thinking Generator Tool particularly useful in helping to systematically break down each stage of the thinking process. It also helped him understand how his emotions and past personal experiences had influenced his beliefs, even toward something like a preferred revision method.

Ali questioned whether the sources of the 'facts' regarding the usefulness of 'Active Recall' were in fact helpful (such as word-of-mouth, YouTube videos). The Thinking Generator Tool provided him with a more critical lens on each stage of his belief. For example, it prompted him to review his understanding of the 'Active Recall' method, where further research showed that there were various approaches to the method itself (such as using flashcards) (A. Humayun, personal communication, March 22, 2023).

Suggestions to Align Skills With the Tool

Teachers can share this checklist with students to support them in identifying their higher-order thinking and social emotional skills.

Table 18.2 Suggestions to align higher-order thinking and social emotional learning skills with the tool.

Critical and Creative Thinking Skills for Problem-Solving		**Social Emotional Learning Skills**
☐ I can analyze and evaluate my ideas, assumptions, prejudices and biases. ☐ I can describe and justify my own thoughts, beliefs, values and actions to identify assumptions, problems and bias.	☐ I can use different creative strategies that make thinking visible. ☐ I make unpredictable or surprising connections between thoughts and ideas. ☐ I create novel ideas and consider new perspectives.	☐ I can recognize and examine my emotions and understand how they impact other people. ☐ I can understand and explore bias and prejudice. ☐ I can manage and communicate my emotions in a thoughtful way. ☐ I am curious and open-minded. ☐ I understand that I have a responsibility to behave in an ethical way. ☐ I can find possible ways to problem-solve for myself and society.

(Continued)

Table 18.2 (Continued)

Critical and Creative Thinking Skills for Problem-Solving		Social Emotional Learning Skills
☐ I can check the accuracy of facts and interpretations and look at multiple perspectives. ☐ I can analyze and evaluate my emotions. ☐ I can develop contrary or opposing arguments.		☐ I can plan for and evaluate what the consequences of my actions will be. ☐ I understand what empathy is and can empathize with others. ☐ I can make decisions that are fair and impartial. ☐ I care about others' feelings and the impact of my actions on them. ☐ I take action to support others' well-being.

Source: Graphic created by the authors.

Questions for Students to Support Higher-Order Thinking Skills

Table 18.3 Questions for students.

Grade 6–8

1. Did the tool get you to think about your bias in a different way? If so, how?
2. Before using the tool, had you ever thought about how other people influence your thinking?
3. Does using the tool help you to be more open-minded? If so, how?

Grade 9–10

1. Did you analyze and evaluate your ideas, assumptions, prejudices and biases in a different way? If so, how?
2. Did exploring your beliefs impact how you felt about the topic?
3. Before using the tool, had you thought about how other people influence your beliefs? Did it help you realize who influences your decisions?
4. Could The Thinking Generator Tool help you problem-solve other issues to do with bias, stereotypes or being more open-minded? Give reasons for your answer.

Source: Graphic created by the authors.

Teacher Reflection

KEY TAKEAWAY: Reflecting critically on your beliefs, bias, ideas and behavior.

- Describe the scenario and classroom context—what was the problem you wanted to address with this tool?
- Did you achieve your goal?
- How did you use the tool to support students' higher-order thinking skills (HOTS)?

Complement With Other Tools

Ethical mindset: The Bias and Fairness Tool, The Circles Tool and The Clock Tool.

Chapter Notes

Use this space to plan and write your personal thoughts, ideas and questions here:

Create your mind-map or sketch out your ideas

The Thinking Generator Tool© Blank Worksheet (available as online support material)

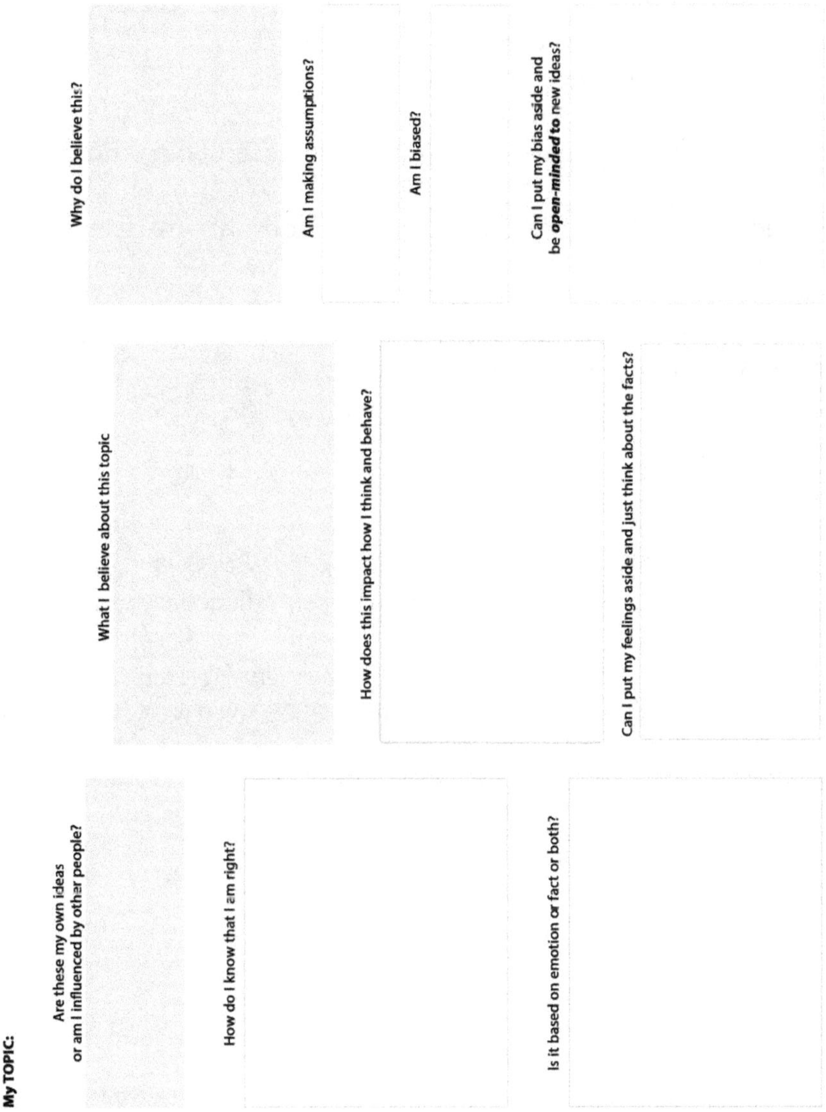
My TOPIC:
Are these my own ideas or am I influenced by other people?
What I believe about this topic
Why do I believe this?
How do I know that I am right?
How does this impact how I think and behave?
Am I making assumptions?
Am I biased?
Is it based on emotion or fact or both?
Can I put my feelings aside and just think about the facts?
Can I put my bias aside and be *open-minded to* new ideas?

Figure 18.6 The Thinking Generator Tool blank worksheet.
Source: Graphic created by the authors.

Definitions

Assumption: belief or feeling that something is true or that something will happen, although there is no proof.
Behavior: the way in which someone behaves, especially toward others.
Bias: a strong feeling in favor of or against one group of people or one side in an argument, often not based on fair judgment.
Emotion: a strong feeling, such as love, anger, fear, etc.
Feelings: how we interpret an emotional state or reaction.
Identity: who you are—a person's name and other facts about who they are.
Open-minded: willing to consider ideas and opinions that are new or different from your own.

The definitions in this list are sourced from Cambridge Online Dictionary (2023) and Merriam-Webster Dictionary (2023).

References

Cambridge University Press & Assessment (Ed.). (2023). *Cambridge online dictionary*. Retrieved November 14, 2023, from https://dictionary.cambridge.org/

Merriam-Webster, Incorporated (Ed.). (2023). *Merriam-Webster dictionary*. Merriam-Webster.com. Retrieved November 15, 2023, from www.merriam-webster.com/

19

The Time Tunnel Tool

Looking Forward, Looking Back

Suggested Grade Level: 8–10

Key Takeaways—Developing student awareness of the impact of their actions on future generations. Fostering empathy and a sense of responsibility for environmental and other global, ethical issues.

Global Skills and Key Themes

Skills: Critical thinking, creative thinking, problem-solving and reflection.
Themes: Citizenship, curiosity, environmental issues, empathy, global themes, imagination, multiculturalism, multiple perspectives and open-mindedness.

Stories

FROM THE CLASSROOM: Possibilities in P.E. and film posters and objects—Grade 10 students.
Definitions: Empathy, ethical values, perspective and philosopher (p. 265).

DOI: 10.4324/9781032664989-20

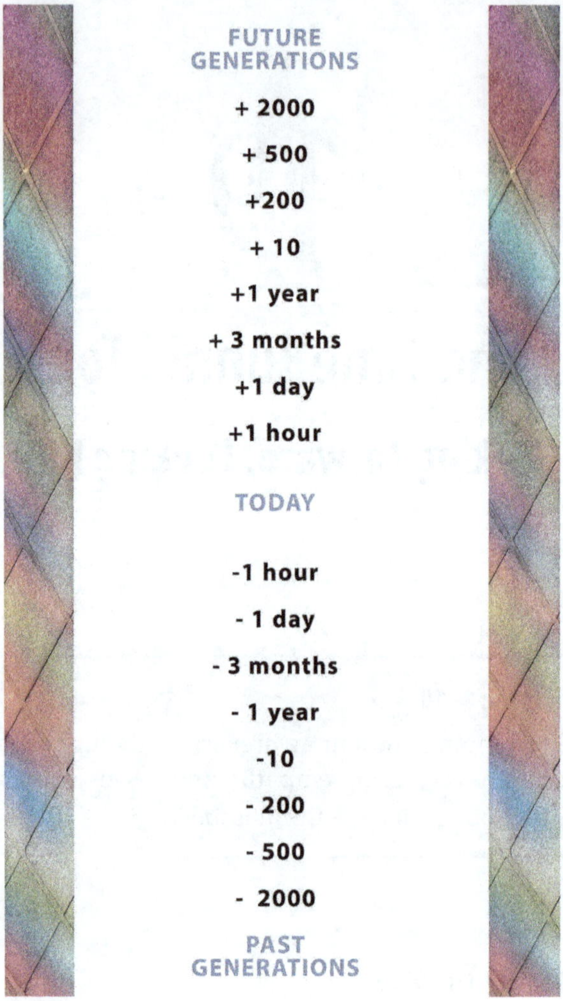
FUTURE
GENERATIONS
+ 2000
+ 500
+200
+ 10
+1 year
+ 3 months
+1 day
+1 hour
TODAY
-1 hour
- 1 day
- 3 months
- 1 year
-10
- 200
- 500
- 2000
PAST
GENERATIONS

Figure 19.1 The Time Tunnel Tool.
Source: Graphic created by the authors.

What Does The Time Tunnel Tool Do?

Explores new perspectives for positive change through imaginative time travel. This tool can inspire students to imagine the past and predict other futures. It can generate discussions about ethical considerations and the human impact on both future and past generations. This tool was inspired by the work of the philosopher Roman Krznaric, author of *The Good Ancestor: How to Think Long Term in a Short-Term World* (Krznaric, 2021).

What does being a 'good ancestor' mean to you?

How can you plan in your lifetime for the benefit of future generations?

The Time Tunnel Tool can help you think of time in a different way and be more empathic. It can be a starting point for discussions about our impact on future generations and also looking backwards to imagine how our ancestors might have thought.

FUTURE GENERATIONS
+ 2000
+ 500
+200
+ 10
+1 year
+ 3 months
+1 day
+1 hour
TODAY
-1 hour
- 1 day
- 3 months
- 1 year
-10
- 200
- 500
- 2000
PAST GENERATIONS

Figure 19.2 The Time Tunnel Tool with questions.
Source: Graphic created by the authors.

How to Use It

1. Choose your topic.
2. Read the different times (plus, minus and today) on the timeline.
3. Respond to the questions in the table. Questions 1–3 require a numerical score. For questions 4–5 students can give two reasons for the benefits of reflecting on time from different time frames.

The Time Tunnel Tool Questions

1. How well can you remember what happened today? . . . ./10
2. Choose one plus (+) number and one minus (–) number from the timeline . . . .
3. How clearly can you imagine the future with the plus number e.g. +200 years ahead? . . . . . out of 10
4. How clearly can you remember the past with the minus number e.g. –3 months ago? . . . out of 10
5. How can imagining the future help us and our world? Give two reasons ....
....
....
....
6. How can reflecting on the past help us and our world? Give two reasons ....
....
....
....

STORIES FROM THE CLASSROOM

P.E. and Health

As a potential line of inquiry, a P.E. teacher felt that students could use the tool to examine issues relating to the decrease of activity levels as a result of industrialization and the development of technology changing the workplace and recreational spaces to be more sedentary. They thought the tool could support critical and creative thinking. For example, the Time Tunnel Tool could engage students to think about long-term fitness and health issues through an ethical lens by plotting goals both for themselves and the wider community (S. Blake, personal communication, May 27, 2023).

Freeze Frame—Grade 10 Media Activity

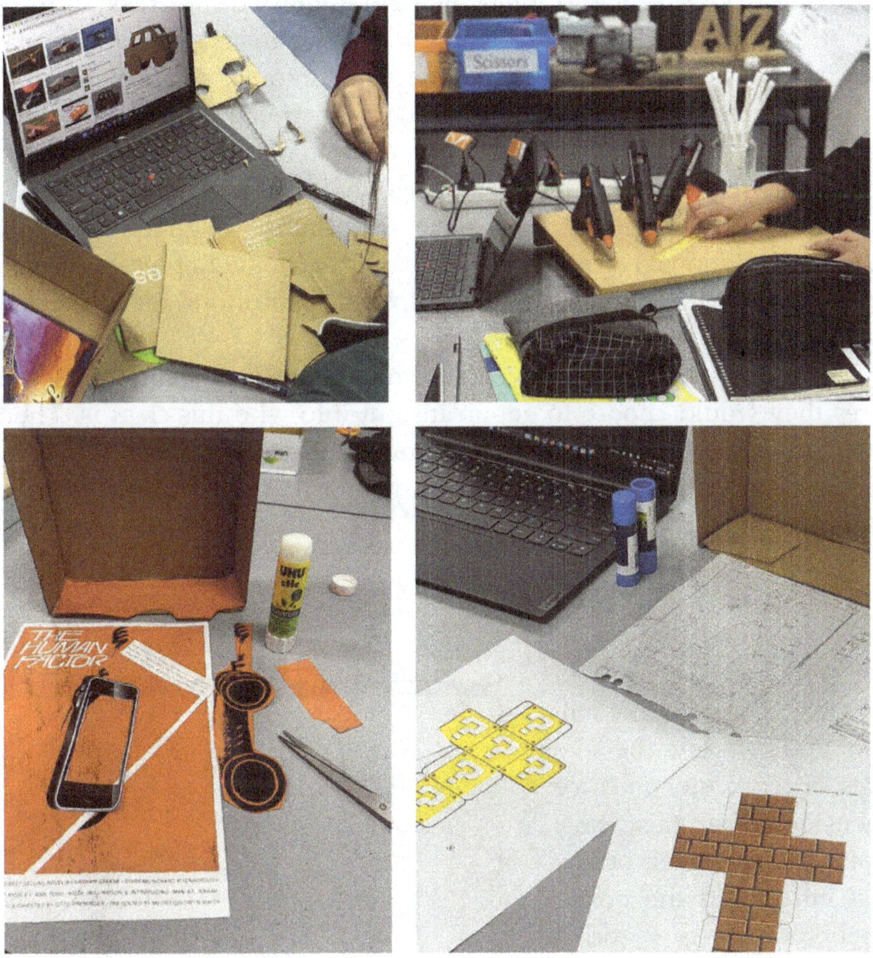
Scissors
UHU
THE HUMAN FACTOR

Figure 19.3 Example of student work.
Source: Image credit Renee Gross-Zylbersztajn.

Teachers can also use this tool as an imaginative time travel activity as described by Renee Gross-Zylbersztajn, a media teacher from South Oakleigh College, Australia.

Using The Time Tunnel Tool with a new class of students effectively added a level of complexity and interest to what could be considered a one-dimensional activity. Even though I love this activity, I wanted to support the students to connect to the task and to the group.

Having only met these students the day before, I used The Time Tunnel Tool as an ice breaker. I was hoping that the outcomes of this activity would allow me to get an understanding of who the students are, how they work together collaboratively and what they are interested in. I needed to build rapport with the students, [to] be able to deliver them a lot of information about the course and engage them at the same time. This class is set up as [a] head start to the new year, even though it is very much the end of the current year. The aim, to capture their attention and hold on to this engagement over the holidays so they return ready and eager to study media.

I introduced them to the study plan, the admin, design information and me, my expectations. I broke down the basics of Media Representation to six media elements: individuals, social groupings, institutions, ideas, events and issues.

The second period students chose a movie poster. I wanted to see what genres they would choose to get an insight into who this class is. The task invited students to dissect the movie poster into layers, parts, elements. To help develop creative thinking opportunities I thought I would restrict the materials they use. They each got the lid of a photocopy paper box; their limitations included the size of their work, an A4 piece of paper size. The outcome will stand and display the elements of the poster in three dimensions or at least three or four different levels or layers. I introduced the poster activity and then I added a hook, a twist. I showed them The Time Tunnel Tool. I said to them that the poster they'd chosen was the initial moment in time. The outcome will require them to consider the current poster and what representation is within that frame. What will help to distinguish the year the movie was set from another? Their job is to identify and describe

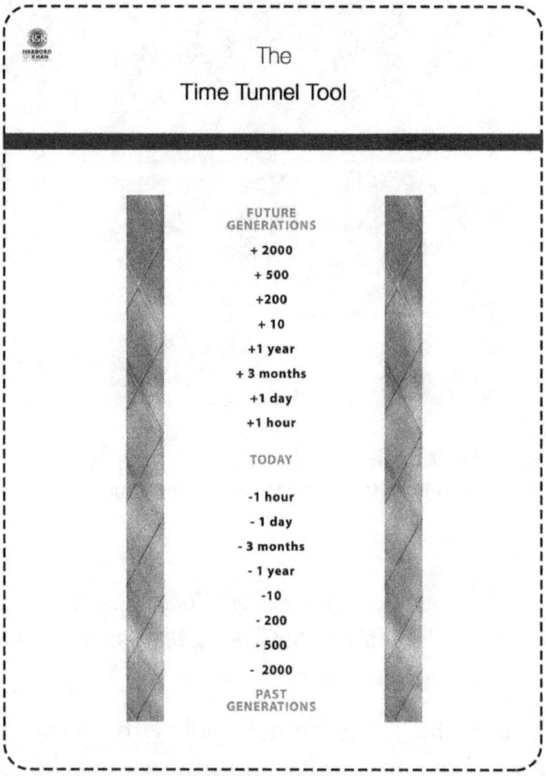
The
Time Tunnel Tool
FUTURE GENERATIONS
+ 2000
+ 500
+200
+ 10
+1 year
+ 3 months
+1 day
+1 hour
TODAY
-1 hour
- 1 day
- 3 months
- 1 year
-10
- 200
- 500
- 2000
PAST GENERATIONS

Figure 19.4 The Time Tunnel Tool card.
Source: Graphic created by the authors.

the mise-en-scène (the whole frame) and to adjust the elements of the movie to a different era; the past or in the future. That's essentially how we used The Time Tunnel Tool. To visualize the opportunities, choices they have are broken down to hours, days, months, years. I loved that they could choose to simply change the time of day or extend their learning to a completely different story element; fashion, product placement, font style.

The students really liked the tool and were very engaged. As they worked I went around and asked them how they were using critical, creative thinking and design thinking using pre-planned suggestions to align with the tool. This is how I hoped to facilitate their progress without interfering.

Some of the types of comments they made were:

> "It's an animation, how might we represent these guys in a different era?"
> "Do we have to change the whole poster or just parts of it to create a sense of the past?"
> "Can we just remove the color and make it black and white?"
> "I actually don't really think the existing poster is effective, but I'm not sure why."
> "Can I put my own face in the poster to make the poster about today?"
>
> (R. Gross-Zylbersztajn, personal communication, November 29, 2023)

What would happen if I was curious and open-minded?

Figure 19.5 Stegosaurus going for a walk.
Source: Artwork by Linda Weil©.

Suggestions to Align Skills With the Tool

Teachers can share this checklist with students to support them in identifying their higher-order thinking and social emotional skills.

Table 19.1 Suggestions to align higher-order thinking and social emotional learning skills with the tool.

Critical and Creative Thinking for Problem-Solving		Social Emotional Learning Skills
☐ I can analyze and evaluate issues and my ideas. ☐ I can identify trends and forecast possibilities. ☐ I can consider ideas from multiple perspectives. ☐ I can imagine multiple viewpoints.	☐ I create novel ideas and consider new perspectives. ☐ I can consider and explore a range of different ideas, including some that may or may not be possible. ☐ I make unexpected or unusual connections between objects and/or ideas. ☐ I can speculate and ask "what if" questions. ☐ I can use different creative strategies that make thinking visible.	☐ I am curious and open-minded. ☐ I understand that I have a responsibility to behave in an ethical way. ☐ I can plan for and evaluate what the consequences of my actions will be. ☐ I understand what empathy is and can empathize with others. ☐ I can make decisions that are fair and impartial. ☐ I care about others' feelings and the impact of my actions on them. ☐ I take action to support others' well-being.

Source: Graphic created by the authors.

Questions for Students to Support Higher-Order Thinking Skills

Table 19.2 Questions for students.

1. Did the tool make you think differently about how your actions might impact future generations? Give reasons for your answer.
2. Can thinking about time in different ways teach us anything about how we want to live and treat other people?
3. Does your culture or community reflect and use past knowledge to guide your decision-making today?

Source: Graphic created by the authors.

Teacher Reflection

KEY TAKEAWAY: Developing student awareness of the impact of their actions on future generations. Fostering empathy and a sense of responsibility for environmental and other global ethical issues.

- Describe the scenario and classroom context—what was the problem you wanted to address with this tool?
- Did you achieve your goal?
- How did you use the tool to support students' higher-order thinking skills (HOTS)?

Complement With Other Tools

Time and multiple perspectives: The Clock Tool and The Detective Tool.

Chapter Notes

Use this space to plan and write your personal thoughts, ideas and questions here:

Create your mind-map or sketch out your ideas

Definitions

Empathy: the ability to understand and share the feelings of another.
Ethical values: the beliefs people have, especially about what is right and wrong and what is most important in life, that control their behavior.
Perspective: a particular way of considering something.
Philosopher: someone who studies or writes about the meaning of life.

The definitions in this list are sourced from Cambridge Online Dictionary (2023) and Merriam-Webster Dictionary (2023).

References

Cambridge University Press & Assessment (Ed.). (2023). *Cambridge online dictionary*. Retrieved November 14, 2023, from https://dictionary.cambridge.org/

Krznaric, R. (2021). *The good ancestor: How to think long term in a short-term world*. WH Allen.

Merriam-Webster, Incorporated (Ed.). (2023). *Merriam-Webster dictionary*. Merriam-Webster.com. Retrieved November 15, 2023, from www.merriam-webster.com/

20

The Transfer Tool

Making Connections

Suggested Grade Level: 7–10

Key Takeaway—Exploring how what is learned at school and what is learned out of school can complement each other.

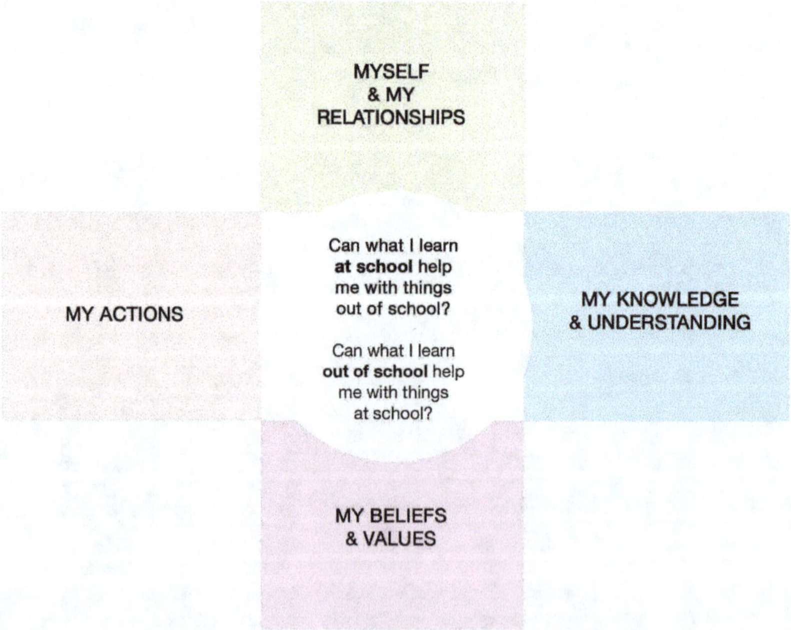

MYSELF & MY RELATIONSHIPS
MY ACTIONS
Can what I learn **at school** help me with things out of school?
Can what I learn **out of school** help me with things at school?
MY KNOWLEDGE & UNDERSTANDING
MY BELIEFS & VALUES

Figure 20.1 The Transfer Tool.
Source: Graphic created by the authors.

DOI: 10.4324/9781032664989-21

Global Skills and Key Themes

Skills: Critical thinking, creative thinking, problem-solving, transfer and making connections.
Themes: Holistic approaches, real-world issues and relationships.

Stories

FROM THE CLASSROOM: Debating example—Grade 12 student.
STORIES FROM THE WORLD: Edible Schoolyard NYC.
DEFINITIONS: Beliefs and values (p 278).

What Does The Transfer Tool Do?

Sometimes students feel their lives at school and out of school are disconnected. They often work just to achieve good grades and don't always perceive (or are not made to feel) the value of learning in their lives that is not assessed. When students are pressured to be concerned only about their grades without a thought for all the other parts that make up who they are, it can frequently lead to a feeling of self-doubt and a lack of confidence.

- Encourages students to develop a more holistic view when reflecting on their identity, knowledge and relationships.
- Helps students think about the connections between their beliefs and values, knowledge and understanding and actions.
- Supports students in recognizing and acknowledging that their skills and experiences out of school have a value and that these could also impact their lives at school. Teachers usually assess the transfer of learning from subject to subject; however, there is also value in exploring the transfer of knowledge and skills from one environment to another.

Benefits for Students

Table 20.1 Benefits for students.

The Transfer Tool can help me:	
Metacognition Support creative and critical thinking, making connections, problem-solving and transfer.	• Make connections between what I do at school and out of school. • Consider how I can use my problem-solving skills in new ways and situations.

(Continued)

Table 20.1 (Continued)

The Transfer Tool can help me:	
Well being Support self-management.	• Develop insights about how different areas of my life impact me and give me more clarity on complex relationships and issues in my life as a whole.
Self-awareness Reflect critically on my beliefs and actions in all areas of my life.	• Reflect on how I can use my knowledge and experiences in a range of situations.
Ethical thinking Support thinking about ethical issues and values e.g. empathy, justice, kindness and open-mindedness, etc.	• Examine my behavior—Do my thinking and actions reflect my values and beliefs?

Source: Graphic created by the authors.

How to Use It

1. Choose your topic and keep in mind the central questions.
2. Read all the different sections, 'Myself and My Relationships', 'My Knowledge and Understanding', 'My Beliefs and Values' and 'My Actions' to see which are relevant to your topic.
3. Select and explore the relevant sections in any order.

EXAMPLE 1 Myself and My Relationships

Students can compare and contrast what they learn from their families and communities with what they learn at school from their teachers and peers.

Table 20.2 Example 1 myself and my relationships.

Myself and My Relationships It is important to take action to help people.		
Out of School	↔	**At School**
It is important to help my neighbor with recycling.	Can help me	It is important to support my school's recycling program.

Source: Graphic created by the authors.

EXAMPLE 2 My Beliefs and Values and My Actions

Consider how students' beliefs about the environment in school and out of school could support each other to make a positive impact.

Table 20.3 Example 2 my beliefs, values and actions.

My Beliefs, Values and Actions It is important to take action to conserve energy.		
At School	↔	Out of School
It is important to turn the lights off when they are not needed.	Can help me	It is important to conserve energy and tell my family about it so we can do the same at home.

Source: Graphic created by the authors.

STORIES FROM THE CLASSROOM

The Impact of Debating

ZR (Grade 12 student) reflected on how the experience of debating at school impacted her in other areas of her life.

- Firstly it forced me to be cognizant of the world around me—in order to do well and win we had to be very aware of current affairs globally, economics and politics. As well as thinking about the consequences of events that otherwise are very easy to gloss over such as voting or other 'big' topics, we had to dissect them in a variety of ways and actually 'weigh out' costs and benefits.
- Secondly it changed the way I think—I find it easier to think on the spot and find refutations and counter arguments on the go as well as finding solutions to problems on the spot.
- I find that I'm able to structure my thoughts much more coherently, and they appear as a list of tiers of argumentation rather than a jumble of various overlapping thoughts.
- You have to think a lot about individual strengths and weaknesses when working with a team, which is also a huge learning process. This made me more patient with myself and others and also forced me to grow out of my comfort zone and adapt to situations where

teammates couldn't understand a point or we didn't see eye to eye on the debate floor. Also, being one of the few all-female teams on a heavily male-dominated circuit meant that we had a lot of confidence issues to work through as well as being seen as a joke and having to try our best regardless.

- I think it made me a lot better at doing embarrassing things, because you sometimes go to the debates floor with information you aren't sure about, and you have to deliver it in a convincing way, often forming your opinion and arguments while you're speaking for eight minutes straight and being judged and critiqued.

(Z. R, personal communication, August 23, 2023)

STORIES FROM THE WORLD

Edible Schoolyard NYC

Edible Schoolyard NYC is a nonprofit organization whose mission is to support edible education for every child in New York City. As every school is different, Edible Schoolyard NYC offers a variety of program models which range in depth and scope. Through their partnership with New York City public schools, they aim "to cultivate healthy students and communities through hands-on cooking and gardening education, transforming children's relationship with food." (Harbord & Khan, 2021).

The director of education, Liza Engelberg commented:

> The best example I have of this is with fourth and fifth graders. These students were part of a "green team" which met weekly at school, and were given the chance to focus on an issue of particular concern to them.
>
> They were interested in the problem of garbage in their neighborhood, which led them to study recycling, which led them to advocate for recycling at their own school.
>
> Getting this off the ground was incredibly challenging, but the students made it happen, and I think that had a positive impact on them and the school at large. This year, when we had remote instruction due to covid, the students wrote to their city council member to ask for more trash and recycling receptacles in their neighborhood.
>
> (L. Engelberg, personal communication, November 10, 2021)

EXAMPLE 3 Recycling In and Out of School

Table 20.4 Example 3 recycling.

MYSELF & MY RELATIONSHIPS + BELIEFS & VALUES + KNOWLEDGE & UNDERSTANDING + ACTIONS			
RECYCLING			
At School	Out of School	At School	Out of School
Being on the school green team.	Garbage in my neighborhood.	Setting up a school recycling program.	Petitioning city council to provide more recycling containers.

Source: Graphic created by the authors.

Applications

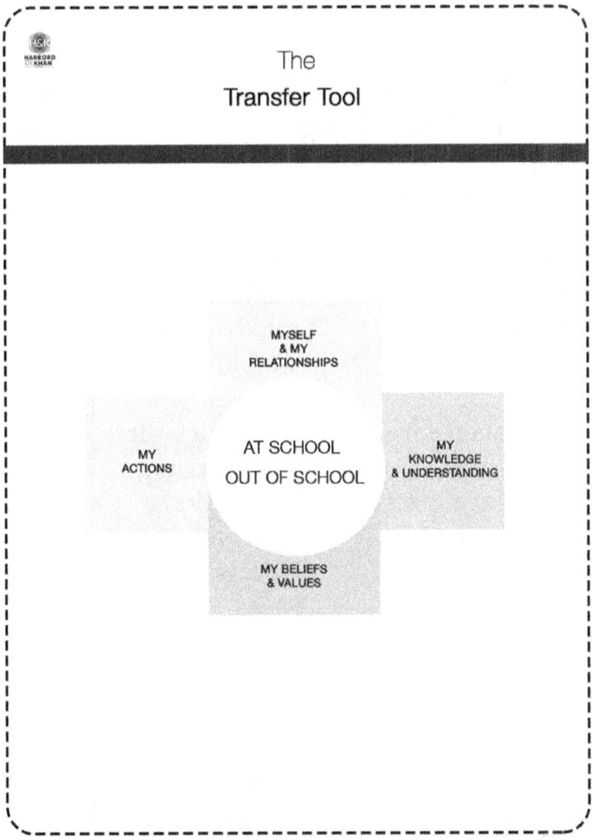

The
Transfer Tool
MYSELF & MY RELATIONSHIPS
MY ACTIONS
AT SCHOOL
OUT OF SCHOOL
MY KNOWLEDGE & UNDERSTANDING
MY BELIEFS & VALUES

Figure 20.2 The Transfer Tool card.
Source: Graphic created by the authors.

'My Knowledge and Understanding' and 'My Actions'

What have I learned at school that could help me with my life out of school?

Debating at school has helped me be more confident meeting new people and striking up a conversation.

'Myself and My Relationships' and 'My Actions'

What have I learned at home that could help me with my life at school?

Having a younger sibling has taught me patience as I have to wait my turn and sometimes they get more attention. This has helped me be better at collaborating with my classmates when we work together.

Suggestions to Align Skills With the Tool

Teachers can share this checklist with students to support them in identifying their higher-order thinking and social emotional skills.

Table 20.5 Suggestions to align higher-order thinking and social emotional learning skills with the tool.

Critical and Creative Thinking Skills for Problem-Solving		Social Emotional Learning Skills
☐ I can analyze and evaluate issues and my ideas. ☐ I can reflect on myself, skills and value. ☐ I can draw reasonable conclusions or generalizations. ☐ I can consider ideas from multiple perspectives, examining different aspects of the topic to support understanding. ☐ I can check the facts and interpretations. ☐ I can use transfer skills to change the context of an inquiry to gain different perspectives.	☐ I can use different creative strategies that make thinking visible. ☐ I make unpredictable or surprising connections between objects and/or ideas. ☐ I can use different creative strategies that make thinking visible.	☐ I am curious and open-minded. ☐ I recognize how critical thinking skills are used in school as well as out of school. ☐ I care about others' feelings and the impact of my actions on them. ☐ I take action to support others' well-being.

Source: Graphic created by the authors.

Questions for Students to Support Higher-Order Thinking Skills

Table 20.6 Questions for students.

Grade 7–8

1. Did the tool help you make connections between what you do at school and what you do out of school? Give reasons for your answer.
2. Did the tool help you use your problem-solving skills in new ways and situations?
   Give reasons for your answer.

Grade 9–10

1. Was the tool useful in helping you think about what you learned at school and how to apply it to your home life? Can you give an example?
2. Reflect on how the tool helped you to transfer your knowledge and experiences from school to home and vice versa?

Source: Graphic created by the authors.

Teacher Reflection

KEY TAKEAWAY: Exploring how what is learned at school and what is learned out of school complement each other.

- Describe the scenario and classroom context—what was the problem you wanted to address with this tool?
- Did you achieve your goal?
- How did you use the tool to support students' higher-order thinking skills (HOTS)?

Complement With Other Tools

Self-regulation and identity: The Myself Tool, The Polka Dot Tool and The Points of View Tool.

Chapter Notes

Use this space to plan and write your personal thoughts, ideas and questions here:

Create your mind-map or sketch out your ideas

Table 20.7 The Transfer Tool Table.

At School	↔	Out of School
MY RELATIONSHIPS		
	Can help me	
MY KNOWLEDGE & UNDERSTANDING		
	Can help me	
MY BELIEFS & VALUES		
	Can help me	
MY ACTIONS		
	Can help me	

Source: Graphic created by the authors.

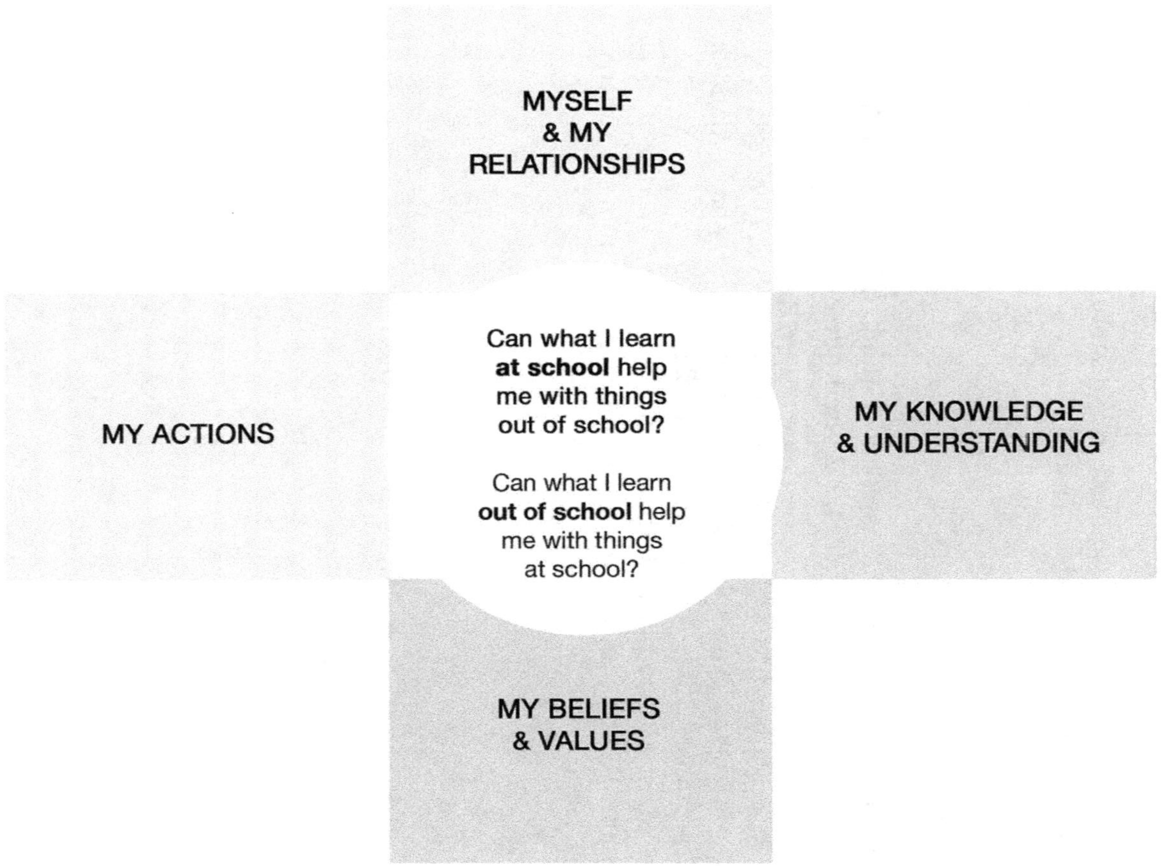
MYSELF
& MY
RELATIONSHIPS
MY ACTIONS
Can what I learn
at school help
me with things
out of school?
Can what I learn
out of school help
me with things
at school?
MY KNOWLEDGE
& UNDERSTANDING
MY BELIEFS
& VALUES

Figure 20.3 The Transfer Tool template.
Source: Graphic created by the authors.

Definitions

Beliefs: the feeling of being certain that something exists or is true.
Values: the beliefs people have, especially about what is right and wrong and what is most important in life, that control their behavior.

The definitions in this list are sourced from Cambridge Online Dictionary (2023) and Merriam-Webster Dictionary (2023).

References

Cambridge University Press & Assessment (Ed.). (2023). *Cambridge online dictionary*. Retrieved November 14, 2023, from https://dictionary.cambridge.org/

Khan, S. R., & Harbord, M. J. (2021). *Edible schoolyard NYC*. Harbordandkhan.com/. Retrieved November 25, 2023, from https://harbordandkhan.com/portfolio/edible-schoolyard-nyc/ret 24/11/23

Merriam-Webster, Incorporated (Ed.). (2023). *Merriam-Webster dictionary*. Merriam-Webster.com. Retrieved November 15, 2023, from www.merriam-webster.com/

21

The Zig-Zag Tool

Everything to Gain

Suggested Grade Level: 8–10

Key Takeaways—Exploring the value of students' tasks. Making unusual connections and imagining different scenarios to generate inquiry. Encouraging different viewpoints and fostering empathy.

Global Skills and Key Themes

Skills: Collaboration, critical thinking, creative thinking and problem-solving.
Themes: Empathy, ethical perspectives, multiple perspectives, imagination, multiculturalism, open-mindedness, self-awareness and self-regulation.

Stories

FROM THE CLASSROOM: Slam dunk poetry with Grade 8 students.
DEFINITIONS: Empathy, ethical perspectives and multiple perspectives (p 292).

DOI: 10.4324/9781032664989-22

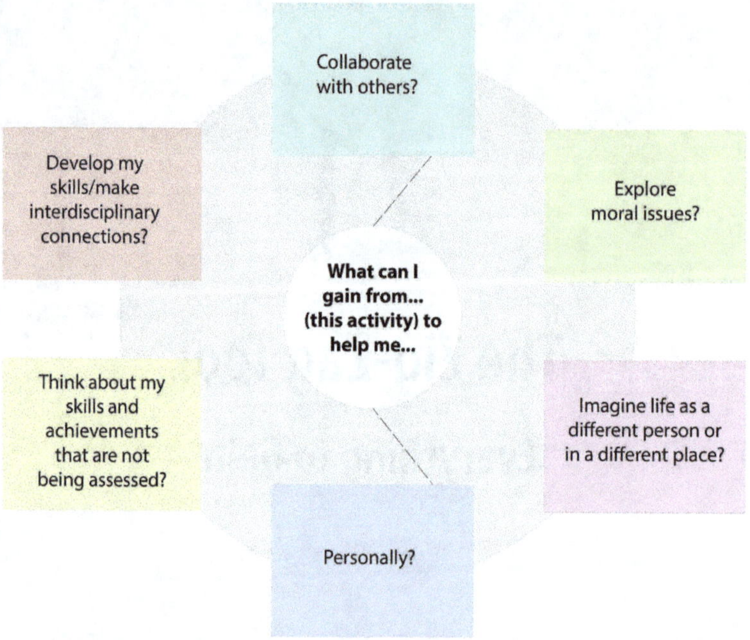
Collaborate with others?
Develop my skills/make interdisciplinary connections?
Explore moral issues?
What can I gain from... (this activity) to help me...
Think about my skills and achievements that are not being assessed?
Imagine life as a different person or in a different place?
Personally?

Figure 21.1 The Zig-Zag Tool.
Source: Graphic created by the authors.

What Does The Zig-Zag Tool Do?

The Zig-Zag Tool can support students in being creative and considering different viewpoints. It gives them the opportunity to think of the learning experience as an opportunity to gain something, instead of just a task. The connections students zig-zag to make can be random and give them unusual perspectives about their learning. Ideas are rarely linear. The Zig-Zag Tool can guide students in making connections between their beliefs and values and how they collaborate and empathize with others. It encourages students and teachers to be more aware of students' skills beyond those that are being assessed. Having conversations about skills that are not often perceived as valuable in the classroom can give teachers a different perspective about their students. Learning about skills and interests of your students helps you develop a better rapport.

How to Use It

1. Choose your topic/activity.
2. Put your topic/activity in the middle circle, 'What can I gain from this activity to help me' . . .?
3. Draw zig-zag lines from the middle circle to two or more of the rectangles. This will give you your questions.

EXAMPLE 1 Spanish Verbs Activity

Topic: Learning about irregular Spanish verbs.

Zig-zag from 'Collaborate with others?' to 'Personally'.

Inquiry: What can I gain from 'Learning about irregular Spanish verbs' to help me 'Collaborate with others' and 'Personally'?

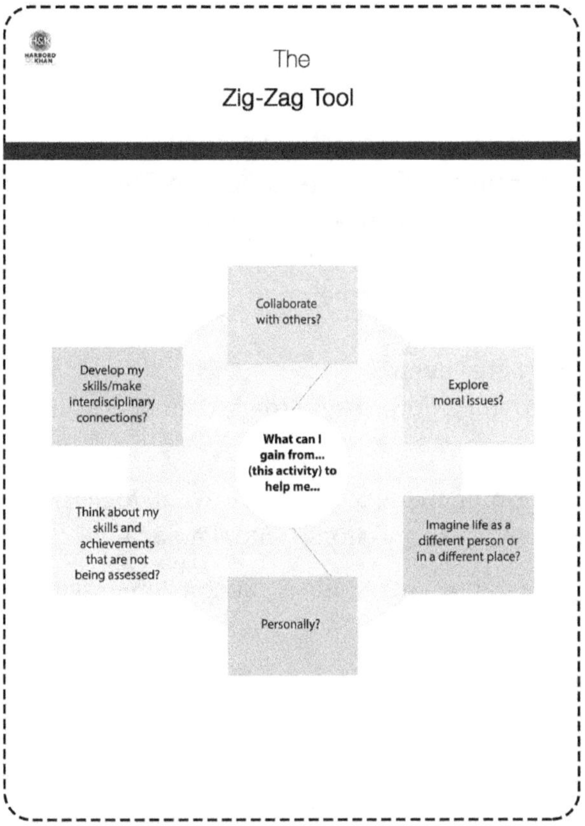
The
Zig-Zag Tool
Collaborate with others?
Develop my skills/make interdisciplinary connections?
Explore moral issues?
What can I gain from... (this activity) to help me...
Think about my skills and achievements that are not being assessed?
Imagine life as a different person or in a different place?
Personally?

Figure 21.2 The Zig-Zag Tool card.
Source: Graphic created by the authors.

Collaborate with others: Learning another language has made me a better listener and a more patient person and given me a better understanding about how learning new things can be hard or challenging. It can help me connect with people in the community who speak Spanish.

Personally: Through my interest in Spanish I have learned playing guitar, which I love doing out of school but it doesn't get me marks for my report card.

EXAMPLE 2 Problem-Based Learning Math Activity

Topic: Analyzing graphs, tables and equations and explaining what is being represented.

Zig-zag from 'Explore moral issues' to 'Develop my skills/make interdisciplinary connections (with math and visual arts and language arts)'.

Inquiry: What can I gain from 'Analyzing graphs, tables, and equations and explaining what is being represented' to help me 'Explore moral issues' and 'Make interdisciplinary connections'?
Students can use their analysis of information on animal rights (moral issues) from graphs and tables (analyzing graphs and tables) to create posters on the topic in a visual arts class.

Students can investigate data manipulation (analyzing graphs and tables) to discuss and debate issues of misinformation (moral issues) in a language arts class.

STORIES FROM THE CLASSROOM

Slam Dunk Poetry

A Grade 8 English teacher, Sim Gray, used The Zig-Zag Tool with her students to explore their concerns about performing in their upcoming Slam Dunk Poetry event. She hoped that by reflecting on the importance of working through tasks they might feel uncomfortable with, students would be able to recognize the value of the tasks and be less apprehensive about their performance.

TOPIC: Performing in the Slam Poetry event.
Zig-zag from 'Develop my skills/make interdisciplinary connections to 'Personally'.

Inquiry: What can I gain from 'Performing in the Slam Poetry event' to help me 'Develop my skills/make interdisciplinary connections?' and 'Personally'?

Students also used the tool to 'Think about my skills and achievements that are not being assessed'.

Poetry Performance

At the end of our first unit 'The Crossover', students are required to perform their chosen poems in front of the class. We assess students on their performance techniques: PVLEGS (Poise, Voice, Life, Eye Contact, Gestures, Speed) and musical techniques, as well as their use of poetic devices and authenticity.

Students have some previous experience performing poetry from 6th grade. However, in 6th grade, students are given poems to perform; they do not perform their own poems. They also do their performances in small groups. However, in 8th grade, performing their own poems and doing it on their own is often a daunting task for many students.

As we were looking at example slam poetry performances in class, a number of students voiced their concerns about the poetry performances. They explained that they were feeling uncomfortable about having to perform in front of the whole class and asked how these skills would be useful in any way outside their English classes. I wanted my students to change their mindsets about the performance task, understand that these skills are transferable and participate in the practice sessions and do their final performances wholeheartedly.

What Could Students Gain From Writing Poetry?

When the students were working on their answers for The Zig-Zag Tool activity, they were chatty and loud. I wasn't sure if they were actually engaged with the task. However, when I started reading their answers at the end of our lesson, I realized that many of them had actually been using their critical thinking skills and showed awareness of the transferable skills that we are aiming for them to gain through this activity. Quite a number of students were also able to identify how writing poetry would help them develop on a personal level, helping them express their emotions and connecting them with other people.

Impact on Student Metacognition

The thinking tool definitely raised awareness of the transferable skills we are aiming to practice with this performance task. Even though students may still feel uncomfortable performing in front of the class, now most of them understand why it is important to push themselves outside their comfort zone to do it.

When students understand why it is important to complete a difficult task, this also impacts their well-being and their attitude toward the learning experience in a positive way. There were no complaints about the final performances throughout the lesson, which in itself was a huge progress (S. Gray, personal communication, November 5, 2023).

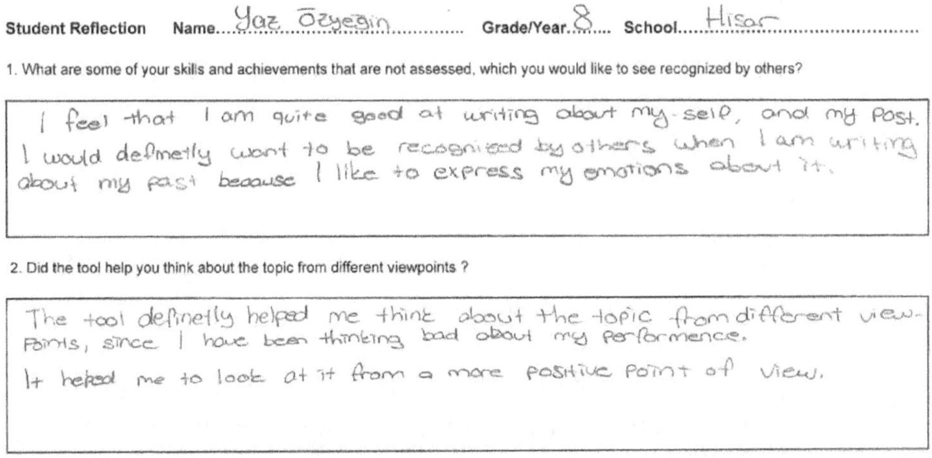

Student Reflection Name: Yaz Özyeğin Grade/Year: 8 School: Hisar

1. What are some of your skills and achievements that are not assessed, which you would like to see recognized by others?

I feel that I am quite good at writing about my-self, and my past. I would defenetly want to be recognized by others when I am writing about my past because I like to express my emotions about it.

2. Did the tool help you think about the topic from different viewpoints ?

The tool definetly helped me think about the topic from different view-points, since I have been thinking bad about my performence.
It helped me to look at it from a more positive point of view.

Figure 21.3 Student reflection by Yaz on using The Zig-Zag Tool.
Source: Image credit Hisar School.

Table 21.1 Table with student responses.

STUDENT	What are some of your skills and achievements that are not assessed, which you would like to see recognized by others?	Did the tool help you think about the topic from different viewpoints?
1. Elif	One of my skills and achievements is singing. I would like my singing to be recognized by others. More of my skills: volleyball, poetry, writing in general, etc.	It helped me realize more about the topic.
2. Yaz	I feel that I am quite good at writing about myself and my past. I would definitely want to be recognized by others when I am writing about my past because I like to express my emotions about it.	The tool definitely helped me think about the topic from different viewpoints, since I have been thinking bad about my performance. It helped me look at it from a more positive point of view.
3.	I would like others to see how much emotion I have and I can express.	Yes, because now I see that slam poetry performances can help me express more feelings in other presentations too.
4.	My behavior, I have improved very much since 6th grade. While I used to be rude to my teachers now I am more polite and have manners.	Yes.
5.	I would like people to see my achievements in sports.	Yes. It helped me so much to think about my task from another view.
6.	Talking and expressing ourselves better. Showing our emotions more effectively.	Yes, I can see where I can use it in my life.
7.	I think that presenting an informative presentation is not assessed, maybe a lot more focus on writing.	Yes, the tool helped me to understand a topic from different viewpoints.

Source: Graphic created by the authors.

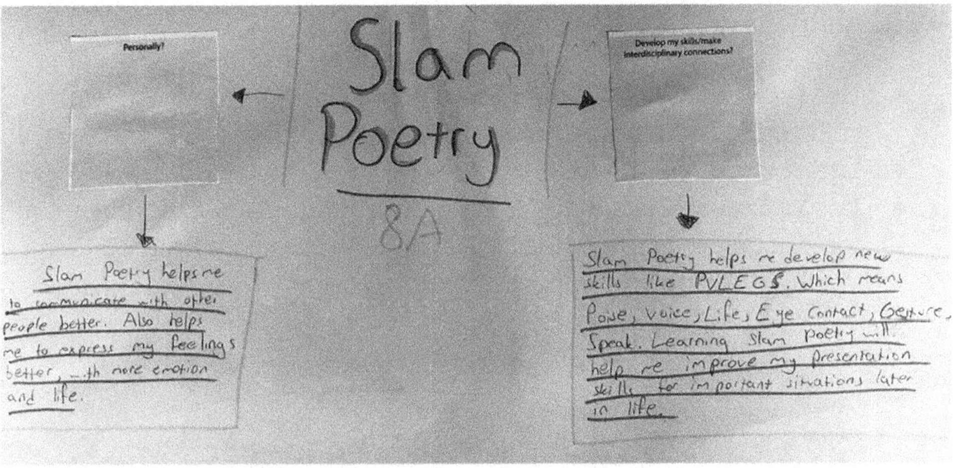
Slam
Poetry
8A

How can performing in the Slam Poetry event help me...

Develop my skills/make interdisciplinary connections?'

Slam Poetry helps me develop new skills like PVLEGS. Which means Poise, Voice, Life, Eye Contact, Gesture, Speak. Learning Slam Poetry will help me improve my presentations skills for important situations later in life.

Personally?

Slam Poetry helps me to communicate with other people better.

Also helps me to express my feelings better with more emotion and life.

Figure 21.4 Slam poetry poster student example.
Source: Image credit Hisar School.

Applications

- Use your creative thinking to connect ideas—create and develop connections and inquiries through visual diagrams.
- Use your critical thinking to analyze and evaluate issues.
- Use your problem-solving skills to find solutions to the problem or topic. e.g. Identify how the work you do in the classroom can help you in other areas of your life.

I make unpredictable or surprising connections between objects and/or ideas.

Figure 21.5 Zig-Zag Dragon.
Source: Artwork by Linda Weil©.

Suggestions to Align Skills With the Tool

Teachers can share this checklist with students to support them in identifying their higher-order thinking and social emotional skills.

Table 21.2 Suggestions to align higher-order thinking and social emotional learning skills with the tool.

Critical and Creative Thinking Skills for Problem-Solving		Social Emotional Learning Skills
☐ I can identify the problem/inquiry question. ☐ I can analyze and evaluate issues and my ideas. ☐ I can identify trends and forecast possibilities. ☐ I can break up complicated ideas into different parts and reassemble them to develop new understanding. ☐ I can find solutions to the problem/inquiry question.	☐ I create novel ideas and consider new perspectives. ☐ I use brainstorming and visual diagrams to create and develop ideas, connections and inquiries. ☐ I make unpredictable or surprising connections between objects and/or ideas. ☐ I create innovative works and ideas. ☐ I transform existing ideas and works and find innovative uses for them. ☐ I can use different creative strategies that make thinking visible. ☐ I can find solutions to the problem/inquiry question.	☐ I am curious and open-minded. ☐ I can make decisions that are ethical based on respect and an understanding of what is appropriate for different cultures. ☐ I recognize how critical thinking skills are used in school as well as out of school. ☐ I understand what empathy is and can empathize with others.

Source: Graphic created by the authors.

Questions for Students to Support Higher-Order Thinking Skills

Table 21.3 Questions for students.

1. What are some of your skills and achievements that are not assessed that you would like to see recognized by others? 2. Did the tool help you think about the topic from different viewpoints?

Source: Graphic created by the authors.

Teacher Reflection

KEY TAKEAWAYS—Exploring the value of students' tasks. Making unusual connections and imagining different scenarios to generate inquiry. Encouraging different viewpoints and fostering empathy.

- Describe the scenario and classroom context—what was the problem you wanted to address with this tool?
- Did you achieve your goal?
- How did you use the tool to support students' higher-order thinking skills (HOTS)?

Complement With Other Tools

Multiple perspectives: The Building Blocks Tool, The Clock Tool, The Detective Tool, The Knowledge Twister Tool, The Points of View Tool and The Time Tunnel Tool.

Chapter Notes

Use this space to plan and write your personal thoughts, ideas and questions here:

Create your mind-map or sketch out your ideas

The Zig-Zag Tool© Template (available as online support material)

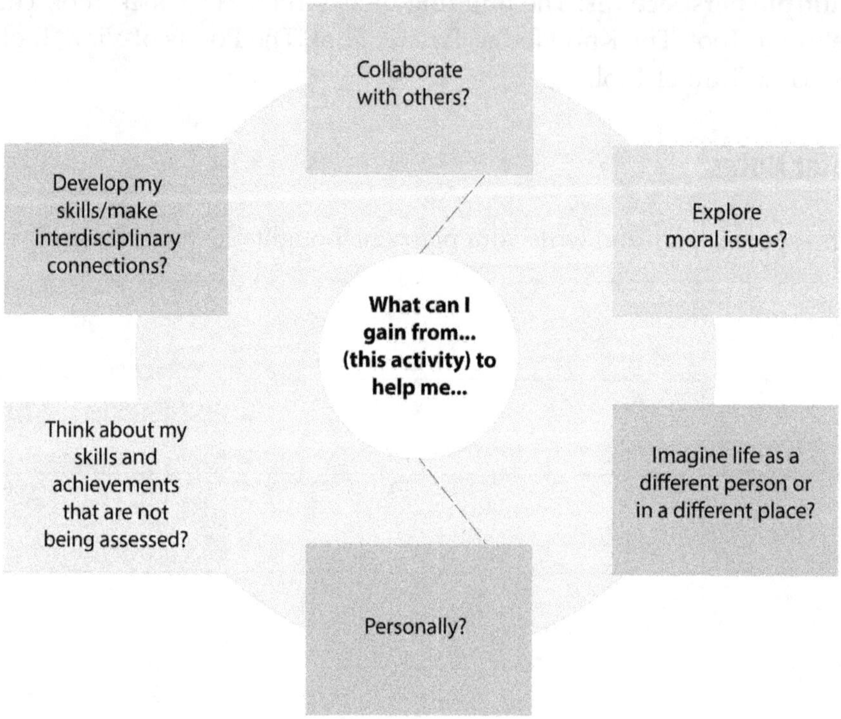
Collaborate with others?
Explore moral issues?
Imagine life as a different person or in a different place?
Personally?
Think about my skills and achievements that are not being assessed?
Develop my skills/make interdisciplinary connections?
What can I gain from... (this activity) to help me...

Figure 21.6 The Zig-Zag Tool template.
Source: Graphic created by the authors.

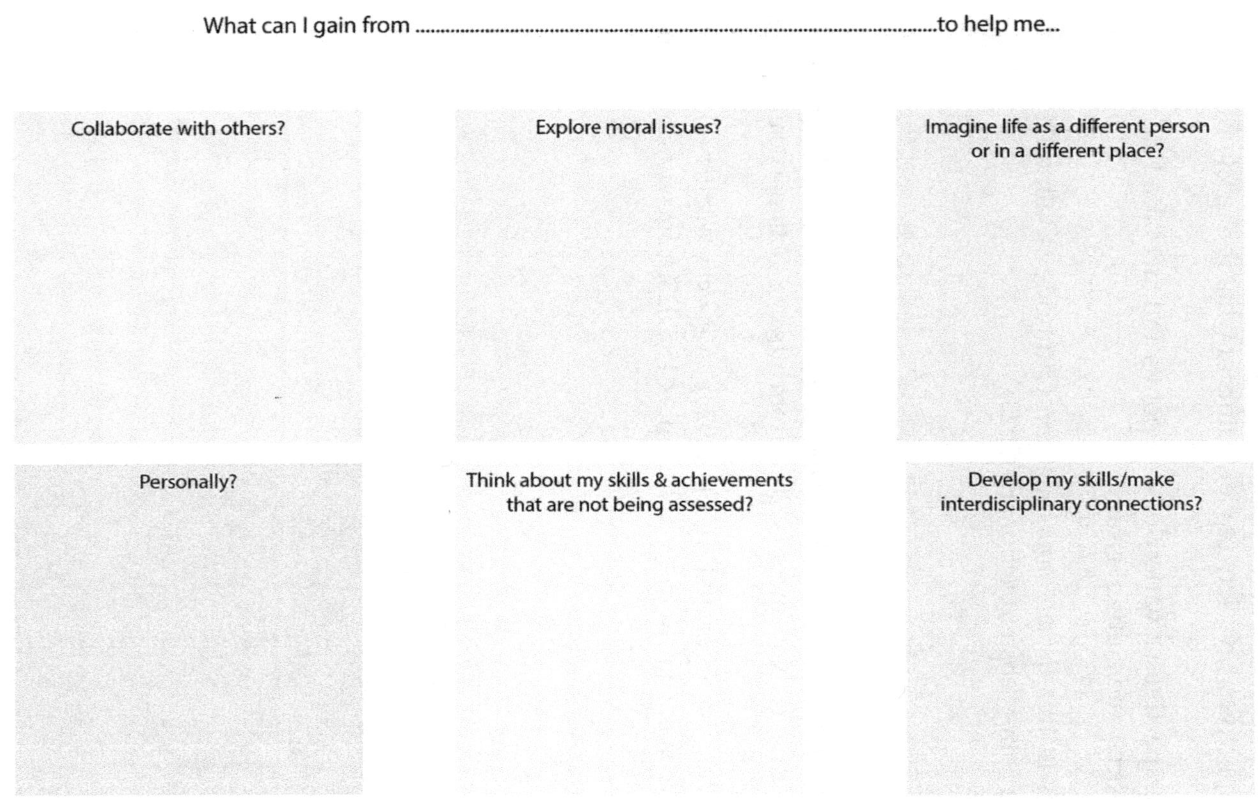
What can I gain from ....to help me...
Collaborate with others?
Explore moral issues?
Imagine life as a different person or in a different place?
Personally?
Think about my skills & achievements that are not being assessed?
Develop my skills/make interdisciplinary connections?

Figure 21.7 The Zig-Zag Tool worksheet.
Source: Graphic created by the authors.

Definitions

Empathy: the ability to share someone else's feelings or experiences by imagining how it would feel to be in that person's circumstances.
Ethical perspectives: a variety of viewpoints of what is morally right and what is not.
Multiple perspectives: a variety of viewpoints and fact-based, accurate sources on social and cultural issues.

The definitions in this list are sourced from Cambridge Online Dictionary (2023) and Merriam-Webster Dictionary (2023).

References

Cambridge University Press & Assessment (Ed.). (2023). *Cambridge online dictionary*. Retrieved November 14, 2023, from https://dictionary.cambridge.org/

Merriam-Webster, Incorporated (Ed.). (2023). *Merriam-Webster dictionary*. Merriam-Webster.com. Retrieved November 15, 2023, from www.merriam-webster.com/

For Product Safety Concerns and Information please contact our EU representative GPSR@taylorandfrancis.com
Taylor & Francis Verlag GmbH, Kaufingerstraße 24, 80331 München, Germany

www.ingramcontent.com/pod-product-compliance
Lightning Source LLC
Chambersburg PA
CBHW060509300426
44112CB00017B/2594
9781032626222